7S

the **FINE WINES** *of* NEW ZEALAND

KEITH STEWART

the *Fine* *Wines* of

NEW *Z*EALAND

KEITH STEWART

GRUB STREET · LONDON

For David

ACKNOWLEDGEMENTS

From the bottom of my heart I thank the wine companies who made their wines available for tasting so that this project could be completed. Offering up wine that at times represented more than a decade of winemaking, of wrestling with soil and climate, and ultimately with the vagaries of critics and public taste, involved them in considerable cost, both financial and emotional, as many saw me passing judgement on their life's work, their passion. I only hope that I have been able to match their faith in me with an honest assessment and fair words.

I also take this opportunity to thank my friends Malcolm Walker and Ian McCallum, who shared some difficult tastings with me and listened with good humour to my raving and mumbling about how painfully demanding the whole project was. The book would never have been finished without their support.

My Godwit publishing team, Brian Phillips, for the original idea, and fierce Jane Connor, for coping with regular deadline extensions beyond reason, have turned this crazy collection of adjectives into a very smart publication that I am proud of. Also to Alison Mudford at the *Listener* who edits my weekly wine column and quietly supports my attempts to tell more of the wine story than is usually apparent.

Finally, but always first, my family, especially Julie, who works so that I may write, and who puts up with the moods and the disappearances, and shares more bottles of great wine with me than anybody else.

Published by Grub Street
The Basement, 10 Chivalry Road
London SW11 1HT

First published in New Zealand by Godwit
Publishing Ltd

Copyright © 1996 Grub Street
Text copyright © 1995 Keith Stewart

The moral right of the author has been asserted.

British Library Cataloguing in Publication Data
Stewart, Keith
The fine wines of New Zealand
1. Wine and winemaking – New Zealand –
Guide Books
I. Title
641. 2′ 2′ 0993

ISBN 1 898697 54 X

Printed and bound by The Bath Press, Bath

CONTENTS

INTRODUCTION   7

CHARDONNAY   11
Ata Rangi Chardonnay   13
Babich Irongate Chardonnay   14
Brookfields Chardonnay Reserve   17
Church Road Chardonnay   18
Cloudy Bay Chardonnay   20
Collards Rothesay Chardonnay   22
Cooks Winemakers' Reserve Chardonnay   25
Coopers Creek Swamp Reserve Chardonnay   26
Corbans Private Bin Chardonnay   27
Delegat's Proprietors Reserve Chardonnay   29
Giesen Reserve Chardonnay   31
Grove Mill Lansdowne Chardonnay   32
Hunter's Chardonnay   33
Kumeu River Chardonnay   35
Martinborough Vineyard Chardonnay   38
Matua Valley Judd Estate Chardonnay   40
Morton Estate White Label Chardonnay   42
Morton Estate Black Label   44
Neudorf Moutere Chardonnay   46
Ngatarawa Alwyn Chardonnay   49
Robard & Butler Chardonnay   50
Stonecroft Mere Road Chardonnay   52
Te Mata Estate Elston Chardonnay   54
The Millton Vineyard Clos de Ste. Anne
        Chardonnay   56
Vavasour Reserve Chardonnay   58
Vidal Reserve Chardonnay   59
Villa Maria Barrique Ferment Reserve
        Chardonnay   61

CHENIN BLANC   63
Collards Dry Chenin Blanc   64
The Millton Vineyard Chenin Blanc   65

GEWÜRZTRAMINER   68
Dry River Gewürztraminer   70
Martinborough Vineyard Gewürztraminer   72
Robard & Butler Gewürztraminer   74

PINOT GRIS   76
Dry River Pinot Gris   77

RIESLING   79
Coopers Creek Riesling   80
Dry River Riesling   81
Giesen Estate Canterbury Riesling   83
The Millton Vineyard Riesling Opou
        Vineyards   84
Grove Mill Marlborough Riesling   86
Martinborough Vineyard Riesling   87
Montana Marlborough Riesling   89
Neudorf Moutere Riesling   91
Ngatarawa Hawke's Bay Riesling   93
Robard & Butler Amberley Rhine Riesling   95
Seifried Estate Riesling   96
Stoneleigh Vineyard Rhine Riesling   98

SAUVIGNON BLANC   100
Cloudy Bay Sauvignon Blanc   102
Collards Rothesay Sauvignon Blanc   104
Corbans Private Bin Fumé Blanc   106
Hunter's Sauvignon Blanc   107

Hunter's Oak Aged Sauvignon Blanc   109
Kumeu River Sauvignon   111
Matua Valley Reserve Sauvignon Blanc   113
Montana Marlborough Sauvignon Blanc   114
Morton Estate Black Label Fumé Blanc   117
Neudorf Fumé Blanc   118
Oyster Bay Sauvignon Blanc   120
Stoneleigh Vineyard Marlborough
    Sauvignon Blanc   121
Te Mata Estate Cape Crest
    Sauvignon Blanc   123
Te Mata Estate Castle Hill
    Sauvignon Blanc   124
Vavasour Reserve Marlborough
    Sauvignon Blanc   126

SPARKLING WINES   128
Cloudy Bay Pelorus   129
Daniel Le Brun Blanc de Blancs   130
Daniel Le Brun Vintage   132
Morton Estate Vintage   133

BOTRYTIS SWEET WINES   135
Corbans Private Bin Noble Rhine
    Riesling   137
Dry River Selection Series   138
Glazebrook Penny Noble Harvest   140
Martinborough Vineyard Late Harvest   142

CABERNET SAUVIGNON AND
PRINCIPAL BLENDS   144
Ata Rangi Célèbre   147

Babich Irongate Cabernet Sauvignon/
    Merlot   149
Brookfields Cabernet Sauvignon Reserve   151
Brookfields Cabernet/Merlot   153
Church Road Cabernet Sauvignon   154
Delegat's Proprietors Reserve Cabernet
    Sauvignon   156
Goldwater Estate Cabernet/Merlot/Franc   158
Kumeu River Merlot/Cabernet   161
Matua Valley Cabernet Sauvignon   164
Ngatarawa Glazebrook Cabernet/Merlot   166
Stonecroft Cabernet Sauvignon-
    Cabernet/Merlot   168
Te Mata Awatea   170
Te Mata Coleraine   173
Vidal Reserve Cabernet Sauvignon   176
Vidal Reserve Cabernet/Merlot   177
Villa Maria Cabernet Sauvignon   179
Villa Maria Reserve Cabernet/Merlot   180

PINOT NOIR   182
Ata Rangi Pinot Noir   184
Dry River Pinot Noir   186
Martinborough Vineyard Pinot Noir   187
Neudorf Pinot Noir   190
Rippon Vineyard Pinot Noir   192

SYRAH   194
Stonecroft Syrah   195

THE WINEMAKERS   197

THE WINERIES   203

INTRODUCTION

THIS BOOK SEEKS TO PROVIDE A VIEW OF THE FIRST YEARS OF THE FINE WINE industry in New Zealand, through the taste of the wines themselves in a series of 'vertical' tastings. These are the most renowned wines in the country, those that have made reputations for their winemakers and the companies who employ them, and for the nation as it shapes its destiny as a fine wine producer.

New Zealand is the latest member of the international fine wine fraternity — those wine-producing regions whose reputations are based on the quality, rather than the quantity, of their wine — and because New Zealand's arrival is so recent — a mere 10 years — the opportunity to taste the wines responsible is unique. Indeed, it could fairly be said that this country's record is still too short to claim fine wine status at all, if it were not for New Zealand wine's stunning elevation to respectability in that time.

The impact of New Zealand wine has, however, been so dramatic, particularly in the influential British market, that it would be inaccurate to contradict its place in the fine wine trade. Its participation is marked not just by sales success, but by the influence of New Zealand Sauvignon Blanc on other fine wines made from this variety. Sauvignon Blanc is a category in which New Zealand wine is generally recognised as setting the international standard, with its strongly aromatic, pure character and consistent high quality, a remarkable achievement in a decade, and one that no other New World region has managed to emulate, in spite of considerably older fine wine histories.

This performance has been supported by critically acclaimed Chardonnays and Méthode Champenoise sparkling wines, as well as a number of less universally fine, but frequently excellent Cabernet Sauvignons, Pinot Noirs, Rieslings and botrytised sweet wines. It is a range that has depth, definably regional character, and very high standards across the range of producers, all significant contributing factors in classification as a fine wine region.

It is also significant that the largest market for New Zealand wine is Britain, which favours relatively high-quality, luxury wines rather than staple beverages, and even here New Zealand wine is not considered to be low either in price or in quality.

Fifteen years ago the first tentative introductions of New Zealand wine to the British wine trade attracted supportive murmurs and comments about the potential of this newcomer to the international wine scene. It was seen as a curiosity, from a small former colony that most people associated with sheep and butter, but with no vinous culture worthy of consideration alongside France, Germany and Italy, or even the New World tyros, California and Australia.

In 1985 all that changed, when critics and trade alike were treated to a sensational tasting at New Zealand House in London, a tasting that impressed those who attended as the seminal event for New Zealand's international reputation. The wines were not just very good, they were memorable, with a character which gave them a special identity — a character derived from strong aroma, pure flavour and refreshing clarity, coupled with the universal signs of fine wine craft.

FINE WINE

Those characteristics alone do not make for fine wine, and nor is a wine reputation made on the basis of one tasting. Single wines may be fine, but to accumulate a reputation that categorises it as a fine wine a label must be of consistently high quality, at least as good or better than its compatriots from each vintage. In the history of wine it is the consistency of performance above all else that defines a wine as fine. Occasionally outstanding, with frequent disappointments, is never enough.

Traditionally, price has been the measure of this consistency, and in the famous classification of the winemaking properties of the Medoc in 1855, it was the principal guide. Those who drew up that system were able to reflect on a much longer trade history than is the case with New Zealand wine. Price in this country is as much a reflection of extreme publicity and tiny size as it is of reliable performance over a number of years.

There is also the question of just what is a reasonable time over which to measure performance. In Europe, or even in California, 20 years is fair, and winemaking reputations are often made, and destroyed, over much greater periods. New Zealand has no wineries with that sort of history of fine winemaking, and few that stretch back even 10 years, but where wines have accumulated a reputation over at least four consecutive vintages, they have been considered for inclusion here.

As trade is the yardstick, so those wine producers who operate outside normal trade parameters struggle to have their products categorised as fine wine. This is especially the case for very small producers, whose reputations are often based on the experience of such a limited group of drinkers it is difficult to rate their status according to the same criteria as those applied to larger producers. The distortions of price caused by limited production are also a factor, when price is such a critical measure of the sustainable quality of a wine producer and attendant vineyards.

Fine wine is also a qualitative assessment, a judgement, and the inclusion of the following wines is made after consideration of the writings and assessments of wine critics Vic Williams, Michael Cooper and Bob Campbell, as well as the Air New Zealand wine competition and its predecessors, and the regular tastings of *Cuisine* magazine. As well as these New Zealand sources, the ratings of overseas publications such as *Decanter*, *Wine*, and *The Wine Spectator*, have also been taken into account.

Finally there has been my experience of the tastings themselves. Some wines originally included did not show the consistency and/or the quality that could reasonably be expected of fine wines, and so were ultimately excluded from this publication.

SELECTION

The wines included here are those that have established a reputation, within New Zealand and abroad, among critics and wine judges as well as the wider wine-drinking public. Some wines with reputations have been excluded where their production is so small they fall outside the influences that define fine wines, as mentioned above. However, in some cases, tiny production wines have been included, where they satisfy the leadership needs of a new developing industry. Wines that give quality direction by leading with new varieties and higher winemaking standards are an essential part of a young industry, and their fine wine status needs to be seen in context. However, as the whole industry improves to meet those standards, so must the small production capacity of experimental winemakers increase to meet the dynamics of the international fine wine trade.

CLASSIFICATONS

The wines are listed under general headings according to the grape varieties from which they are made. This is the method of labelling wines in New Zealand, and varietal names are those by which each wine is known.

For each wine the details of the vineyard source of the grapes, harvest date, variety(ies) used and winemaking treatment are included where individual producers have been happy to supply such information and for it to be published.

Other than alcohol content, details such as total acidity, pH and sugar at harvest have been excluded in the belief that these are of interest only where they influence taste and as such should be apparent in the wine and the tasting notes.

THE TASTINGS

The wines for each tasting were provided by the producers themselves, and were taken from their stocks. This ensured, as far as possible, that they were aged under similar conditions at source, and that the winemakers were aware of the conditions in which they matured.

With the exception of two wines, all tastings were held between June and December 1994, so that the age of each wine, per vintage, is similar.

Every effort has been made to let the wines themselves tell their own story; the notes are descriptive rather than judgemental.

Assessments of the expected longevity of each wine are general, and made on the basis of one bottle tasted, in one particular situation, at a specific time.

As an aid to those who wish to make contact with the wine producers mentioned in this book, the addresses for each are given at the end, as well as the addresses of their British agents.

In acknowledgement of the efforts made by a number of winemakers in advancing the standards of New Zealand wine, and their influence on fine wine production in particular, brief biographical notes on selected winemakers are also included at the end of the tasting notes.

CHARDONNAY

CHARDONNAY HAS RAPIDLY BECOME THE LEADING FINE WINE STYLE IN NEW Zealand. No other body of wines has shown the consistent high standard, sophistication of winemaking technique and capacity to improve with bottle age. Indeed, the question over the aging potential of New Zealand wines now seems resolved, at least for Chardonnay, with the proven longevity of the oldest wines in this group.

New Zealand Chardonnay now has a group of winemakers who have produced high-quality styles consistently over the decade since 1984, styles that have improved steadily to the point where the best are now of top international standard. They have gradually been joined by others who have lifted their standards and have found solutions to particular regional winegrowing problems.

These are all wines showing sophisticated winemaking skills that have been adapted to suit the intense fruit flavours of New Zealand-grown grapes. Although this process is not yet complete in some wineries, and in others no start has been made at all, the standard of the leading group is very high, and quite diverse styles have been successfully developed. Some of these have been driven entirely by the demands of regional grape differences, others have their roots in strong winemaking philosophies but, in all the best wines, harmony between winemaking and grape character is a feature of their success. For a number of improving producers, particularly those in the South Island, this process has been hampered in the early 1990s by difficult vintages, so it has been hard to get a true measure of their progress. Given better weather, it is likely we shall see a flowering of Marlborough Chardonnay in the last years of the 20th century.

These points considered, however, it would be inaccurate to say that regional styles of Chardonnay have been established in New Zealand, or that they are ever likely to emerge. A comparison between the Kumeu/Huapai/ Waimauku-sourced Chardonnay wines of Bruce Collard and Michael Brajkovich reveals both high quality and extreme stylistic differences and, in spite of fine tuning over 10 years, the most recent vintages of both show no significant narrowing of the style gap between them.

The vertical tasting exercise *does* show that winemakers who have a consistent source of fruit for their Chardonnay have produced more

11

harmonious, and consequently better-quality, wines than those whose grape supply varies from region to region, or even between vineyards. It is also clear that differences between grapes are often just that, differences, and given that wines of quality are made from them, judgements about regional characteristics are purely subjective rather than statements of fact.

Judging by James Busby's favourable opinion of the Chardonnay cuttings he took to Australia from Europe in 1833, it is possible that Chardonnay was among the vines he brought to New Zealand and established at his vineyard in Waitangi. If that is the case, it may be that the first wine made in New Zealand was at least partly a Chardonnay, a 'light white wine, very sparkling and delicious to taste', according to the French explorer, Dumont D'Urville in 1840.

There is, however, little evidence of Chardonnay growing in New Zealand before the 1920s, when there was an introduction from California, but the performance of this vine was so poor that no serious winemaking was attempted until another ex-Californian clone was introduced in 1971. Brought across from the CSIRO in Australia, the McCrae clone, as it was known, was never popular with contract grape growers because of its low production and irregular berry size, with large numbers of very small berries among a smattering of regular ones. These were just the attributes winemakers needed, however, although few were looking for them intentionally. The concentrated flavours of the juice from the tiny berries produced a level of intensity in wine that laid a foundation on which high-quality wines could be produced.

After research by Dr Richard Smart identified this as originally a Californian clone, it was rechristened Mendoza, and is the most important quality winemaking vine in the country, a major component of every significant premium Chardonnay made in New Zealand. It is somewhat ironic that, as New Zealand's Chardonnay reputation flourishes on the basis of Mendoza's special attributes, this clone was rejected by both the Californian and Australian wine industries.

There are now some 20 clones of Chardonnay in New Zealand, and more are being introduced regularly as winemakers seek to improve their Chardonnay performance in the vineyard, and consequently in the winery. Other clones of interest to premium Chardonnay makers are RUA1 and UCD15.

Currently, more area in New Zealand is planted in Chardonnay than in any other wine variety and, with almost 25 per cent of the total vineyard area, it is by far the dominant fine wine variety. Much of this is from high-yielding (in Chardonnay terms) vines and is used for lesser Chardonnays, blending and for sparkling wine production.

ATA RANGI CHARDONNAY

Ata Rangi originally gained its reputation and momentum from its very good red wines, but in recent years this tiny Wairarapa company has been making very poised, slightly understated Chardonnays of real class. They are wines that appear to be well harmonised with the character of the fruit the winemaker takes from Martinborough vineyards.

1989

*13.5% alc/vol; 100% Chardonnay, Mendoza clone;
Martinborough district, Wairarapa region; 100% barrel
fermentation in new 225-litre French oak;
5 months in same oak; 20% malolactic.
Winemaker: Phyll Pattie
Best drinking: 1995–97*

Brassy butter-yellow colour, clear and bright. The bouquet is starting to show some mellow, bottle age characters among its smoky, sawdusty, slightly creamy fragrances, with a small measure of green oak. The taste does not, however, quite live up to the promise of the bouquet, being more workmanlike than refined, but it does have some very agreeable, sweet fruit in the mid-palate, in partnership with a mellow, mealy flavour, and a certain jolly briskness throughout that

makes for attractive drinking. Bits of it are good, some bits less than fine, but it is sweet and plump enough for pleasure.

1990

*12.5% alc/vol; 100% Chardonnay, Mendoza clone;
Martinborough district, Wairarapa region; hand picked
2–13 April, 100% barrel fermentation in new 225-litre
French oak; 5 months in same oak; 30–40% malolactic.
Winemaker: Phyll Pattie
Best drinking: 1995–97*

A light, clear, soft, brassy yellow wine, still with a tinge of green. The nose has elements of herbaceousness, and a hearty measure of toasty oak embroidered with traces of lime juice. Feels quite firm in the mouth, with lovely fruit texture to match the creamy, mealy tone and hints of nuts, a feel and flavour that linger beautifully right through the graceful finish. The whole wine gives a wonderfully harmonious impression of svelte creaminess and fragrant poise. Very fine.

1991

*13% alc/vol; 100% Chardonnay, Mendoza clone;
Martinborough district, Wairarapa region; hand picked
9–12 April, 100% barrel fermentation in new 225-litre
French oak; 5 months in same oak; 30–40% malolactic.
Winemaker: Phyll Pattie
Best drinking: 1996–2001*

Still showing a youthful green cast to its light, yellow-straw hue, this wine has a delightful fragrance of clotted cream and hazelnut kernels. Fine, careful and pretty with sweet waves of fruit, it offers a mouthful of silky texture almost like crème anglais, but beautifully worked with expensive oak to a far more savoury character that the bouquet enlivens, lingering on like a whiff of lime blossom. The overall impression is quite beautiful, especially as it lingers so harmoniously, its distinctive air of freshness mellowed and enriched by warmth of flavour. It promises to gain even more subtlety and complex flavours with bottle age, and should be quite superb at about five years old, the epitome of graceful Chardonnay.

1992

13% alc/vol; 100% Chardonnay, Mendoza clone;
90% Hawke's Bay region, 10% Martinborough; hand
picked 10 April (Hawke's Bay), 21 April (Martinborough);
100% barrel fermentation in new 225-litre French oak;
5 months in same oak; 30–40% malolactic.
Winemaker: Phyll Pattie
Best drinking: 1996–98

A clear, soft, light yellow wine with a big caramel and oak bouquet that boasts a hearty chunk of grapefruit-like aroma. Bigger, more assertive wine than the previous, or later vintages, with sweet fruit to the fore throughout, kept company at all times by a sturdy measure of oak. Finishes quite warm, and just a little short, but the intensity of flavour at the heart of the wine keeps everything in pleasant form, aided by a soft hint of creamy texture. Good, well-crafted but atypical wine.

1993

13% alc/vol; 100% Chardonnay, Mendoza clone; 15%
Hawke's Bay, 85% Martinborough; hand picked 23 April
(Hawke's Bay), 25–26 April (Martinborough);
100% barrel fermentation in new 225-litre French oak;
5 months in same oak; 30–40% malolactic.
Winemaker: Phyll Pattie
Best drinking: 1996–2000

Looks pretty with its fresh, green-tinged straw colour, and it has a bouquet to match: gentle, softly washed with oak and perfumed with fragrances of lime blossom. With a heart of fruit intensity and supple, lightly creamy palate with spicy, hokey pokey oak flavours and some austere oak textures, it is not powerful wine, but alive with promise and delightful flavours. Very, very pretty, again notable for its poise and harmony.

BABICH IRONGATE CHARDONNAY

Made exclusively from Chardonnay grown in the shingly, dry soils of the Irongate Vineyard in Gimblett Road, Hawke's Bay, this wine has become a leader of the austere, racy Chardonnay style in New Zealand. It is not, however, a wine lacking in fruit, for its characteristically intense flavour, suitably grapefruit-like in true Hawke's Bay fashion, is one of its distinctive features. The flavour invariably has great clarity, and is usually strong enough to support the style without requiring the winemaker to resort to extravagant use of malolactic fermentation or heavy oak.

1985

12.7% alc/vol; 100% Chardonnay, Mendoza clone;
Irongate Vineyard, Gimblett Road, Hawke's Bay; hand
picked 19 March 1985; fermented in 225-litre French oak
barriques; aged on yeast lees for 6 months, and aged for a

further 18 months in bottle before release.
Winemaker: Joe Babich
Best drinking: 1995–96

Bright, very pretty, pale gold wine, with a lovely bouquet of fragrant oak, toast and limy grapefruit, mature yet fresh, with an entrancing shadow of intensity. Beautiful wine to drink, light, almost tender, with subtle savoury delicacies and a keen edge of intense, limy, citrus fruit flavour that is the backbone of the wine, holding its lacework of flavour nuances together and imparting a sense of lively continuity. A lovely glass of wine, not big, but displaying its maturity with an effortless sense of poise.

1986

12% alc/vol; 100% Chardonnay, Mendoza clone; Irongate Vineyard, Gimblett Road, Hawke's Bay; hand picked 25 March 1986; fermented in French 225-litre oak barriques; aged on yeast lees for 6 months, and aged for a further 18 months in bottle before release.
Winemaker: Joe Babich
Best drinking: 1995–97

Light golden colour, and an aromatically toasty, straightforward nose. It has an immediate, sweetly intense wave of fruit in the mouth, an intensity that holds right through to a razor-sharp finish, moderated nicely by a seasoning of oak. This still seems very young, with a charred edge to the oak, and a racy enthusiasm that tingles with limes and grapefruit, but rather fades off at the end. It gives the impression that it will last forever, steadily becoming more subtle, more intricate, less enthusiastic.

1987

12% alc/vol; 100% Chardonnay, Mendoza clone; Irongate Vineyard, Gimblett Road, Hawke's Bay; hand picked 31 March 1987; fermented in French 225-litre oak barriques; aged on yeast lees for 6 months, and aged for a further 18 months in bottle before release.
Winemaker: Joe Babich
Best drinking: 1995–98

The moderate, golden colour and vaguely burnished appearance of this wine imply more depth and richness than are apparent on the nose, which is quite delicate. Its nuances of toast and oak complement the background aroma of syrupy limes, but there is no suggestion of the cuttingly intense fruit flavours that

the wine holds, a piercing core of limes and grapefruit graced by toastiness and vanilla-oak in a fine-grained palate that holds on, lingering beautifully like some vinous mezzo-soprano at the close of a sad aria.

1988

12% alc/vol; 100% Chardonnay, Mendoza clone; Irongate Vineyard, Gimblett Road, Hawke's Bay; hand picked 13 March 1988; fermented in French 225-litre oak barriques; partial malolactic fermentation; aged on yeast lees for 6 months, and aged for a further 18 months in bottle before release.
Winemaker: Joe Babich
Best drinking: 1995

Light, burnished copper-gold with a rolling, aromatic, mealy-creamy bouquet that is forthright but lacking in focus. Some intensity on the palate, however, with a kernel of orange peel flavour, a neatly soft texture and a lot of fascinating, furry, honey-edged flavours. Its lightness is never, however, compensated for by weight of flavour, leaving it rather hollow, flat, reducing its many subtleties to interesting asides, rather than the decoration on something sound.

1989

12% alc/vol; 100% Chardonnay, Mendoza clone; Irongate Vineyard, Gimblett Road, Hawke's Bay; hand picked 25 February 1989; fermented in French 225-litre oak barriques; aged on yeast lees for 6 months, and aged for a further 18 months in bottle before release.
Winemaker: Joe Babich
Best drinking: 1995–2000

From this light, gold-coloured wine wafts a subtle, toasty, steady bouquet which is fragrantly gentle, again with the core of fruit intensity that gives a piercing quality to the grapefruit-lime fruit characteristics. It is a feature that imparts a cool elegance to this wine, completed by a fiercely fruit-driven finish that leaves a sense of uncompromising flavour and vigorous freshness that is almost ethereal. The oak, slightly mealy-nutty yeast subtleties, and mellow hints of bottle age are all very carefully crafted into a supporting role, but it is the fruit, so fine, so elegant, so intense, that holds onto your attention and memory.

1990

13.5% alc/vol; 100% Chardonnay, Mendoza clone; Irongate Vineyard, Gimblett Road, Hawke's Bay; hand picked 3 April 1990; fermented in French 225-litre oak barriques; aged on yeast lees for 6 months, and aged for a further 18 months in bottle before release.
Winemaker: Joe Babich
Best drinking: 1995–96

Moderately deep, golden colour, with a ripe grapefruit and cream nose, laced with aromatic toast and nuts in a style of easy opulence. It does have some fruit intensity lingering in its sensual depths, but this is forward rather than subtle, a creamy-textured, sexy style quite different from the earlier vintages, saved from being loose by a finishing twist of astringency and some clever oak treatment. Glowing with friendliness and warm succulence, it is a very pleasant glass of wine indeed.

1991

12% alc/vol; 100% Chardonnay, Mendoza clone; Irongate Vineyard, Gimblett Road, Hawke's Bay; hand picked 26 March 1991; fermented in French 225-litre oak barriques; aged on yeast lees for 6 months, and aged for a further 18 months in bottle before release.
Winemaker: Joe Babich
Best drinking: 1995–2002

Quiet wine, from its pale, vaguely burnished colour to its persistently delicate lingering finish. There are hints of minerals and creamy nuts among the aromatic oak and ripe grapefruit characters of the bouquet, well-turned details that enhance the confident fruit aromas which run deep and emerge as intense but never obvious flavours in the mouth. These are graced by silky, rounded textures and suggestions of nuts, yeast, rolled oats and other mellowing influences that hang around to the very end, never getting lost in the fruit. Very, very smart wine, lifted to beautiful elegance by its faultless sense of proportion and quiet reserve.

1992

13.5% alc/vol; 100% Chardonnay, Mendoza clone; Irongate Vineyard, Gimblett Road, Hawke's Bay; hand picked 26 March 1991; fermented in French 225-litre oak barriques; aged on yeast lees for 6 months, and aged for a further 18 months in bottle before release.
Winemaker: Joe Babich
Best drinking: 1996–2003

Pale gold, its bouquet touched with a glimmer of intense fruit, spiced oak, washed by an unusual, fruity perfume. Warm on the palate, with big fruit flavours that hint at grapefruit, slightly creamy and concentrated with a mellow slide of oak, it is big wine that leaves your mouth abuzz. Ripe and sensual, it is saved from pure decadence by clever winecraft and a restraining element of intensity that gives it an air of grace, but this wine really is awash with fruit right to the very end.

1993

12.5% alc/vol; 100% Chardonnay, Mendoza clone; Irongate Vineyard, Gimblett Road, Hawke's Bay; hand picked 8 April 1992; fermented in French 225-litre oak barriques; partial malolactic fermentation; aged on yeast lees for 6 months, and aged for a further 18 months in bottle before release.
Winemaker: Joe Babich
Best drinking: 1997–2005

Moderate pale gold, its aromatic oak and butter nose is backed by a shadowy fruit intensity that is almost tropical in character. The palate is based on this heart of intensity, fiercely fruity in a clarion call of ripe Chardonnay that is pure and very, very lively. Fine, fresh, razor-edged stuff that promises to last forever if it ever gets over being so terribly eager, keeping up the intensity from the first sniff to the last, lingering finish.

BROOKFIELDS CHARDONNAY RESERVE

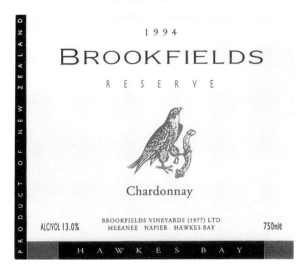

A soft, very appealing Chardonnay style with warmth and lively Hawke's Bay fruit characteristics that are typically grapefruity. A solid quality performer that, through increasingly sensitive oak handling, has steadily gained in sophistication with each vintage.

1989

12.3% alc/vol; 100% Chardonnay, Mendoza clone; 100% Hawke's Bay region, Fernhill district.
Winemaker: Peter Robertson
Best drinking: 1995–96

Beaten gold colour, buttery and ripe on the nose, with mellow-sweet bottle age characters, and a measure of milky oats. Fine, with a linseed oil richness of texture and even, fresh palate that has plenty of small flavours for interest and pleasure. A charming wine, not delicate, but subtle, with a silvery quality and an abundance of detail that is very satisfying.

1990

12.5% alc/vol; 100% Chardonnay, Mendoza clone; 100% Hawke's Bay region, Fernhill district; harvested last week in March 1991; 100% barrel fermentation, new French 225-litre Nevers oak barriques; 66% malolactic fermentation; 8 months in new oak barriques.
Winemaker: Peter Robertson
Best drinking: 1995–96

A light and clear yellow-gold wine, it has the aged bouquet reminiscent of old oak furniture with an underlying sweetness of fruit that is both fresh and mellow. Quite stringy oak flavours, and the fruit flavours are rather light after a promising hint on the bouquet, but they hang on well to the finish to complete a pleasant wine.

1991

12.2% alc/vol; 100% Chardonnay, Mendoza clone; 100% Hawke's Bay region, Fernhill district; harvested 27 March 1991; 100% barrel fermentation, new French 225-litre Nevers oak barriques; 66% malolactic fermentation; 8 months in new oak barriques.
Winemaker: Peter Robertson
Best drinking: 1995–97

Gold-brass-tinged colour, hearty looking, and the bouquet has delicious aromas of fine, sweet oak that hints at warm toast, with a suggestion of richness in the creamy, nutty smells of yeast and fermentation. Ripe tasting, it is also warm with flavour, but light in body, and has an interesting clarity of fruit flavour that tastes for all the world like perfumed grapefruit. Very tidy, pretty wine with plenty of charm. Again, highly satisfying.

1992

13.5% alc/vol; 100% Chardonnay, Mendoza clone; 100% Hawke's Bay region, Fernhill district; harvested 10–12 April 1992; 100% barrel fermentation, new French 225-litre (50% Nevers, 50% Alliers) oak barriques; 40% malolactic fermentation; 6 months in new oak barriques.
Winemaker: Peter Robertson
Best drinking: 1995–99

Bright, light, green-gold. Soft and spicy bouquet, with a dash of summer milk, mellow fruit and some nutty creaminess that has the ripe fragrance of yeast. Beautifully creamy on the palate, supple and sexy, with flavour and a suave, strokable texture, this is very succulent wine with plenty of heart and a smorgasbord of flavour nuances to complement its feel. Big and cuddly, it hangs around all soft at the end, with a freshness of acidity that prevents it from cloying and promises to keep it delicious for a few more years yet.

1993

13.7% alc/vol; 100% Chardonnay, Mendoza clone; 100%
Hawke's Bay region, Fernhill district; harvested 10 April
1993; 100% barrel fermentation, new French 225-litre
Alliers oak barriques; 75% malolactic fermentation;
6 months in new oak barriques.
Winemaker: Peter Robertson
Best drinking: 1996–2001

A piercing bouquet of intense fruit and oak that is mellow, spicy and fine shows up the fierceness of the fruit which persists throughout this wine. The oak contributes a five spice powder, Oriental dimension that the juicy fruit flavours have not quite come to grips with, although there is a measure of harmony in the vaguely lemony fragrance that pervades the wine. The bits are impressive, but the whole is still just a collection of parts rather than something complete, and the piercing fruit drives right through the middle, dominating the other components.

CHURCH ROAD CHARDONNAY

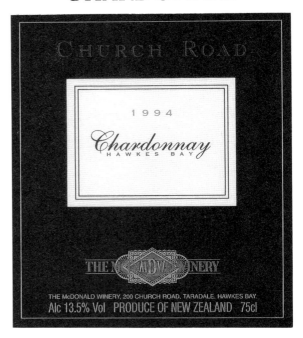

Montana's Church Road winery in Hawke's Bay is a latecomer to New Zealand's fine wine collection, but the Church Road Chardonnay has quickly taken a place among the country's premium Chardonnays with its easy, sophisticated style. Through its well-established Gisborne Chardonnay, Montana has long had a reputation for making honest, fruit-driven Chardonnays that are remarkably good value, and, through nationwide distribution, has introduced many New Zealanders to Chardonnay wine. This label is a logical development of Montana's traditional Chardonnay programme.

1990

12.5 % alc/vol; 100% Chardonnay, various clones;
Hawke's Bay region.
Winemaker: Tony Prichard
Best drinking: 1995–96

Light, green-gold colour, young and fresh. The bouquet is rich, laden with oak and alive with mealy, nutty aromas laced with fruit. The oak again stands out on the palate, giving the wine an assertive, sweet and toasty character, with hints of char and a soft, buttery texture. An easy, attractive style, pleasantly flavoured and slightly rough at the end.

1991

12.5 % alc/vol; 100% Chardonnay, various clones;
Hawke's Bay region.
Winemaker: Tony Prichard
Best drinking: 1995–97

Fresh-looking wine, bright with green and gold hues, it has a fine, limy fragrance shot with toasty oak, hints of butterscotch and marmalade grapefruit. A very creamy, sweet palate that suggests ripe peaches and more butterscotch, now with some toasted coconut, makes this a very appealing, supple wine. Its soft, slick texture enhances the inviting character of those complex flavours, but it is just a little short at the finish. Still, however, full of life and enjoyment.

1992

13.5% alc/vol; 100% Chardonnay, various clones;
Hawke's Bay region.
Winemaker: Tony Prichard
Best drinking: 1995–99

Pretty, lemon-yellow colour. The hints of lime juice, nut kernels and coconut underneath a robe of sweet, hearty oak aromas give interest to the bouquet, leading on to an oaky but very clean, clear palate. Edgy concentration and strength are the features of this quite angular wine, moderated somewhat by sweet oak and some lively grapefruit characters that run deep. Again, just a little on the short side for a wine of top class, but it promises to unleash a fusillade of flavour nuances — oatmeal, butterscotch, toast and marmalade — as it reaches maturity.

1993

13% alc/vol; 100% Chardonnay, various clones;
Hawke's Bay region.
Winemaker: Tony Prichard
Best drinking: 1995–2000

Light lemon-yellow in colour, bright and fresh, but in contrast the bouquet is a cramped concentration of aromas — mostly toasty oak, creamy nuts and oatmeal, with a splash of butter. The palate, too, is intense at first, with fresh, bold fruit that is somehow a blend of ripe grapefruit and lavish tropicals supported by a fine oak texture and flavour. It emerges as a deeply flavoured, neatly structured wine with some real finesse and a sense of luxury. Juicy, succulent and confident, there is enough length of flavour to complement its bouncy nature, its obvious strength, and it should bottle age well for a least five years.

CLOUDY BAY CHARDONNAY

As a partner to the famous Cloudy Bay Sauvignon Blanc, this wine was much heralded when the first vintage, 1986, was released, but the early wines never quite matched the Cloudy Bay reputation, in spite of the careful wine-making lavished on them. In recent years, however, this label has claimed a place among the élite Chardonnays of Marlborough and New Zealand, with a sequence of beautifully crafted, finely tuned wines. This welcome development reflects the time it has taken for wine producers to come to grips with the unique characteristics of Marlborough-grown Chardonnay, a difficulty that nothing but experience can overcome.

1986

13.5% alc/vol; 100% Chardonnay, Mendoza clone; Marlborough region; 100% fermented and aged in new 225-litre French oak barriques.
Winemaker: Kevin Judd
Best drinking: 1995

Bright straw colour, with a slightly canned peas character on the bouquet, just kept in check by some fragrant, luxurious oak aromas. The peas remain right through the palate, again corralled by strong oak flavours, and a pretty core of sweetish, citric fruit. There is plenty of alcohol here, but it tastes disjointed, a bit on the rough side, and altogether too austere and lightly flavoured for a top-class Chardonnay.

1987

13.5% alc/vol; 100% Chardonnay, Mendoza clone; Marlborough region; 100% fermented and aged in new and used 225-litre French oak barriques; a small proportion of malolactic fermentation.
Winemaker: Kevin Judd
Best drinking: 1995

Bright straw colour, with the bottle-aged character of sweet vanilla biscuits, peas and minty nuances on the nose, well covered by oak. A easy, pleasant, fresh-edged, slightly citric wine, again with an abundance of alcohol, but lacking in flavour and mid-palate juice. Awkward.

1988

13.8% alc/vol; 100% Chardonnay, Mendoza clone; Marlborough region; 90% fermented in new and used 225-litre French oak barriques; 10% malolactic fermentation; aged in new and used 225-litre French oak barriques.
Winemaker: Kevin Judd
Best drinking: 1995–96

The delicate, peasy, sawdust-littered bouquet has a pleasant dash of vanilla and some lime fragrance to give it charm, and the palate is attractively fine-grained, with nuances of ripe hay and touches of lime. Tastes more like fine wine, with neat subtleties of flavour, good length and no alcohol abrasions, but its weight overcomes the fruit, and in the end it is a bit too skinny to be gorgeous.

1989

14.5% alc/vol; 100% Chardonnay, Mendoza clone; Marlborough region; 75% fermented in new and used 225-litre French oak barriques; 25% stainless fermented, including malolactic; aged in new and used 225-litre French oak barriques.
Winemaker: Kevin Judd
Best drinking: 1995–99

Light straw colour, clear and bright, with a bouquet that is all delicate elegance, finely detailed with flavour nuances that have noticeable moments of lime juice, sweet, creaming soda fruit, camembert cheese, clear oak and just a trace of oatmeal. Delicately wrought flavours repeat the impression of elegance, with the palate texture starting soft and sweet and progressing through a sweet, chewy, mealy, warm middle to finish long and warm, and just a trifle hard. Impressive wine, big but never flamboyant, it is delicately wrought from beginning to end, but has a friendly, succulent heart that delivers generosity as well as elegance.

1990

14% alc/vol; 100% Chardonnay, Mendoza clone; Marlborough region; harvested 1–22 April 1990; 60% fermented in used (75%) and new 225-litre French oak barriques; 40% fermented in stainless steel; aged 12 months on yeast lees, and a further 6 months before bottling.
Winemaker: Kevin Judd
Best drinking: 1995–98

Clear, light straw wine that is so bright it almost sparkles. Fine, lime-like bouquet with some appealing spicy oak characters, clean, light and elusively attractive. The sweet fruit palate is also light, but suavely creamy in texture, with a tight acid finish and a collection of fine flavours embedded in its creamy body. This wine is more complete, with fewer diverse parts and a unifying texture that sweeps from beginning to end with a seductive stroke. Very fine, delicately flavoured, warm, poised wine with a lovely range of detail. Top-class winemaking.

1991

14% alc/vol; 100% Chardonnay, Mendoza clone; Marlborough region; harvested 2–11 April 1991; 60% fermented in used (75%) and new 225-litre French oak barriques; 40% fermented in stainless steel, including full malolactic; aged 12 months on yeast lees, and a further 6 months before bottling.

Winemaker: Kevin Judd
Best drinking: 1996–2001

A straw-coloured wine with a proud bouquet strong with oak and sweet, ripe fruit, nicely detailed with yeast fragrances and other sophistications. Excellent fruit weight on the palate, based on a sweet, hearty core that maintains a momentum of fruit flavour and texture right through, helped by a superb supporting cast of oak, yeast, meal and nut characters. This wine is all about balance and proportion, each part supporting the others, with flavour generous enough to constrain the alcohol's worst intentions and still act in harmony with that lovely texture. It is a classic against which other Marlborough Chardonnays could well be measured, a wine of great style and controlled abundance.

1992

14.5% alc/vol; 100% Chardonnay, Mendoza clone; Marlborough region; harvested 2–24 April 1992; 60% fermented in used (80%) and new 225-litre French oak barriques; 40% fermented in stainless steel; 50% malolactic; aged 12 months on yeast lees, and a further 8 months before bottling.
Winemaker: Kevin Judd
Best drinking: 1997–2001

A lifted, sweet fruit and oak bouquet with hints of coconut and limes. Fine but strong-bodied wine of the deep, quiet, handsome type, it is vigorous, with a heart of concentrated fruit and the tension of youth. With suave texture, creaming soda fruit characters and littered with yeast, it is crafted so that it oozes style, and the lingering fragrance of the finish, shot as it is with shadows of sweetness from its wealth of fruit, suggests a glamorous future.

1993

14% alc/vol; 100% Chardonnay, Mendoza clone; Marlborough region; harvested 20 April–6 May 1993; 75% fermented in used (75%) and new 225-litre French oak barriques; 25% fermented in stainless steel; 60% malolactic; aged 12 months on yeast lees, and a further 6 months before bottling.
Winemaker: Kevin Judd
Best drinking: 1998–2003

Fragrant lime blossom bouquet, laced with oak and hints of soft, sweet cheese, it is both delicate and deep. The lime edge trims the palate too, with creamy nut flavours, a beautiful silky texture and a hard-core concentration of creaming soda fruit, glossed here and there by a glaze of soft milkiness. Taut, fresh as morning and lingering crisp, it is a big wine with as yet untouched depths of flavour, the appearance and feel of a thoroughbred, crafted for style.

COLLARDS ROTHESAY CHARDONNAY

Unquestionably one of the élite Chardonnays of New Zealand, this wine has always been an outstanding example of excellent winecraft, from vineyard to winery. It invariably shows off its fruit characters to best advantage, and has consistently displayed a superb balance that is the mark of masterful winemaking.

Early on, there was always a tendency for the simple excellence of the vineyard to put in a solo performance, and the fruit had little obvious support from the winery, but in recent years a greater proportion of winemaker influence has been noticeable, to the immense benefit of the whole wine. This progress has been made without any loss of balance, however, and Collards Chardonnay wines are reliably poised, well-mannered beauties that give their seamless, lithe performances without any evidence of sweat or effort.

1983

13% alc/vol; 100% Chardonnay, Mendoza clone; Rothesay Vineyard, Waimauku district, Auckland region; hand harvested 30 March 1983.
Winemaker: Bruce Collard
Best drinking: 1995–96

Pretty, lemon-gold wine that is charming to look at, and even more charming to smell, its bouquet lavish with subtleties of mellow shortbread, toast, fresh fruit and ripe fruit, even traces of spice, and still full of such lively freshness it seems only half its age. The palate is full to the brim with sweet fruit that is clean and absolutely delicious, showing a wonderfully charming wine that is so lit up with flavour complexities, warm, convivial alcohol and the glossy texture of matured, ripe fruit that it does not seem to need any winemaking sophistications. A chaotic collection of aromas and flavours that somehow create harmonious delight, this wine is still youthful in taste and in spirit, a real treasure from the earliest days of New Zealand Chardonnay.

1984

12.5% alc/vol; 100% Chardonnay, Mendoza clone; Rothesay Vineyard, Waimauku district, Auckland region; hand harvested 26–27 March 1984.
Winemaker: Bruce Collard
Best drinking: 1995–96

Clear, clean gold with rich yellow lights, this is attractive-looking wine. The bouquet has definite toast and broad bean characters in its aromatic gridlock of complexities, and the palate is similarly complex, while still emerging clear and fresh in character. It is nice wine, still young and a bit simple with only its fruit to live off, but its warm, fruit-filled finish is succulent and pretty persuasive, tinged with toasty characters and showing itself in perfect condition. Most enjoyable, and proof, if it is needed, that Chardonnay grown in Auckland can really last the distance.

1985

12.5% alc/vol; 100% Chardonnay, Mendoza clone; Rothesay Vineyard, Waimauku district, Auckland region; hand harvested 10 April 1985.

Winemaker: Bruce Collard
Best drinking: 1995

Yellow, tending towards gold in colour, with an intriguing, light, fresh bouquet of oak and olive aromas amid a range of other subtleties that seem to come from deep within the wine. Lovely sweet fruit on the palate lifts it above its simple, fresh texture, adding succulence and an element of richness in the bottle age warmth that the fruit has gained. The oak is beginning to show through as a slightly austere character, but the fruit is still keeping it at bay. Wholesome wine, still fresh and full of clean living, it is long and easy. Great drinking now.

1986

12% alc/vol; 100% Chardonnay, Mendoza clone; Rothesay Vineyard, Waimauku district, Auckland region; hand harvested 1–2 April 1986.
Winemaker: Bruce Collard
Best drinking: 1995–96

Yellow gold in colour, very pretty. The bouquet is a simple oak and fruit creation that is aging gracefully, with an abundance of fresh toast to keep the fruit sweetness company. Sweet, clean, light and easy on the palate, this wine's charm lies in the fruit and in the subtleties bequeathed by age, subtleties that linger at the finish. Still full of life, it is a very pleasant bottle, nicely made, fresh and comfortable, showing the advantages of high-quality grapes and bottle aging Chardonnay.

1987

13% alc/vol; 100% Chardonnay, Mendoza clone; Rothesay Vineyard, Waimauku district, Auckland region; hand harvested 2 April 1987.
Winemaker: Bruce Collard
Best drinking: 1995–2000

This light, happy gold-coloured wine has a fascinating bouquet that immediately conjures up ideas of wedding cake, concentrated, with the intensity of dried fruit and sweet, slightly almond-tinted icing, all held inside a frame of neat oak and restrained from sweet excess by a slightly abrasive note. Fascinating stuff, kept going by an equally enchanting palate which, in spite of its cleanliness, has a decadent feel to it, with lashings of sweet, concentrated fruit and a background flavour that continues to recall some exotically iced fruitcake

with a garnish of spiced nuts. Again, all is kept in check, this time by elements of oak and a grainy, subtle astringency, but the sweetness remains pervasive, sending fruit shivers down your spine, and leaving the impression of voluptuous beauty with more than a touch of class.

1988

12% alc/vol; 100% Chardonnay, Mendoza clone; Rothesay Vineyard, Waimauku district, Auckland region; machine harvested after hand selection, 25 March 1988.
Winemaker: Bruce Collard
Best drinking: 1995

A pretty, moderately golden wine with an interesting, grainy, aromatic bouquet that is unusually perfumed with orange peel characters among the toast and oak. Fresh, clean, neatly made, but without the fruit weight to carry it through to the end, it finishes dry and lean. A nice drink, with interesting complexities.

1989

13% alc/vol; 100% Chardonnay, Mendoza clone; Rothesay Vineyard, Waimauku district, Auckland region; hand harvested 29–30 March 1989.
Winemaker: Bruce Collard
Best drinking: 1995–2002

Sweet-smelling, with aromas that are reminiscent of a freshly baked orange cake, this plump yellow wine is flush with fruit fragrances and hints of freshly whipped cream. The mellow tones of bottle age can be clearly found in the palate, too, in touches of toast and shortbread that mingle with the sweet patterns of maturing fruit, warm alcohol and gently supporting oak. Like some rare piece of Chippendale furniture, craftsmanship is part of the beauty of this finely wrought wine, combining with a charming, light succulence to make every swallow an invitation to the next mouthful. Warm and very, very persuasive.

1990

13.5% alc/vol; 100% Chardonnay, Mendoza clone; Rothesay Vineyard, Waimauku district, Auckland region; hand harvested 26–28 March 1990.
Winemaker: Bruce Collard
Best drinking: 1995–1999

A perfect yellow colour and a nose full of milky lanoline, sweet fruit and trim, spicy oak introduce a wine that is just beginning to show the shortbread characters of bottle age. Sweet and mellow yet deliciously brisk in the mouth, this is an energetic Chardonnay, layered with abundant sweet fruit and delectable traces of mealiness. Very suave, neatly complex, with a tough departure that is deftly lined with sweet fruit, it comes across like a prince with attitude.

1991

12.5% alc/vol; 100% Chardonnay, predominantly Mendoza clone, some clone 15 and clone 6 at low crop levels; Rothesay Vineyard, Waimauku district, Auckland region; hand harvested 3 and 10–12 April 1991.
Winemaker: Bruce Collard
Best drinking: 1995–2000

Pretty, bright, clear yellow, with an aromatic oak and sweet fruit bouquet that is positively ebullient after the restraint of the later vintages. Still it is gently done, upfront yet clear and beautifully balanced. This is lighter wine with a gently attractive character borne out by soft, sweet, vanilla-embossed flavours that have an air of self-confident prettiness, but with essential prerequisites of well-mannered elegance: tasteful oak, mouth-filling texture and subtle strength. Smart wine.

1992

13.5% alc/vol; 100% Chardonnay, predominantly Mendoza clone, some clone 15 and clone 6 at low crop levels; Rothesay Vineyard, Waimauku district, Auckland region; hand harvested 13–14 April 1992.
Winemaker: Bruce Collard
Best drinking: 1996–2005

Light, attractive yellow wine, bright and clear to look at, it is so precisely balanced and restrained that it smells clear and deceptively easy. In the mouth the fruit flavours immediately take over, welling up from deep within and laced with elegant oak, creamy, nut kernel flavours and distant hints of lemon. Very complex wine, beautifully fused together into a round, suavely juicy mouthful that has the intensity and texture of fine Chardonnay, but manages to hide its true power and depth behind sweet, bouncy fruit that serves as a delicious front for a very serious wine.

1993

14.5% alc/vol; 100% Chardonnay, predominantly Mendoza clone, some clone 15 and clone 6 at low crop levels; Rothesay Vineyard, Waimauku district, Auckland region; hand harvested 13–15 April 1993.
Winemaker: Bruce Collard
Best drinking: 1997–2007

Green-lit, clear, bright wine with clarity the dominant feature of a bouquet that is not aromatic but manages to imply hidden depths of power behind its tracery of fine oak and vaguely sweet, ripe fruit. The palate also has a clear, fresh perspective, carefully precise and with effortless, smooth Rolls-Royce power lurking behind its graceful pirouettes of sweet succulence and oaky spice. In among a smooth, dense, wide-bodied, vinous robe of close-grained flavour can be found promising flickers of limes, oatmeal and a tender creaminess that follows flavour to the very end. This is superb stuff, its sunshine clarity leaving a shimmer and glow on everything.

COOKS WINEMAKERS RESERVE CHARDONNAY

Once one of the most sought-after Chardonnays in the country, this premium Cooks wine has always had a strong oak influence and rather lush, peachy characteristics. Never subtle, it is a friendly, slightly coarse style, delivered with gusto.

1983
CHARDONNAY
13.5% alc/vol; 100% Chardonnay; Gisborne region.
Best drinking: 1995

A perfect gold colour, bright and shiny, this wine has the distinct aroma of canned asparagus dominating its finer, nutty, creamy points. Full and juicy with a lively edge of acid and a long, long, warm finish, it is very jolly, ebullient wine that comes with a froth of softness and delicious matured flavours. Quite delicious, but marred by the jarring nature of its asparagus aroma.

1984
GISBORNE CHARDONNAY
12% alc/vol; 100% Chardonnay; Gisborne region.

A mature-looking wine, bright, mellow gold, with a tender bouquet that holds aromas of toast and old furniture, and more than a dash of asparagus. Supple, butter-soft wine, light and pretty, it is fading away quite quickly, with even the nuances of age disappearing.

1985
PRIVATE BIN HAWKE'S BAY CHARDONNAY
12.2% alc/vol; 100% Chardonnay; Hawke's Bay region.
Best drinking: 1995

A greenish, hay-like colour that looks very young still, an impression also conveyed by the slightly citrus tone to the bouquet, which is light and vaguely creamy. On the palate it is fat and buttery with a chunk of grainy oak well embedded, and some hints of citrus among the peach-like fruit flavours. Finishing a bit short, it feels lighter than its flavours would suggest. A real peaches and cream wine, fresh and positively delightful.

1986
RESERVE HAWKE'S BAY CHARDONNAY
13.2% alc/vol; 100% Chardonnay; Hawke's Bay region.

Deep gold, with a flat, broad nose that has little fragrance or hints of bouquet. Short on flavour other than oak and a vague suggestion of peach-like fruit, this is a dry, mean bottle well past its drink-by date.

1987
11.8% alc/vol; 100% Chardonnay; Hawke's Bay region; aged one year in 225-litre French and American oak.
Best drinking: 1995–96

A tinkle of tiny bubbles in this wine makes it seem very young, but its light gold colour shows its true age. A very toasty bouquet that is big and florid, with lashings of butter and rich-seeming fruit, but the palate is lighter than this grandstanding leads you to believe, although the fine, silky texture makes up somewhat for a lack of warmth. Flavours of citrus and mature, shortbread bottle age are enhanced by a sense of freshness throughout, and a nice feeling of balance that lingers with the finish.

1989

13.5% alc/vol; 100% Chardonnay; Hawke's Bay region; aged one year in 225-litre French and American oak. Best drinking: 1995

Fresh asparagus and canned peas aroma disturb the bouquet, which is solid with oak and has a jolly, fat dimension to it. Feels soft and lumpy and tastes warmly alcoholic, but it dries out to an austere finish with a parting hint of vanilla.

1990

13% alc/vol; 100% Chardonnay; Hawke's Bay region; aged 10 months in 225-litre French and American oak. Best drinking: 1995

Light golden wine, with a delicately fragrant bouquet that has all the sophistication of rolled oats mealiness and a persuasion of sweet butter aroma. Lean on the palate, but measured rather than mean, it has a lime-citrus freshness, warmth and nut kernel richness of flavour, well larded with butterscotch and a trace of vanilla. The palate texture is even, soft and almost smooth in balance with the fresh acid, a feeling that lasts right through the finish and adds to the impression of complexity. Soft in style, this wine has a fresh appeal that makes for very good current drinking.

1991

13% alc/vol; 100% Chardonnay; Hawke's Bay region; fermented in oak for half fermentation; 10 months on lees in 225-litre French and American oak. Best drinking: 1995–97

A very oaky, vanilla and sawdust bouquet that has some deeper fruit and a healthy measure of lime and butter aromas. Very supple, slightly juicy fruit flavours are kept at bay by a furry collar of oak that never allows the softer aspects of the wine through, to the point where the finish is slightly resinous and vanilla flavour almost squeezes the sweet fruit into oblivion. Could respond positively to some more time in bottle.

COOPERS CREEK SWAMP RESERVE CHARDONNAY

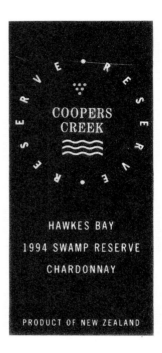

A very hearty, brawny style of Chardonnay made from the best Hawke's Bay grapes available to Coopers Creek each year. A regular award winner in competitions, it is made with the intention of buyers giving it some bottle age to soften out its somewhat hairy-chested youthful nature.

1986
HAWKE'S BAY SWAMP ROAD CHARDONNAY

13.3% alc/vol; 100% Chardonnay; Hawke's Bay region.

Light, golden colour, but an unfortunate sulphur character on both bouquet and palate detract from the potential pleasure in this wine.

1987

HAWKE'S BAY SWAMP ROAD CHARDONNAY

13% alc/vol; 100% Chardonnay.
Best drinking: 1995

A bright, yellow-gold tinged with green, this is a warm, rich wine, with a strange bouquet that is milky and slightly dusty-spicy, but with a fresh air to it. In the mouth it is warm and immediate, a friendly, moderately rich wine with a hearty finish and more of that unusual milky spiciness.

1989

HAWKE'S BAY SWAMP ROAD CHARDONNAY

13.5% alc/vol; 100% Chardonnay; Hawke's Bay region;
100% barrel fermentation; 11 months on lees in French oak; 25% malolactic.
Best drinking: 1995–96

Light, ripe, yellow-green colour, with a whiff of peas on the nose, but wads of oak and butterscotch underneath. A creamy, ripe, rich, mellow wine, with an acid backbone that provides a fresh, lingering finish, it gives the impression of being solid and tasty with more than enough warmth.

1990

13% alc/vol; 100% Chardonnay; Hawke's Bay region.
Best drinking: 1995–97

A good looker in golden yellow, its fresh toasty bouquet shot with yeast, charry oak and lively citrus fruit, completes an attractive introduction. Ripe, just a tad peasy, with a texture that is slightly graining like good chocolate, it comes across as a tough, strong wine, complete with the structural components of acid, astringency and alcohol, matched by a dense collection of flavours. Just becoming creamy around the edges, it should shake down into another generous Chardonnay with fire in its belly.

1992

13.5% alc/vol; 100% Chardonnay; Hawke's Bay region.
Best drinking: 1996–2000

Light, soft, yellow-straw wine with a rich fruit and oak bouquet that wells up softly, ingrained with lime and custard hints and a strong spice of oak. The palate has waves of creamy nuts, rolled oats and oak, in a fresh, vigorous frame of lively fruit with citrus tones, but it calms down somewhat towards the end. A big wine, with softer edges than in past vintages, but with a warm heart to complement its vigour.

CORBANS PRIVATE BIN CHARDONNAY

Regularly a top performer at wine competitions, this wine has strong claims to being the leading Chardonnay from the Marlborough region. Invariably beautifully crafted, it has a winemaking component that is a carefully wrought complement to the fresh but tender creaming soda fruit flavours produced in Marlborough-grown Chardonnay. A fine, elegant style of wine that is never overstated in spite of its significant winemaker contribution.

1984

12.5% alc/vol; 100% Chardonnay; Marlborough region;
harvested 11 April 1984; fermented in new 500-litre French oak; aged in same for 5 months.
Best drinking: 1995–97

Light, polished gold tinged with gentle green, this wine is clear and bright with a rich confectionery bouquet that is mellow with maturity. A blissful bouquet that is at once subtle and strong, with an air of freshness seasoned by some fine fragrances of old oak furniture and sweet, shortbread-like fruit. Together they make a ravishingly beautiful, fine-grained whole that shimmers with lacy aromas. The palate touches, holds, lingers in the sweetly gentle way of great wine, persuading with hints of many flavours in a deep well of softness and clarity that is the heart of Chardonnay fruit. Suave, perfectly silky-light and effortlessly fine, it is certainly superb wine, worthy of its reputation as one of the great New Zealand Chardonnays of the first decade.

1986

13.5% alc/vol; 100% Chardonnay; Marlborough region; harvested 19 April 1986; fermented in new 500-litre French oak, aged in same for 11 months.
Winemaker: Glenn Thomas

This old, subtle wine is a faint recollection of what it was, from its fresh gold colour to the short, whispering finish. It is at best mild and pleasant, but hardly fine Chardonnay .

1987

13.5% alc/vol; 100% Chardonnay; Marlborough region; harvested 3 April 1987; fermented in 225-litre French oak, aged in same one year.
Winemaker: Glenn Thomas
Best drinking: 1995–97

Wine of a mature, golden colour, it retains a green, youthful cast and the nose, too, is fresh and limy, with a suggestion of boiled sweets and splinters of aromatic oak. Very sweet oak on the palate, too, with the fruit and other assorted flavours dashing about out of control, making it seem very young and gawky. The confectionery character reasserts itself at the finish, along with a hearty dash of astringency, making this a most unusual, angular wine.

1988

13.6% alc/vol; 100% Chardonnay; Marlborough region; harvested 4 April 1988; aged 11 months in 225-litre French oak.
Winemaker: Glenn Thomas
Best drinking: 1995–99

Golden green in colour, with fine oak aromas and ripe citrus-like fruit that is just starting to show the mellow tones of bottle age, this is emerging as an elegant, fragrant wine with real depth. The palate is equally fine, again with a fresh clarity of sweetish, ripe citrus flavours and even-handed, fragrant oak that gives the wine a very svelte texture right through its lightly concentrated, complex flavours to the graceful finish. A wine that is the epitome of elegant winemaking, elevating clear fruit flavours into the realms of something very special—poised, beautiful, swift, but with a generous heart that exudes warmth throughout.

1989

13.5% alc/vol; 100% Chardonnay; Marlborough region; harvested 22 March 1989; aged 9 months in 225-litre French oak.
Winemaker: Alan McCorkindale
Best drinking: 1995–97

Fresh, bright wine that is a light, green-gold colour. There is an air of limy freshness about the toasty, coconut bouquet, a characteristic that is also noticeable in the palate, where the lime is more subtle, but the feel of freshness gives this rather warm wine a cool edge. Freshness that is balanced by some mellow, creamy, nutty nuances, but the understated fruit never quite matches the strength of alcohol. Good wine, racy, with its sinews showing through, especially at the finish where there is a touch of almost bitter astringency. Possibly could be improved with more bottle age mellowness.

1990

13% alc/vol; 100% Chardonnay; Marlborough region; harvested 7 April 1990; aged one year in 225-litre French oak.
Winemaker: Alan McCorkindale
Best drinking: 1995

Light, bright, fresh wine lit with green from beginning to end, from colour to palate. Lime and sweet oak on the nose, and a hearty slug of sweetness in the front of the palate. This is refreshed by limy characters, aromas, flavours, a tingle of enthusiasm that keeps the fine oak company and gives an air of frivolity to a very pleasant glassful. Pretty stuff.

1991

13.5% alc/vol; 100% Chardonnay; Marlborough region; harvested 20 March 1991; malolactic fermentation; aged one year in 225-litre French oak.
Winemaker: Alan McCorkindale
Best drinking: 1995–2003

Glossy-looking wine, plump with ripe, light yellow hues touched by a trace of green. Bright, toasty oak aromas and delicate nuances of lime juice, and creamy, nut kernel and rolled oats complexities in a gentle, very attractive bouquet that has the charm of fragrance and the presence of careful craft. Fresh lime juice and fine oak on the palate, this wine tastes very expensive, for it is long and lean, with a kernel of concentration and the silky cream texture of yeasty nuts and meal to counterbalance its lime freshness. Deep, warm and rather crisp, it has appealing shades of flavour throughout, as well as a lingering, graceful finish that marks it as an aristocrat.

1992

14% alc/vol; 100% Chardonnay; Marlborough region; malolactic fermentation; aged one year in 225-litre French oak.
Winemaker: Alan McCorkindale
Best drinking: 1997–2000

Green, light, clear and bright, with an aroma of old milk, fresh linen and spicy oak that is rather unusual. Very hard, appley flavours, with traces of cream and sweet spice, complete a hard, clean wine that is closed tight at present, but does hint at depths which may yet unfold from its sweet heart and expensive trim of oak. Although it feels very powerful, this strength is not matched with suitably rich, energetic flavours; it seems to be expecting a lot to happen with bottle age.

DELEGAT'S PROPRIETORS RESERVE CHARDONNAY

Delegat's were one of the pioneers with strapping, woody Chardonnays back in the early 1980s when John Hancock was their winemaker. They have evolved that style into the carefully crafted, plump, deceptively easy wines that now carry their top Proprietor's Reserve label with distinction.

1986

12.8% alc/vol; 100% Chardonnay, Mendoza clone; Gisborne region; harvested 20 March 1986; 100% tank fermented; aged one year in new and used 500-litre French Nevers oak puncheons.
Winemaker: Brent Marris
Best drinking: 1995

Old, brassy colour, but clear, with honey, orange peel and oodles of toast on the nose. The palate, fading away, is still fresh and clean, but the flavours have lost all their enthusiasm to a gently nutty-toasty shadow. Still pleasant, mildly interesting company.

1987

12.5% alc/vol; 100% Chardonnay, Mendoza clone;
Gisborne region; harvested 1 April 1987; 100% tank
fermented; aged 10 months in new and used 500-litre
French Nevers oak puncheons.
Winemaker: Brent Marris
Best drinking: 1995

Polished golden wine, bright, with a big, mature nose that is well seasoned with mellow, toasty characters and some hints of orange peel. Quite fine, and carefully balanced, retaining an element of palate freshness, it is a light, fragrant style, with the neatly crafted pieces still doing their stuff with fading, but still pretty grace.

1989

HAWKE'S BAY CHARDONNAY

13% alc/vol; 100% Chardonnay, Mendoza clone; Hawke's
Bay region; machine harvested 30 March 1989; 90% tank,
10% barrel fermented in new 225-litre French Nevers oak
barriques; aged 9 months in 50/50, new/used Nevers
barriques.
Winemaker: Brent Marris
Best drinking: 1995–97

Light, shiny gold wine, it has an enchanting bouquet of toasted coconut and orange peel, spiced with aromatic coffee. A plump, sweetly prim wine, freshly scrubbed and carefully measured, it has a stylish, limy detail to its palate, and some delicate, interesting flavours for decoration.

1990

13.1% alc/vol; 100% Chardonnay, Mendoza clone;
Hawke's Bay region, Vicarage Vineyard; machine harvested
8 April 1990; 50% barrel fermented and lees stirred; 10%
malolactic fermentation; aged 9 months in 50/50, new/used
225-litre French Nevers oak barriques.
Winemaker: Brent Marris
Best drinking: 1995–97

Light, flashy gold, very pretty and polished, this is rather beautiful wine. The bouquet, toasted and grapefruity, is given weight by a nice trim of oak and distinct rolled oats characters, which also support the fresh, limy palate with its mellow tones and sweet fruit. Another neatly balanced wine, with a soft, malleable character and pleasant intensity, it feels light for Chardonnay, but that may be a result of its careful balance, for it certainly seems substantial and it has a satisfying collection of flavours right to the end.

1991

13% alc/vol; 100% Chardonnay, Mendoza clone; Hawke's
Bay region, Vicarage Vineyard; machine harvested
28 March 1991; 50% barrel fermented and lees stirred;
10% malolactic fermentation; aged 9 months in 50/50,
new/used 225-litre French Nevers oak barriques.
Winemaker: Brent Marris
Best drinking: 1995–99

A punchy bouquet with strong oak influence, minerals and lime sets this wine up as a virile, intense young thing that is not yet showing any bottle age at all. Limy right from the first sip, its fruit intensity is moderated by some mealiness and a light, creamy texture, but its vigour is still in charge, youthful zest hiding the balance of structural components and the sweetness of Chardonnay fruit. Cleverly wrought, highly promising wine.

1992

13.5% alc/vol; 100% Chardonnay, Mendoza clone;
Hawke's Bay region, Vicarage Vineyard; machine harvested
3 April 1992; 50% barrel fermented and lees stirred; 12%
malolactic fermentation; aged 9 months in 50/50, new/used
225-litre French Nevers oak barriques.
Winemaker: Brent Marris
Best drinking: 1996–2000

Pale, brassy straw colour, bright, with a rich bouquet that has fine oak and a grapefruit note on the nose along with creamy tones and some vanilla-tinged spice. A very supple, easy palate seems initially forward, but the moderately rich flavours and intensity suggest that, given time, there is much more to come. Soft in parts, with clearly buttery influences, and a vague lemon fragrance to the citrus dimension, the wine has an abundance of flavour variety to build on, and that easy balance imparts charm. The best part is its finish, which is long and given a nice furriness with a modicum of astringency. Graceful stuff.

GIESEN RESERVE CHARDONNAY

The Red Curtain by Edward Bullmore

Canterbury
Burnham School Road
CHARDONNAY
RESERVE

Vintage
1990

e 750ml.
12.5%
Vol.

**Produced and bottled by
GIESEN WINE ESTATE, Christchurch
PRODUCT OF NEW ZEALAND**

Initially made to show the best of Canterbury-grown Chardonnay, this wine has steadily built a name for Giesen as reputable Chardonnay makers. Essentially quite racy, the wines have been good, with many winemaking embellishments, and are growing in confidence, but have yet to clearly define a style for the label, especially since the move from Canterbury to Marlborough grapes in 1992 and 1993.

1989

*13.9% alc/vol; 100% Chardonnay, Mendoza clone;
Canterbury region, Burnham district; picked on 20 April
1989; 100% barrel fermentation in new and used French
225-litre barriques; 100% malolactic fermentation;
12 months barrel age; partial lees contact.
Winemaker: Marcel Giesen
Best drinking: 1995–1999*

All the wines in this line-up displayed almost identical, light, polished gold colour. Very creamy, buttery, toasty bouquet, slick and trimmed with lime, coffee and a faint suggestion of oatmeal. A big, sweet, buttery thing, with butterscotch flavours and tough oak right through the palate, it is very much a grandstand wine that lacks subtlety and fruit presence, but does have flavour, length and a lot of vigour.

1990

*12.5% alc/vol; 100% Chardonnay, Mendoza clone;
Canterbury region, Burnham district; picked on 30 April
1990; 100% barrel fermentation in new and used French
225-litre barriques; 100% malolactic fermentation;
12 months barrel age; partial lees contact.
Winemaker: Marcel Giesen
Best drinking: 1995–97*

A plump, richly appointed wine with a buttermilk nose embellished with grainy, vanilla oak. Has pleasant fruit, clear yet subtle, lime-like and quite juicy, with a sweet fruit texture that complements the creaminess of its mellow yeast and butter characteristics. Its pleasant balance between flavour and texture makes it an easy, moderately weighted wine that is attractive drinking.

1991

*13.3% alc/vol; 100% Chardonnay, Mendoza clone;
Canterbury region, Burnham district; picked on 22 April
1991; 100% barrel fermentation in new and used French
225-litre barriques; 100% malolactic fermentation;
12 months barrel age; partial lees contact.
Winemaker: Marcel Giesen
Best drinking: 1996–2001*

Very taut from bouquet to finish, this wine is really starting to show finesse in winemaking and some palate elegance. Lemony, oaky aromas decorate a rather austere, fresh nose, and the initial palate is similarly tight and hard-edged, with a tinge of lemon, but it gradually reveals depth and riper textures, a subtle fruit sweetness and impressive length, all of which suggest that time will reveal some fine flavours and subtle, open fragrances. Offering more promise than performance, it feels better than it tastes at present.

1992

*13.6% alc/vol; 100% Chardonnay, Mendoza clone;
Marlborough region; 100% barrel fermentation in new and
used French 225-litre barriques; 100% malolactic
fermentation; 12 months barrel age; partial lees contact.
Winemaker: Marcel Giesen
Best drinking: 1996–2002*

A toasty banana and oak bouquet, with a sprinkling of delicate milkiness, introduces this beautifully textured wine with a cream custard feel, the vigour of freshness and warm alcohol, and long delicate flavours that are based on pineapple-like fruit. It is close-grained, slick, with a reservoir of energy within it that almost makes it shimmer, a feature which is nicely counterpoised by the deft texture.

1993

13% alc/vol; 100% Chardonnay, Mendoza clone and clone UCD 5; Marlborough region; 100% barrel fermentation in new and used French 225-litre barriques; 100% malolactic fermentation; 12 months barrel age; partial lees contact.
Winemaker: Marcel Giesen
Best drinking: 1997–2005

Strangely fragrant wine, with a silvery dimension and a zesty, lemonish sort of nose decorated with a trace of fragrant oak that hints at aromatic Oriental spices. Quick, fresh feeling with depth of flavour but no juicy heart, although it does have intensity and serious length. Built up with a careful measure of creamy, nut kernel and oatmeal yeast character for richness, and some mellowing butter nuances, this is a finely crafted but highly strung wine.

GROVE MILL LANSDOWNE CHARDONNAY

Lansdowne Chardonnay arrived with a flourish, winning gold medals and trophies at major wine competitions with the very first, 1989, vintage. Thankfully, winemaker David Pearce was not seduced by the prizes, and has steadily refined the initial big, oaky style to a less overt but still boisterous Chardonnay that is infinitely more sophisticated but still bold enough to divide drinkers into love it or hate it camps.

1989

13.5% alc/vol; 100% Chardonnay, 100% Mendoza clone; 80% Gisborne region, 20% Marlborough region; 100% barrel fermented in 225-litre new oak barriques, 40% American oak, 60% French oak; aged 6 months in oak.
Winemaker: David Pearce
Best drinking: 1995–97

Light, palish gold colour, and a big, aromatic bouquet that is chock-full of oak, lean and dry with shades of butter, toast and vanilla for interest, remarkably like the smell of a drawer in a piece of old oak furniture. Resinous, and coarse with alcohol, it lacks fruit flavour and sensuality. Short, unusually oily and aggressive.

1990

13.5% alc/vol; 100% Chardonnay, 100% Mendoza clone; Marlborough region; 100% barrel fermented in 225-litre new oak barriques, 20% American oak, 80% French oak; aged 10 months in oak, on yeast lees.
Winemaker: David Pearce
Best drinking: 1996–99

Light gold, with a honeyed nose and abundant but finer oak aromas. This wine also has an abrasive tone to it, but it is lighter, more aromatic, and the softening influence of creamy nuts and butter is more apparent on the nose and in its softer texture. Although its citrus, lemon-lime flavours give the impression of lightness, it is still big wine, with a nice touch of nutty creaminess, and it swaggers beneath its coat of oak like a slick dealer in an Italian suit.

1991

*13.5% alc/vol; 100% Chardonnay, 50% Mendoza, 50%
clone RUA1; Marlborough region; 100% barrel fermented
in 225-litre French new oak barriques; 25% full solids
fermentation; aged 10 months in oak on yeast lees.*
Winemaker: David Pearce
Best drinking: 1996–2005

Light gilded wine that has a bouquet of fine oak aromas
laced with lime blossom and milky softness, which has
a most appealing and pleasing ripeness, imparting an
easy buoyancy to the otherwise fresh-edged fragrances.
In this wine the oak presence is beautifully matched
by the sweetness of ripe fruit, a sort of creaming soda
character that is delicious but not precisely fruity.
Blended with the creamy nuttiness of yeast, it feels and
tastes wonderful, making the whole more mellow,
richer, deeper and infinitely more interesting. The
finish shows off the structure as it should, with acid
and alcohol showing through, keeping the flavours
hanging on. A big, beautiful, hearty character of a
wine.

1992

*13.5% alc/vol; 100% Chardonnay, 100% clone RUA1;
Marlborough region; 100% barrel fermented in 225-litre
oak barriques, 25% used; 40% full solids fermentation; 10%
American oak, 90% French oak; aged 10 months in oak
on yeast lees.*
Winemaker: David Pearce
Best drinking: 1996–2000

Light golden wine with a limy nose that is decorated
to the edges with a tracery of oak and a yeasty-creamy
background note. At its heart there is concentration
of fruit flavour, lime and creaming soda, as well as
sweetness and a vanilla-charged banana custard
character that has flavour as well as texture. The feel
and flavour seem to concentrate around the middle
of the wine, giving it a rather clipped, orderly air,
suggesting a lithe rather than a boisterous future.

HUNTER'S CHARDONNAY

Hunter's was the first producer regularly to
meet the challenge of Marlborough-grown
Chardonnay fruit with suitably sophisticated
winemaking, and so produce high-class
Chardonnays that were worthy of the region's
rapidly created reputation as a winegrowing
region of international standing. Early on
Hunter's achieved wine that had the sweetness
of ripe fruit as well as generosity of flavour and
texture to match the fresh acidity and austere
inclinations of Marlborough Chardonnay.
They were the first to match coolness with
warmth, and this tempting winecraft paradox
remains the basis of Hunter's style.

1986

*13.5% alc/vol; 100% Chardonnay, Mendoza clone;
Marlborough region; fermented 8 weeks, partly in oak,
partly in stainless; aged in new 225-litre French oak
barriques for 5 months.
Winemaker: John Belsham
Best drinking: 1995–96*

Ripe, glossy, yellow-gold wine, with a light bouquet that suggests cachous, and savoury as well as herbaceous characters in the wings. The palate is notable for its sweet, creaming soda fruit and slightly glossy texture. All this is disturbed by a disruptive little kernel of herbaceousness that is related to fresh beans, and a slightly bad-mannered finish that slinks off without saying where it is going. Still, that fruit centre is lovely, and the wine still has plenty of heart and the required portion of oak.

1987

*13.5% alc/vol; 100% Chardonnay, Mendoza clone;
Marlborough region; harvested 11 April 1987; fermented
70% in stainless, 30% in oak; aged in new and year-old
225-litre French oak barriques.
Winemaker: John Belsham
Best drinking: 1995–97*

Pretty and yellow, with a hint of ripe straw about it, this wine is almost as pleasant to look at as it is to drink. However, the savoury, sweet bouquet and easy, fresh palate just have the edge for charm. These fine textured succulent flavours, a whiff or two of old oak drawers and a fresh, zingy finish that leaves you looking for another sip, win the day for the taste buds. Gracious, charming wine that is built on style in the way of old aristocrats.

1988

*13.5% alc/vol; 100% Chardonnay, Mendoza clone;
Marlborough region; harvested 21 April 1988; aged in new
and year-old 225-litre French oak barriques for 6 months.
Winemaker: John Belsham
Best drinking: 1995–99*

Quiet, almost sullen on the nose, this wine has a lightish, pale gold colour, tinged with green, and an overall air of freshness. In spite of the reticent bouquet, the lemon-lime flavours fair leap down your throat, washed by a wave of sweet, creaming soda fruit, with oak kicking in very nicely at the end, helped by a gentle squeeze of furriness that somewhat elevates the level of sophistication. There is some bottle maturity emerging in various places, but this wine is very much a river of fruit, with oak and age as mere seasoning. Quite delicious.

1989

*13% alc/vol; 100% Chardonnay, Mendoza clone;
Marlborough region; harvested 29 March 1989; partially
barrel fermented; partial malolactic fermentation; aged in
new and year-old 225-litre French oak barriques for
8 months.
Winemaker: John Belsham
Best drinking: 1995–2000*

Light, greenish gold. Aromatic, fragrant toasty-creamy nut kernels and hay create the bouquet, with the help of an oak drawer or two. There is neat tension throughout the palate, between fresh liveliness and a heart of sweet, creamy, concentrated fruit that is layered with grainy oak. Each is supported, respectively, by lime and other citrus characters, slightly furry astringency, and by oak and silky texture. Grand wine, intriguing to drink, surprisingly full, yet light.

1990

*13% alc/vol; 100% Chardonnay, Mendoza clone;
Marlborough region; harvested 21 April 1990; partially
barrel fermented; partial malolactic fermentation; aged in
new and year-old 225-litre French oak barriques.
Winemaker: John Belsham
Best drinking: 1995–96*

A lime cordial and oatmeal nose introduces this light, greenish gold wine that has a strain of limy intensity running through it, and a sweet fruit presence. Tidy wine with lovely fruit and a long, dry finish, it makes attractive, happy drinking to the point that you could miss its finer attributes of careful balance, depth and a lingering finish. Light, but no lightweight, it is fine and succulent, a sensualist's delight.

1991

*13.5% alc/vol; 100% Chardonnay, Mendoza clone;
Marlborough region; harvested 7 April 1991; partially
barrel fermented; partial malolactic fermentation; aged in
new and year-old 225-litre French oak barriques.
Winemaker: Gary Duke
Best drinking: 1995–2005*

Light green-gold with touches of straw, this wine is as pretty to look at as it is to smell, with a bouquet that is juicy with fruit fragrance, a lively sweetness that is modulated by some spicy oak, savoury touches and a background of mealy, nut kernel richness. The palate is immediately marked by a fine intensity and a lovely, creamy texture perfectly dovetailed with the grain of oak, sweet lime juice, warmth and quiet power, a complexity that it accomplishes with ease and elegance. This wine is all class, from that first moment to the last touch of a suitably furry, strongly flavoured, lingering finish. It is fine and clear like a Debussy piano piece, with gorgeous embellishments, a style that perfectly harmonises coolness with warmth. Certainly one of the great New Zealand Chardonnays of this decade.

1992

13% alc/vol; 100% Chardonnay, Mendoza clone;
Marlborough region; harvested 4–22 April 1992;
40% barrel fermented in 225-litre French oak barriques;
10% malolactic fermentation; 40% aged in new and year-
old 225-litre French oak barriques for 8 months.
Winemaker: Gary Duke
Best drinking: 1996–2005

Light, green-straw in colour with a creamy, buttery, mealy, oaky nose and the aroma of concentrated, limy fruit. A neat, creamy texture, with some sweet fruit, but it is fiercely crisp, piercing, its oak and mealy touches just suggestions against the race of fruit and acid. Smartly made, but short on soul.

1993

13% alc/vol; 100% Chardonnay, Mendoza clone;
Marlborough region; harvested 4–12 May 1993; 45%
barrel fermented in 225-litre French oak barriques; 15%
malolactic fermentation; aged in new and year-old 225-litre
French oak barriques for 8 months.
Winemaker: Gary Duke
Best drinking: 1996–2003

Light, green-straw with a limy, creamy bouquet complemented by a neat layer of oak and fragrant spice. Pretty, lighter wine, with sweet fruit, a nice texture and some concentrated lime juice flavours, it finishes brisk and clear and vigorously youthful.

KUMEU RIVER CHARDONNAY

Michael Brajkovich caused quite a controversy among the New Zealand wine community with the launch of his first Kumeu River Chardonnay in 1986, because it deviated so much from the reductive, clean, fruit-based styles that were then the norm. The wine was criticised for being 'over the top' in its collection of winery-introduced characters gained from wild yeasts, barrel fermentation, full malolactic and other non-intervention techniques.

It was claimed to be, among other things, short-lived, dirty, unrecognisable as Chardonnay, and heavy-handed, but wine drinkers around the world disagreed, and instead found great complexity, subtlety and sophistication in the wine, which has subsequently become one of the country's most illustrious. It has also set an example to other Chardonnay makers as a viable alternative to those simple oak and fruit techniques that dominated winemaking here until the mid-1980s.

1985

12.5% alc/vol; 100% Chardonnay, Mendoza clone only; Kumeu/Huapai district, north-west Auckland; hand picked 20 March 1985, 100% barrel fermented in new 500-litre French oak; 100% malolactic fermentation; aged in 225-litre French oak, 9–10 months.
Winemaker: Michael Brajkovich
Best drinking: 1995–97

Light, freshly polished, golden colour with no hint of brown at all. What an inviting wine, sending out a clear, lilting bouquet that is ripe, richly mellow, with a tang of soft cheese and oak, and delicate traces of subtle, fig-like fruit fragrance in among orange peel and hints of honey. Wonderfully intricate and almost floral, it leads on to a wine that is every bit as complex, mature and poised. Cascades of subtlety reveal marmalade, toast, nuts, oatmeal and other nuances, embedded in a lightly creamy, supple whole that is as golden in nature as it is in colour. Quietly strong, it retains supporting freshness and warmth, excellent depth and length, leaving a memory of great delicacy and effortless charm.

1986

12.5% alc/vol; 100% Chardonnay, Mendoza clone only; Kumeu/Huapai district, north-west Auckland; 100% barrel fermented in new 500-litre French oak; 100% malolactic fermentation; aged in 225-litre French oak, 9–10 months.
Winemaker: Michael Brajkovich
Best drinking: 1995

Brightly golden with a yellow hue, this wine has a pungent aroma that suggests ripe camembert, bold oak and sun-sweet figs, all mixed into a body of oatmeal. Solid wine, fat and chunky with more than a touch of marmalade, some toasty flavour aspects and an underlying toughness. Ends soft and a little short, with a flush of fruit flavour, nicely matured and ripe, attractively layered with toastiness, but showing paradoxical lightness for a wine that seems so sturdy at the beginning.

1987

13% alc/vol; 100% Chardonnay, Mendoza clone only; Kumeu/Huapai district, north-west Auckland; hand picked 25–30 March 1987, 100% barrel fermented in new 225-litre French oak; 100% malolactic fermentation; aged in 225-litre French oak, 9–10 months.
Winemaker: Michael Brajkovich
Best drinking: 1995–97

A burnished, golden wine, its energetic bouquet alive with toasty oak, orange peel, honey and a fatness of buttery, fig-like fruit. Bold, strong stuff, broad and generous in character, with a liqueur-like intensity and viscosity, but never lacking in the subtleties that fine wine drinkers seek, nor the depth that gives substance to such a brave wine style. As well as its warmth and soft bounty, this wine has an intriguing edge of freshness throughout, a freshness that keeps it lively while it balances those mellow tones provided by bottle age, a freshness that lingers with the remains of toast and fruit, on to a long, long finish. Outstanding wine of the highest quality, with a fine sense of style and luxury.

1989

13% alc/vol; 100% Chardonnay, Mendoza clone only; Kumeu/Huapai district, north-west Auckland; hand picked 6–22 March 1989, 100% barrel fermented in new 225-litre French oak; 100% malolactic fermentation; aged in 225-litre French oak, 9–10 months.
Winemaker: Michael Brajkovich
Best drinking: 1995–2001

Polished, bright wine, alive with lemon-gold colour, but the bouquet is less forthcoming, although it has impressive timbre of richness and substance. Hints of camembert and grapefruit push through, and there is fine, ever present oak from the first whiff to the last lingering whispers of flavour. Immediately mouth-filling, although never overt, this wine is a deep, silent type, with superb texture, simultaneously soft and tense, creamy and fresh, spiced with that toasty oak to a long, harmonious finish. A most impressive thoroughbred that is not yet ready to race, but should be spectacular when it does.

1990

12% alc/vol; 100% Chardonnay, Mendoza clone only; Kumeu/Huapai district, north-west Auckland; hand picked 19–22 March 1990, 100% barrel fermented in new 225-litre French oak; 100% malolactic fermentation; aged in 225-litre French oak, 9–10 months.
Winemaker: Michael Brajkovich
Best drinking: 1995–99

Pretty, yellow-gold wine that is deliciously fragrant,

supple and satisfying. The bouquet is an enticing potpourri of toast and marmalade, warm and soft with butter, laced with sleek oak to impress. It tastes as quick, as juicy and delicious as it smells, with a bright network of flavours, combining lively fruit, oak, creamy nuts and butterscotch, that hangs on until it passes away with a sigh at the end of a graceful finish. Lovely wine, complex and deceptively easy.

1991

12.5% alc/vol; 100% Chardonnay, Mendoza clone only; Kumeu/Huapai district, north-west Auckland; hand picked 14 March–15 April 1991, 100% barrel fermented in new 225-litre French oak; 100% malolactic fermentation; aged in 225-litre French oak, 9–10 months.
Winemaker: Michael Brajkovich
Best drinking: 1995–2002

A light, golden straw colour with lemon highlights. From the beginning this is impressive wine, solid at first as it is just evolving for itself a bouquet from aromas of camembert, yeasty oatmeal and a healthy chunk of sweet, dense oak. The flavour, too, has a solid dimension, a density of finely textured and flavoured oak, creamy, nut kernel, yeast flavours, and the rich fruit presence of ripe figs. It also has a slight mineral tang to it, and a freshness without apparent acidity that grows with warmth to finish on a vigorous, clear note which complements gracefully long, persistent flavours and the glossy, suave texture that binds the whole wine together. In total it exudes an air of sensual balance, an elegant, expectant poise that waits on bottle age to reveal itself fully.

1992

13% alc/vol; 100% Chardonnay, Mendoza clone only; Kumeu/Huapai district, north-west Auckland; hand picked 25 March–7 April 1992, 100% barrel fermented in new 225-litre French oak; 100% malolactic fermentation; aged in 225-litre French oak, 9–10 months.
Winemaker: Michael Brajkovich
Best drinking: 1996–2004

Clear and fresh, with a light straw colour just hinting at gold, this wine is pretty to look at, but then becomes an example of power rather than delicacy. From the bouquet to the long, intense finish the impression is of sublime power and abundance, but restrained within carefully defined boundaries. It smells of spicy, toasty oak, fresh figs and creamy porridge, leading to a

mouthful that gives an immediate impression of intense fruit flavour, figs and melons, clear, deep, forceful, which are in turn invaded by a mealy vinosity and sweet, camembert character that add interest and balance. As the flavours linger they appear to build up a galaxy of various nuances, massed points of taste that glitter against a body of creamy richness and warmth, keeping the wine alive well after the last swallow. Superb Chardonnay that seems to combine the best of pure fruit flavour and the complex manipulations of winemaking, it should prove to be a classic and, with bottle age, will grow in character almost as much as its reputation will.

1993

13% alc/vol; 100% Chardonnay, Mendoza clone only; Kumeu/Huapai district, north-west Auckland; harvested 22 March–15 April 1993; 100% barrel fermented in new 225-litre French oak; 100% malolactic fermentation; aged in 225-litre French oak, 9–10 months.
Winemaker: Michael Brajkovich
Best drinking: 1997–2005

Clear and bright, the colour of ripe straw, this wine has fruity aromas of figs and babacos that have a fragrant, Oriental spice twist which is youthful and intriguing. Rich with tropical fruit flavours that evoke loquats, melons and other jungle identities, it has a lush, creamy heart with a frame of intensity and some familiar almond and oatmeal characters wafting about. Deep, clean, long and extremely young, it is an impressive wine that offers considerable pleasure even in its angular, slightly abrasive youth, but the future holds much more. With time—years rather than months—this should become another superbly complex, poised wine with the soft clarity of its forebears.

MARTINBOROUGH VINEYARD CHARDONNAY

Martinborough Vineyard has been the flag waver for Martinborough-grown Pinot Noir wines since winemaker Larry McKenna joined the company, and his track record with Chardonnay has been no less spectacular, although in this field he has had more competition from wine grown in other regions. These must be seen as the white wine equivalents of Martinborough Vineyard Pinot Noir, complex, superbly shaped wines based as much on sophisticated winemaking as on high-quality fruit. They make a major contribution to this tiny company's reputation as one of the class acts of New Zealand winemaking.

1984

13% alc/vol; 100% Chardonnay; Martinborough district, Wairarapa region; hand harvested 15 April 1984. Winemaker: Russell Schultz

Light, greenish gold, it looks surprisingly young for a 10-year-old wine. Its musty, dusty, funny oak nose does not appear promising, but although the wine is rather coarse and clumsy, it is fresh enough and there are some rather good fruit flavours in there, and a quite soft, silvery texture. An interesting drink, in context.

1985

12% alc/vol; 100% Chardonnay; Martinborough district, Wairarapa region; hand harvested 27 March 1985. Winemaker: Larry McKenna

Lightish gold with just a trace of brown, this wine is lightly oxidised, vaguely toasty, soft and flat. Nice bones of once delicious Chardonnay fruit still show through.

1986

13.3% alc/vol; 100% Chardonnay; Martinborough district, Wairarapa region; hand harvested 18 April 1986. Winemaker: Larry McKenna Best drinking: 1995

Light, bright gold, with a herbaceous nose reminiscent of canned peas that overpowers everything else the bouquet may have had to offer. Sweet and limy on the palate, with a twist of herbaceousness, easy strength and a long, citrus-tanged finish, it is much better than the nose implies, with some very attractive flavour complexities and big character. Fresh and clean, quite mellow for all its lively acidity, it lingers well but the finish is not quite sure. Interesting, but not persuasively fine.

1987

12.2% alc/vol; 100% Chardonnay; Martinborough district, Wairarapa region; hand harvested 5 April 1987. Winemaker: Larry McKenna Best drinking: 1995

Pretty wine, clear, golden, with a big, soft bouquet aromatic with toasty bottle age and the lingering fragrance of honey. The intense, very fresh impression of concentrated lime flavour is striking on the palate, and it has a lovely feel of freshness and suave, vinous textures that are imprecise but vaguely mellow, complementary to its zest, but not quite keeping it in balance. The oak is a little clunky, not entirely integrated, but this is still a very refreshing bottle of wine.

1988

14% alc/vol; 100% Chardonnay; Martinborough district, Wairarapa region; hand harvested 5 April 1988.
Winemaker: Larry McKenna
Best drinking: 1995–97

A richly complex, fascinating wine, from its polished, light gold colour to its last, lingering flavours, it seemed at its perfect best for this tasting. The bouquet is delightful, complex and fragrant, heavy with the aroma of toast and hazelnuts, a dab of concentrated lime juice standing out from the myriad other smells. The palate, too, is a wonderful harmony of taste and texture, nut kernel cream and silky butterscotch, seasoned with, among a dozen other delicacies, mildly spicy oak and a hint of camembert cheese. Delicately lively, its heart is sweetish fruit, lightly intense so that it is focused but does not overpower the other features of the palate, and the wine flowers in the glass like a genuine bouquet of fragrances and flavour subtleties. A gorgeous, intricate thing of great subtlety.

1989

14% alc/vol; 100% Chardonnay; Martinborough district, Wairarapa region; hand harvested 13 March 1989.
Winemaker: Larry McKenna
Best drinking: 1995–96

Wine that is a light yellow-gold, tinged green, it has an inviting bouquet of fresh oak underlaid by lime-concentrated fruit, and supported by nut kernel creaminess with just a whiff of alcohol and smoky char. Soft, supple wine, with a juicy soul of grapefruit flavour and warmed up by its hearty charge of alcohol. Sweet from the middle to its mildly astringent, grapefruit-like end, it is big wine, not fierce but proud of its strength, and with almost enough fruit to match it. Something of a doughnut, rather soft in the middle, but a very pleasurable bottle in spite of this.

1990

12.5% alc/vol; 100% Chardonnay; Martinborough district, Wairarapa region; hand harvested 26 March 1990.
Winemaker: Larry McKenna
Best drinking: 1995–96

A rather mellow wine after the previous two, but its light yellow-gold colour and toasty, quietly fragrant bouquet are very pleasant, the latter in spite of its dab of canned peas. Sweet fruit on the palate, with a limy intensity and a fresh but charmingly soft middle, it finishes light and clean, with a neat twist of astringency to give it carry, making it a most attractive bottle, neatly fashioned to best effect.

1991

14% alc/vol; 100% Chardonnay; Martinborough district, Wairarapa region; hand harvested 10 April 1991.
Winemaker: Larry McKenna
Best drinking: 1995–99

This is a lovely wine, fine and gentle, but not weak, its strength in its even pace, depth and power. The colour is light greenish gold, and the bouquet has just a touch of sweet ripeness about it that gives its lime-edged fragrance and spicy, creamy, oak and yeast aromas a patina of warmth. In the mouth it is a cascade of sweet fruit, creamy textures and cleverly layered flavour complexities that swirl on through a wine which is lively, fresh and ripe with alcohol. A big wine with years of life before it, it is tense but balanced, with all the subtleties you could expect of such young wine, but held in reserve so that it feels understated rather than bold. A very classy wine that feels elegant and already tastes superbly poised.

1992

13% alc/vol; 100% Chardonnay; Martinborough district, Wairarapa region; hand harvested 10 April 1992.
Winemaker: Larry McKenna
Best drinking: 1996–99

Pale, golden straw in colour, it has a whey-cream cheese-mozzarella character on the nose, some fragrant citrus notes and a mellowness of spicy oak reminiscent of cognac. Its lime juice fruit intensity is keen, but managed by a strong oak presence on the palate, good length and a seasoning of nutty-cheesy elements. Very young and angular wine, it is fine, and has a core of piercing flavour, but is still rather too lively to be as enjoyable as it could be. Another couple of years of maturity would improve it no end.

1993

13% alc/vol; 100% Chardonnay; Martinborough district, Wairarapa region; hand harvested 24 April 1993.
Winemaker: Larry McKenna
Best drinking: 1996–2001

A light lime-tinged straw colour, this wine also has a lime juice intensity from its first fragrance to the last trace of flavour. Fresh and lively on the nose, with more of those citrus qualities that are quite delicate as fragrance, but the lime juice surges into the palate, with a flush of sweet oak and an undercurrent of mealy, yeasty richness to help balance its crisp acidity. Fresh and extremely young, it has some quite subtle complexities already, good depth and length of flavour and a nice texture of astringency, all of which suggest a candidate for some very profitable bottle aging.

MATUA VALLEY JUDD ESTATE CHARDONNAY

Judd Estate
CHARDONNAY
1994
PRODUCE OF NEW ZEALAND
PRODUCED & BOTTLED BY
MATUA VALLEY WINES LIMITED, WAIKOUKOU ROAD, WAIMAUKU
e750mls 12.0% Vol

Judd Estate Chardonnay has been Matua Valley's flagship white wine for a decade, and although never a big award winner, it has proven that consistency is as valuable an asset to fine wine drinkers as trophy winning. A quietly respected label that has a strong following among local Chardonnay aficionados.

1985

11.5% alc/vol; 100% Chardonnay, Mendoza clone;
Gisborne region.
Winemaker: John Belsham
Best drinking: 1995

Healthy golden colour, bright, clear. A big oily bouquet, alive with the toasty, biscuit-like aromas of bottle age enlivened with a suggestion of fragrant fruit. A lovely tang of intensity in the mouth, pure, clear, like essence of Chardonnay grapes at the heart of the wine, with a delicate waft of lime juice that stays right through to a graceful, soft finish. There are subtleties of oak and toast, even a vague hint of marmalade, all serving to substitute fading beauty for lost vigour. A lovely old charmer that still has a few pleasures left.

1986

12% alc/vol; 100% Chardonnay, Mendoza clone;
Gisborne region.
Winemaker: John Belsham
Best drinking: 1995

A light, fresh golden colour, green enough to front up like something much younger, but the wine itself shows all the benefit of fine, bottle-aged Chardonnay. A beautifully mellow nose, suggestive of all those sweetly mealy things—round wine biscuits, toast, cornmeal—with just a hint of butterscotch for extra interest. The palate is suave, smooth in texture, yet remarkably fresh and juicy, but the lingering kernel of concentrated fruit becomes rather too crisp for the subtle characters at the end, tending to blow away the gentle nuances of age in a draught of freshness. Lovely to drink, and still full of life.

1987

12% alc/vol; 100% Chardonnay, Mendoza clone;
Gisborne region.
Winemaker: Mark Robertson
Best drinking: 1995–97

A jolly, bright, gold wine charged with the aroma of charred oak and a certain plump fruit character. Nice and slick, fat, in the mouth, giving a well-covered feel, and although it does have the sweetness of fruit it lacks any specific fruit-like flavours. Very bright and fresh in character, with a certain citric intensity that appears remarkably youthful, but showing enough bottle age toastiness to suggest that complexity and subtlety are slowly emerging. A nice long finish reinforces this view, and this could turn out to be a very long-lived wine that is currently going through an in between stage.

1989

11.8% alc/vol; 100% Chardonnay, Mendoza clone;
Gisborne region.
Winemaker: Mark Robertson
Best drinking: 1995–99

Golden in the glass, this wine looks, smells and tastes ripe, with aromas of marmalade and mellow toastiness, lush, mouth-watering flavours and a virile, poised feel that lingers on in the delightfully persistent finish. Overtly a marmalade and toast wine, it also has an impressive complexity of flavours and nuances, easy balance and a counterpoint of fresh and creamy textures that make for very special drinking. Neither florid nor too powerful, it is a finely textured, graceful wine that promises to last at least another three years in its present sparkling form.

1991

12% alc/vol; 100% Chardonnay, Mendoza clone;
Gisborne region.
Winemaker: Mark Robertson
Best drinking: 1995–98

An attractive, yellow-gold colour, this wine has a fragrant bouquet that is toasty and vaguely sweet, with suitable suggestions of oak and fruit. Beautifully fresh and juicy to taste, there are hints of tropical fruit salad, babaco and such like that build up throughout until the finish is alive with exotic flavours and lingering fragrances. A bouncy, creamy-textured, delicious wine that has a strong heart of alcohol and the sense of poise which is the mark of elegance. All fruit and texture at present, it promises much.

1992

13% alc/vol; 100% Chardonnay, Mendoza clone;
Gisborne region.
Winemaker: Mark Robertson
Best drinking: 1996–2002

Bright, light golden colour. The bouquet is an intriguing meld of vanilla, rich nuttiness and fragrant fruit that suggests a tropical island jungle, with a whiff of charcoal. Although there is a wave of fresh, succulent fruit in the mouth, concentrated, juicy and ripe, it gives the impression of being a light, rather frivolous wine, but the warmth and depth of flavour at the finish and its lingering presence imply that it is merely biding its time, building complexity and bottle age to add to its concentration and already varied collection of flavours. Still very fresh and bright, this is a wine that seems set for the long haul.

1993

12% alc/vol; 100% Chardonnay, Mendoza clone;
Gisborne region.
Winemaker: Mark Robertson
Best drinking: 1996–2000

A yellowish straw colour, clear and fresh. Lemon sorbet and oak aromas characterise the bouquet, which is still quite simple and aromatic. Beautifully creamy in texture, it is fresh and clean, with an abundance of supple, suave flavour that at the moment is simply delicious, but it has all the parts needed for an illustrious career: sweet fruit, fine oak, and a neat balance of structural components such as acid, alcohol and just an interest of astringency.

MORTON ESTATE WHITE LABEL CHARDONNAY

This was originally created as the second of Morton Estate's Chardonnay labels, and although it has always been less rich and had fewer winemaking embellishments than its partner, it has consistently proven to be one of the better New Zealand Chardonnays. A more restrained style, but never austere or thin, it is invariably a sturdy, satisfying wine.

1983

13% alc/vol; 100% Chardonnay, various clones; Gisborne region; tank fermented; aged in 500-litre French oak barrels for 9 months.
Winemaker: John Hancock

Bright, polished, light colour, with a keen, plump, toasty nose and an oily hint and more than a suggestion of canned peas. Clear, clean, fresh to taste, slightly abrasive and spaced out, without much fruit presence and a fresh, light finish. Still clear and bright, with a modicum of bottle age complexity for interest, but past its best.

1985

12.1% alc/vol; 100% Chardonnay, various clones; 90% Hawke's Bay, 10% Gisborne regions; tank fermented; aged in 225-litre French oak barriques for 9–12 months, 30% new oak.

Winemaker: John Hancock
Best drinking: 1995

Very bright, light, brassy-edged gold in colour and a moderately rich bouquet with some toasty aromatics. Clear and pure, with a pleasant freshness and lingering, light, toasty complex of flavours. Pleasant and pretty.

1986

12.3% alc/vol; 100% Chardonnay, various clones; 85% Hawke's Bay, 15% Gisborne regions; 90% tank fermented, 10% barrel fermented in new 225-litre French oak barriques; aged 9–12 months in 225-litre French oak, 30% new.
Winemakers: John Hancock and Steve Bird
Best drinking: 1995

A very pretty bouquet sets up this attractively bright, yellow-gold wine, its fine, lime-like, toasty nuances mellowed by bottle age to a delicate toast and marmalade character that is very appealing. Fresh on the palate, the marmalade characters continue in a wine that is notable for its bell-like clarity. Shortish at the finish, this is an attractive, interesting bottle that is fading, but retains plenty of charm.

1987

12.5% alc/vol; 100% Chardonnay, various clones; 75% Hawke's Bay, 25% Gisborne regions; 85% tank fermented, 15% barrel fermented in new 225-litre French oak barriques; aged 9–12 months in 225-litre French oak, 30% new.
Winemakers: John Hancock and Steve Bird
Best drinking: 1995

Light, bright and yellow with a herbal pungency that is lifted by aromatic toasty characters. Very fresh, citric and light on the palate, it is a lean, racing form of wine that has neat flavour complexity, length and fragrance, but lacks in succulence and warmth. Would still make a pleasurable mealtime companion.

1988

12.5% alc/vol; 100% Chardonnay, various clones; 75% Hawke's Bay, 25% Gisborne regions; 70% tank fermented, 30% barrel fermented in new 225-litre French oak barriques; aged 9–12 months in 225-litre French oak, 50% new.
Winemakers: John Hancock and Steve Bird
Best drinking: 1995

Ripe, golden yellow wine, fresh and very clear to look at, and packed with evocative fragrances that suggest creamy, yeasty, orange-citric flavours, ground hazelnuts and toast. The citrus emerges on the palate as orange peel, and there is more than a hint of honey in this complex but lean wine that finishes rather short. Not a classic, but the complex flavours make it very interesting in spite of its lightness.

1989

12.5% alc/vol; 100% Chardonnay, various clones; 85% Hawke's Bay, 15% Gisborne regions; 70% tank fermented, 30% barrel fermented in new 225-litre French oak barriques; aged 9–12 months in 225-litre French oak, 30% new.
Winemakers: John Hancock and Steve Bird.
Best drinking: 1995–99

Glossy to look at, with a light, bright lemon-yellow colour. Fragrant with a touch of toast, citrus peel, some sweet, vanilla-like oak and an overall character of mellow, creamy, nuttiness, this wine is fine and supple, its warmth balanced by a nice twist of grapefruit citrus character that lingers right through to the long, pleasing finish. Very satisfying wine, with the interesting complexities of bottle age showing up, some hints of yeast and a very fine texture throughout.

1990

13% alc/vol; 100% Chardonnay, various clones; 90% Hawke's Bay, 10% Gisborne regions; 100% barrel fermented in new and old 225-litre French oak barriques, 25–30% new; aged 9–12 months in 225-litre French oak, 30% new.
Winemakers: John Hancock and Steve Bird
Best drinking: 1995–97

Fresh, light lemon-yellow, clear and bright. A fulsome fragrance that is both ripe and fresh at once, seeded with fine oak aromas, a whiff of toast, mealy, yeasty, nut kernel characters and an edge of citrus-grapefruit. Fresh in the mouth, the citrus flavour is plump like ripe grapefruit, fat and sweet with clear, pure flavours. Texture is enlivened by the freshness, and is just creamy enough to soften it a degree to harmonise with the wine's warmth. Good stuff, with lovely flavours and lively character, enhanced by a texture that is just sufficiently smooth.

1991

13.5% alc/vol; 100% Chardonnay, various clones; 100% Hawke's Bay, 90% from Riverview Vineyard; 100% barrel fermented in new and old 225-litre French oak barriques, 25–30% new; aged 9–12 months in 225-litre French oak, 30% new.
Winemakers: John Hancock and Steve Bird
Best drinking: 1995–2001

A light, bright, pale lemon-yellow colour and a creamy, fragrant bouquet give this wine instant appeal. The juicy, ripe-smelling nose is embellished with aromas of vanilla-toast, oak, grapefruit and hints of sweet nut kernels. Lively, plump, juicy wine with a neat texture enhanced by a lovely astringency that seems to run through the middle, completed beautifully by a long, yeasty, oaky finish which signs off with a sweet dash of grapefruit. This is big wine, supported by deep and lengthy flavours and a heart of richness that acts as a balance to its astringency and acid freshness. A long and lovely melody on grapefruit, oak and cream.

1992

13% alc/vol; 100% Chardonnay, various clones; 100% Hawke's Bay, 90% from Riverview Vineyard; 100% barrel fermented in new and old 225-litre French oak barriques, 30% new; 100% malolactic fermentation; aged 9–12 months in 225-litre French oak, 30% new.
Winemakers: John Hancock and Steve Bird
Best drinking: 1996–2002

Light, fresh lemon-yellow with a fine fragrance that is decorated with creamy, mealy tones and the intense aroma of fresh grapefruit. A concentration of fine fruit flavour dominates the palate as well, producing a fierce intensity of freshness seasoned with yeast and toasty oak complexities. Always deeply flavoured, intense and fragrant to the end of its long finish, this is still very young wine with a lot of promise.

1993

12% alc/vol; 100% Chardonnay, various clones; 100% Hawke's Bay, 90% from Riverview Vineyard; 100% barrel fermented in new and old 225-litre French oak barriques, 30% new; 100% malolactic fermentation; aged 9–12 months in 225-litre French oak, 30% new.
Winemakers: John Hancock and Steve Bird
Best drinking: 1995–99

A jolly, polished, light yellow colour and an attractive bouquet introduce this as a lively, pretty wine without the serious dimension of the previous three vintages. Quite grapefruity in character, with buttery notes and a fresh palate, it is light in style, but well crafted to make the best of itself.

MORTON ESTATE BLACK LABEL

The big, flamboyant, oak-hung style that winemaker John Hancock pioneered at Delegat's was continued and refined at Morton Estate in the now famous Black Label Chardonnays. Although they swaggered somewhat in the early years, tending to be clamorous, overt wines, they have carried bottle age well, and have been regularly among the Chardonnay elite in New Zealand. With the arrival of Chardonnay grapes from the company's own Hawke's Bay vineyards in the 1990 vintage, this label has taken on a new dimension of elegance, adding finesse to its character and securing its place among the very best Chardonnay company.

1984

13% alc/vol; 100% Chardonnay, predominantly Mendoza clone; 100% Hawke's Bay region; 100% machine harvested; 100% barrel fermented in new 225-litre French oak barriques; 100% lees aged for 12 months in new French oak barriques.
Winemaker: John Hancock

A light gold colour, bright with yellow lights, and a very toasty, biscuity aroma indicate a wine getting on in years and, although there is an element of freshness about it, it lacks depth and richness to complete a balanced palate. Short, light and toasty, it is now past its best.

1985

13.1% alc/vol; 100% Chardonnay, predominantly Mendoza clone; 100% Hawke's Bay region; 100% machine harvested; 100% barrel fermented in new 225-litre French oak barriques; 100% lees aged for 12 months in new French oak barriques.
Winemaker: John Hancock
Best drinking: 1995–96

Pretty wine, its sweetly florid, fragrant, toasty nose supporting a charming golden colour, and a flavour that is all sweet fruit and vanilla-tinged complexities. There is a lot of ripe, mellow grapefruit flavour here, well matched with toast in abundance and a warm, lingering sawdust and citrus finish that is quite cleansing in character. A jolly good drink, refreshing, with chunky flavours and a fresh counterbalance to its sweetness, this is convivial Chardonnay.

1986

13% alc/vol; 100% Chardonnay, Mendoza clone; 100% Hawke's Bay region; 100% machine harvested; 100% barrel fermented in new 225-litre French oak barriques; 100% lees aged for 12 months in new French oak barriques.
Winemakers: John Hancock and Steve Bird
Best drinking: 1995

Flashing yellow wine, bright and clear with a full, fragrant bouquet that is mellowed by maturity. The palate is tense, fresh, with some bitter grapefruit characters and attractive underlying flavours of ripe fruit. The bitterness tends to coarseness, however, undermining the appeal of fruit and toasty oak and upsetting the finish. A shame because the fruit flavours and depth appear to be very good.

1987

13% alc/vol; 100% Chardonnay, Mendoza clone; 100%
Hawke's Bay region; 100% machine harvested; 100% barrel
fermented in new 225-litre French oak barriques; 100% lees
aged for 12 months in new French oak barriques.
Winemakers: John Hancock and Steve Bird
Best drinking: 1995

Pretty, clear, bright yellow wine, with a mellow, bottle-aged bouquet of delicate fruit fragrances and aromatic, toasty oak that is quite fine and elegant. The fresh, piercing, very long, strong palate is a neat balance between fresh clarity and deep, tangy flavour with a limy edge to it and some nice details of grapefruit and toast. Very fine and tidy, it would be lovely with food, but it lacks a dimension of richness to be a really classy performer.

1989

13% alc/vol; 100% Chardonnay, Mendoza clone; 100%
Hawke's Bay region; 100% machine harvested; 100% barrel
fermented in new 225-litre French oak barriques; 100% lees
aged for 12 months in new French oak barriques.
Winemakers: John Hancock and Steve Bird
Best drinking: 1995–99

Light, clear yellow colour. The nose is very ripe, grapefruity and mealy, larded with toast and sweet nuts in an ebullient but still fine bouquet that is overflowing with warmth. Lovely, expensive-tasting oak keeps company with plump, citrus fruit-ripe grapefruit flavours and wafts of complex fragrances that well up from the depths of plump, juicy fruit. This is a generous, straightforward wine full of oak and sweet, ripe fruit that is given an element of excitement by a bright spine of acidity. A lavish, extravagant thing that offers class, and a good time.

1990
HAWKE'S BAY CHARDONNAY

12.9% alc/vol; 100% Chardonnay, Mendoza clone; 100%
Hawke's Bay region; 100% machine harvested; 100% barrel
fermented in new 225-litre French oak barriques; 100% lees
aged for 12 months in new French oak barriques.
Winemakers: John Hancock and Steve Bird
Best drinking: 1995–2000

Quite fragrant, with characters that suggest grapefruit and short, sweet biscuits, this lemon-yellow wine has a slight oaky abrasiveness on the nose, but its sweet tone

more than compensates. Neatly balanced, with depth, an impressive heart of grapefruit intensity, and a creamy feel to the palate, its tightly knit, complex flavours and warmth are held together within an elegant but generous character that remains right through to the end of the long finish. Comely wine, with an air of softness that adds charm to its obvious class, completed by a final twist of vinosity.

1990
RIVERVIEW CHARDONNAY

12.7% alc/vol; 100% Chardonnay, Mendoza clone; 100%
Hawke's Bay region, Riverview Vineyard; 100% hand
picked; 100% barrel fermented in new 225-litre French oak
barriques; 100% lees aged for 12 months in new French
oak barriques.
Winemakers: John Hancock and Steve Bird
Best drinking: 1995–2000

Richly fragrant with toasty oak and aromatic lime-grapefruit nuances, a bright, straw-coloured wine with tints of yellow that promises a fine mouthful. Round and full on the palate, alive with grapefruit characters and quite bold oak that come across as a juxtaposition of sweetness and astringency that alternate by degrees. This is big wine, almost stroppy, but sweet enough to keep a steady keel, helped by its ever-present astringency and lingering, delicate fruit flavours. Quite scrumptious.

1991
HAWKE'S BAY CHARDONNAY

14% alc/vol; 100% Chardonnay, 80% Mendoza clone,
20% clone UCD6; 100% Hawke's Bay region, Riverview
Vineyard; 100% machine harvested; 100% barrel fermented
in new 225-litre French oak barriques; 100% lees aged for
16 months in new French oak barriques.
Winemakers: John Hancock and Steve Bird
Best drinking: 1995–2005

Light lemon-yellow, bright and clear. The bouquet is simply beautiful, and a fine, graceful harmony of fruit, oak and nuttiness that seems young in its vigour is given a new dimension on maturity by its effortless balance. This balance continues at different levels throughout the wine, generally being a clever amalgamation of sweet and savoury characters, within which are partnerships between oak and fruit flavours, creamy nuts and fresh acid, plump fruit sweetness and dry astringency. It is the epitome of poise, each feature part of a beautifully patterned whole that is finely textured, deep, powerful and rich, the flavours building towards the end rather than fading. In spite of its youthful vigour, it is already developing the detail of extra flavour nuances, which fit perfectly into the harmonious body of the wine, and are never overwhelmed by its overall strength. It is a full-frontal, sensual assault that concerns itself with pleasurable abandon rather than intellectual precision.

1992

13% alc/vol; 100% Chardonnay, 80% Mendoza clone, 20% clone UCD6; 100% Hawke's Bay region, Riverview Vineyard; 100% machine harvested; 100% barrel fermented in new 225-litre French oak barriques; 30% malolactic fermentation; 100% lees aged for 9 months in new French oak barriques.
Winemakers: John Hancock and Steve Bird
Best drinking: 1996–2003

Pretty, light lemon-yellow colour, with a bouquet that is yeasty, fruity and oaky by turns. The fruit clarity on the nose is repeated on the palate, supported by a solid portion of savoury, spicy oak and some buttery characters that meld well with the grapefruit fruit and mealy nuttiness of yeast. Fine, beautifully measured wine that holds a lot of promise in its deep fruit flavours and edge of concentration, carefully as these are seasoned with oak and butter and yeast. A deep, long, freshly resonant wine that should be very accommodating by the end of the decade.

1993

12.5% alc/vol; 100% Chardonnay, 80% Mendoza clone, 20% clone UCD6; 100% Hawke's Bay region, Riverview Vineyard; 100% machine harvested; 100% barrel fermented in new 225-litre French oak barriques; 100% malolactic fermentation; 100% lees aged for 9 months in new French oak barriques.
Winemakers: John Hancock and Steve Bird
Best drinking: 1997–2003

Very pretty-looking wine, bright, light and fresh with suggestions of yellow, and a young, oaky, fruit fresh bouquet against a backdrop of creamy, mealy aromas and a suggestive sniff of camembert-like cheese. Suave in the mouth, with a lot of new, lively oak, it has a succulent, vigorous edge to it although it is light, and finishes with a light sandpapering burr. Not yet harmonious, but it should come together into a very tidy, interesting wine.

NEUDORF MOUTERE CHARDONNAY

From the first vintage, this Nelson-grown Chardonnay has had a warm and elegant heart, onto which winemaker Tim Finn has subsequently crafted a superb display of richly textured winemaking art. The herbaceousness of early vintages has been overcome by intelligent viticulture, and the complex, infinitely sensual wines of the 1990s have given Neudorf Chardonnay a national reputation second to none. In spite of their inherent style and refined, careful shaping, they remain wines of great eloquence and character, speaking clearly of vineyard, craft and the inimitable ripe pleasure of Chardonnay wine.

1986
VINEYARDS CHARDONNAY
13% alc/vol; 100% Chardonnay, Mendoza clone; hand harvested 28 April 1986; 50% barrel fermented in a mix of

used 500-litre puncheons and new 225-litre barriques,
100% French oak.
Winemaker: Tim Finn
Best drinking: 1995–96

Still pretty in its youthful shimmer of lemon-tinted yellow, this wine has a bouquet that is an aromatic mixture of freshly cooked green beans, dust and lemon sorbet which is strangely fine for all its herbaceous overtones. Still beautifully fresh to taste, with rivulets of succulence and fruit sweet flavours among the tang of beans and a passing furry brush of tannin. Toast, too, is beginning to creep into this medley of flavours, and creaminess adds to the texture, making a fresh, complex wine that is friendly, warm and still deliciously inviting, although it is just drying out a bit at the end. The herbaceous characters will have purists screaming, but there is no clumsiness here as the wine has real style, never getting out of balance or being subverted completely by its flavours.

1987

13% alc/vol; 100% Chardonnay, Mendoza clone; hand harvested 15–24 April 1987; 35% barrel fermented in a mix of used 500-litre puncheons and new 225-litre barriques, 100% French oak; small portion malolactic fermentation.
Winemaker: Tim Finn
Best drinking: 1995–97

Light, polished, lemon-yellow colour and a light, savoury oak and mellow peas bouquet that is held by echoes of limes, toast and creamy nut kernels in a very finely textured shape. The palate feels fine and succulent from the very beginning, building to little peaks of sweet, juicy fruit flavours right through, highlights that are laced with the old furniture character of mature oak and interspersed with an elusive flicker of creamy texture and the limy intensity which enhances the impression of freshness. Clear, almost bold, yet delicately intricate, it is a juicy, inviting wine that keeps calling you back for another sip, but it is never more than pretty, lacking the substance to balance its fresh focus.

1988

13% alc/vol; 100% Chardonnay, Mendoza clone; hand harvested, 33% some shrivelled berries, 19 April, 67% 5 May 1988; 100% barrel fermented in a mix of used and new 225-litre barriques, 100% French oak.
Winemaker: Tim Finn
Best drinking: 1995

The fresh, toasty, oak drawer and toffee nose with its mandarin freshness confirms its brassy, light golden copper colour, for this wine is a harder character, with rather brittle flavours in spite of a trace of fruit sweetness in the middle of the palate. Drier and meaner at the finish than earlier vintages, it has a clean living feel but lacks any sense of fun. All freshness and subtle nuances without warmth.

1989

13% alc/vol; 100% Chardonnay, Mendoza clone; hand harvested 17 April 1989; 100% barrel fermented in a mix of used and new 225-litre barriques, 100% French oak; 15% malolactic; lees stirred.
Winemaker: Tim Finn
Best drinking: 1995–2000

This big, succulent wine is a come-on from the first glance at its flashy, light buttery-gold colour, the sniff of succulent fruit and the expensive perfume of oak, and a taste that is dripping with sweet, juicy fruit, stroking with the creamy silk of nuts and exotic dairy luxuries. For aficionados there is grainy, vanilla-tinged oak, frills of orange peel, warmth and the comfort of mellow, mealy flavours, and a measure of astringency to complement the sensuality of it all, but this bold wine never quite allows subtlety to interfere with its sometimes brash appeal to pure hedonism.

1990

13% alc/vol; 100% Chardonnay, Mendoza clone; hand harvested 17 and 26 April 1990; 100% barrel fermented in a mix of used (30%) and new 225-litre barriques, 100% French oak; 15–20% malolactic; lees stirred.
Winemaker: Tim Finn
Best drinking: 1995–2005

From the flickering green of yellow-gold to the whispering sweet elegance of its passing, this wine is the epitome of graceful Chardonnay. Its fine, fragrant nose has many hints of a bouquet inlaid with aromatic jewels: spicy oak, vanilla, hazelnut kernels, oatmeal, delicate crème anglais and a fruit salad of tropical and ripe citrus. Like the equally intricate palate, however, these are never things apart, and must be looked for within the body of the wine, which is a beautifully integrated whole, a sweet, succulent buoyant thing alive with its own gentle warmth and fresh exuberance. Chardonnay Mozart, with trills of creamy detail, sweet harmonies and a lingering melody of faultless clarity that rings on and on, it is quite gorgeous, deftly completed by a perfectly pitched counterpoint of humid astringency to add a balancing tone of strength and firmness. Superbly proportioned and integrated, its youthfulness suggests even more exquisite detail when the subtleties of bottle age are incorporated.

1991

13.5% alc/vol; 100% Chardonnay, Mendoza clone; hand harvested 27 April 1991; whole bunch pressed; 100% barrel fermented in a mix of used (30%) and new 225-litre barriques, 100% French oak; 15–20% malolactic; 10 months in oak on yeast lees.
Winemaker: Tim Finn

Very light, sandy-straw yellow in colour, it looks and smells young, its bouquet still restrained, but extremely deep, with a seamless clarity and tone that is as elegant as it is effortless. It moves between implications of citrus and cream, sweet fruit and savoury spice and nuts, but you are never able absolutely to identify them before your nose is drawn to the next detail. The palate arrives in waves of sweet, succulent, satin-textured fruit, layered with cream, spiced with oak and alcoholic verve. Quite magnificent, it is a work of art, its multifarious parts singing in harmony with an accompaniment that is the texture of perfect crème anglais. Suave, sophisticated, refined, but never cool, its warmth and depth are seemingly endless, and its power of sensual satisfaction is moderated by the juxtaposition of a teaming swarm of abrasive particles. It is the embodiment of intensely pure New Zealand fruit character, lush texture and the sure touch of talented winecraft.

1992

14.5% alc/vol; 100% Chardonnay, Mendoza clone, some from first year crop; hand harvested 2–4 May 1992; whole bunch pressed; 100% barrel fermented in a mix of used (40%) and new 225-litre barriques, 100% French oak; no malolactic; 10 months in oak on yeast lees.
Winemaker: Tim Finn
Best drinking: 1996–2007

Very light, greenish tinted, sandy yellow colour. The nose offers a thrill of sensual promise, with fine, fragrant oak wafting gently across a deep well of fruit and nut kernel creaminess, tinged with lime, vanilla and an ever-present liquid power. Big, sweet, strapping fruit, restrained by a certain cool elegance and oak

formality, but never hiding the effortless Ferrari power that lies at the heart of the wine, fuelling its warmth and vigour while not subverting the succulent fruit and svelte texture that reaches to the end of the very long finish. The abundance of flavour, fruit, meal, cream, oak, spice and nuts threatens to overflow, but never does, offering various character paradoxes — of generosity and reserve, calmness and energy, rich complexity and intense simplicity. Still very young, it does not have the integration or effortless sensuality of 1991, showing a more thrilling surge of animal passion, a rock 'n' roll soul in a finely bred body.

1993

14% alc/vol; 100% Chardonnay, 45% Mendoza, 55% 2/23 clone; hand harvested 14 May 1993; whole bunch pressed; 100% barrel fermented in a mix of used (40%) and new 225-litre barriques, 100% French oak; 25% malolactic; 10 months in oak on yeast lees.
Winemaker: Tim Finn
Best drinking: 1997–2005

Very light, green-tinged and slightly sandy in colour, this wine offers a bouquet that is a fragrant package of limy, cream cheese, nuts and oak characters which smell expensive and promise delicious form, but still show a naive lack of co-ordination. More cream and nuts on the palate, and less energy than the atomic proportioned 1992, but certainly graceful like the harmonious 1991, this wine beggars precise description, other than in comparison with its Neudorf predecessors. Still short on integration, on harmony and consequential finesse, it has a deep well of fruit and a warm, convivial heart poised to give and glow. Exquisitely long, its classy parts are even now running into each other as the integration process proceeds, giving a message of elegance and breeding, and the promise of another spectacular wine in the future.

NGATARAWA ALWYN CHARDONNAY

The top of the range Chardonnay from this prestigious Hawke's Bay producer has never been a high-profile wine, in spite of its meticulous winemaking. Over the years, however, the quality winemaking craft at Ngatarawa has shone through, and this complex, sophisticated, always interesting wine has quietly maintained its presence among the high-quality, satisfying Chardonnay labels.

1987

13% alc/vol; 100% Chardonnay, Mendoza clone; 100% Hawke's Bay, estate grown, Ngatarawa; 100% barrel fermented; yeast lees aged 10–12 months.
Winemaker: Alwyn Corban
Best drinking: 1995–97

Golden, brassy colour, clear and clean. Fresh toast with honey and some traces of oak on the bouquet, which is showing mature, sweet biscuit characters and an echo of guava-like tropical fruit. Carefully balanced wine with great clarity and freshness, it is a little light in the mid-palate, but has a most attractive barrage of flavour nuances and complexities, and finishes with an ethereal cloud of aged delicacies and a slightly furry texture. Fine, clear, keen.

1988

13% alc/vol; 100% Chardonnay, Mendoza clone; 100% Hawke's Bay, estate grown, Ngatarawa; 100% barrel fermented; yeast lees aged 10–12 months.
Winemaker: Alwyn Corban

Deep colour and a rich, orange peel bouquet that is broad and dusty, with hints of honey and a queer, fresh clarity. This freshness is even more obvious on the palate, where the light flavours have a water-like clarity to them, and a collar of dry oak. Light, simple, past its best.

1989

13% alc/vol; 100% Chardonnay, Mendoza clone; 100% Hawke's Bay, estate grown, Ngatarawa; 100% barrel fermented; yeast lees aged 10–12 months.
Winemaker: Alwyn Corban
Best drinking: 1995–2000

Darkish, brassy, golden colour that looks bright, clear and inviting. So, too, is the bouquet, rich with suggestions of biscuits and butterscotch, laced with the warm aroma of toasted rolled oats and larded with chunks of deep, lingering fruit. A wonderful, big wine, aristocratic but earthy enough to be seductive, its inviting warmth evokes impressions of creamy silk, succulent fruit, home baking and other remembered pleasures, the sort of wine you keep returning to because it feels as good as it tastes. Among the simply lovely bits are also twists of texture, slight touches of abrasion or hints of sour milk that provide balance and keep the wine in check, leaving its invitation open. A complex, self-confident classic.

1990

13% alc/vol; 100% Chardonnay, Mendoza clone; 100% Hawke's Bay, estate grown, Ngatarawa; 100% barrel fermented; yeast lees aged 10–12 months.
Winemaker: Alwyn Corban
Best drinking: 1995–98

Lemon-honey yellow and fresh with a graceful, delicate bouquet, this wine is on the boundary of ripe, fresh fruit and the mellow tones of bottle age. Showing a shadow of oak, a touch of lime and traces of milk and ginger biscuits, its parts are disparate but not without charm, and seem on the verge of a certain harmony that will turn them from prettiness to elegance. A gentle, graceful character should become something quite lovely with a bit more time, for it has a fine texture and lingering, flavoury finish that fades into memories of butterscotch.

1991

13% alc/vol; 100% Chardonnay, Mendoza clone; 100% Hawke's Bay, estate grown, Ngatarawa; 100% barrel fermented; yeast lees aged 10–12 months.
Winemaker: Alwyn Corban
Best drinking: 1996–2001

Pretty, light straw colour with a hint of green. The bouquet, fresh and tense, has no overt fruit characters, but there are hints of limes and melons deep inside the sweet-seeming oak and 'winey' aroma. Has a nice feel to it, very even and balanced, with lovely soft flavours and traces of mealiness and dust, but it is rather muddled at the moment, more of a meal than a drink, like Chardonnay porridge in an oak bowl, enlivened with a splash of acidity. There is real depth here, however, and momentum that suggests it is quietly awaiting its time.

1992

13% alc/vol; 100% Chardonnay, Mendoza clone; 100% Hawke's Bay, estate grown, Ngatarawa; 100% barrel fermented; yeast lees aged 10–12 months.
Winemaker: Alwyn Corban
Best drinking: 1996–2003

A bright, clean, straw-gold colour without a hint of green makes this wine look older than it is, but it smells and tastes like a real juvenile. The bouquet is based on piercing, deep fruit aromas, with gobs of butterscotch and a border of fragrant oak. Very quiet to taste, it has a supple feel, but the intense grapefruity fruit hovers in the background, nervy and very fresh. In spite of its freshness, this is not an angular wine, but rather has the tense quality of spring steel, moderated by a vague creaminess and suggestions of nuts. The finish is excellent, long, with lingering grapefruit flavour, warmth and a pleasing twist of grainy austerity.

ROBARD & BUTLER CHARDONNAY

This juicy Chardonnay has been a pillar of the luscious Gisborne style since 1987, since when it has been made exclusively from Gisborne-grown fruit. Its supple style makes it a particularly attractive wine when young, but it usually matches this with a balancing structure that allows its abundant fruit full scope, and the potential to evolve with bottle age.

1986
PRIVATE ESTATE CHARDONNAY

12.5% alc/vol; 100% Chardonnay; Marlborough region; fermented in French Nevers oak puncheons.
Winemaker: Glenn Thomas
Best drinking: 1995

Gold colour, turning brassy, with a very oaky-toasty bouquet. Lean and oaky on the palate, clean, with a strong oak presence throughout and a pleasant, quiet finish. Still holding an edge of freshness, this is simple, mildly attractive, mature wine.

1989
ROBARD & BUTLER GISBORNE CHARDONNAY

13.5% alc/vol; 100% Chardonnay; Gisborne region; 40% fermented in new French 225-litre oak barriques;

*100% malolactic fermentation; aged 9 months on lees
in French barriques.
Winemaker: Simon Waghorn
Best drinking: 1995–98*

Fresh, clean, pure gold colour with a flash of green. Fat, buttery and full of fruit with lashings of oak and butterscotch throughout, and flavour waves of luscious guava and melon fruit that are moderated by the biscuity tones of bottle age. Lingers to a butter and cream finish that is sweet and fresh with some nice savoury nuances and a warm glow. Good wine, straightforward and gay.

1990

*13% alc/vol; 100% Chardonnay; Gisborne region;
73% fermented in new French 225-litre oak barriques;
40% malolactic fermentation; aged 10 months on lees
in French barriques.
Winemaker: Simon Waghorn
Best drinking: 1995–99*

Ripe, gold, glossy wine with a bountiful bouquet, fragrant with toast and the aromas of buttered oak and juicy fruit. Immediately delightful from the first sip, which gushes with the juicy fragrance of tropical fruit flavours, at once delicate and full-bodied like a sun-ripened melon. This is simply delicious wine with all the best features of Chardonnay-making craft woven around a fat fruit core that positively glows with ripe Chardonnay and alcoholic warmth, wine that holds your interest to the very end with its freshness and succulence. Delicious but never frivolous, it is archetypal Gisborne Chardonnay.

1991

*13% alc/vol; 100% Chardonnay; Gisborne region;
fermented in new French and American 225-litre oak
barriques; 80% malolactic fermentation; aged 10 months
on lees in barriques.
Winemaker: Simon Waghorn
Best drinking: 1995–2000*

Light gold colour and a little on the pale side, this is another fruit-centred wine, with an aromatic bouquet dominated by buttery sweet oak, the juicy fruit coming into its own once the wine is in your mouth. The fruit palate has forceful strands of oak and acid running through it and a vague suggestion of lime juice that hangs on to the very end, but is generally supple in a somewhat jangled melange of textural characteristics.

Fruit sweetness is ever present, however, and the angular nature of the wine could be a feature of its youth, and a reason for optimism about its future.

1992

*13% alc/vol; 100% Chardonnay; Gisborne region;
fermented in new French and American 225-litre oak
barriques; 55% malolactic fermentation; aged 10 months
on lees in barriques.
Winemaker: Simon Waghorn
Best drinking: 1995–99*

Pale green-gold wine with fresh, buttery, sweet oak aromas and some very attractive melon-like fruit on the nose. Clean, very fresh, even jolly wine, with an abundance of fruit and enough oak to have you imagining you can feel the grain with your tongue. Supple and creamy in texture, but this is somewhat suppressed by the freshness of citric-acid characters, and the jungly fruit. Not a subtle wine, but warmly vigorous, and alive with fruit-lovers' delights.

STONECROFT MERE ROAD CHARDONNAY

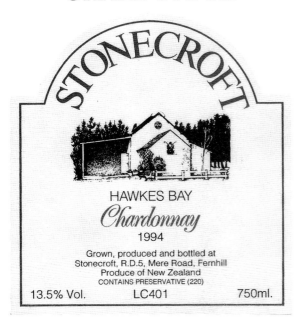

Stonecroft appeared quietly on the winemaking scene at about the time more established wine producers were starting to make a serious effort at producing quality wine. Although this small producer has never quite arrived with a fanfare, not being an entrant in competitions, wine enthusiasts have quickly taken to the Stonecroft label, for it has come to mean reliably honest wines made with passion and an unerring sense of quality. After a solid start in the first two vintages, Stonecroft has now clearly emerged as a real Chardonnay force with a series of high-class performances in wines that are deeply flavoured and vigorous with classic Hawke's Bay style.

1987

12.5% alc/vol; 100% Chardonnay, Mendoza clone; Hawke's Bay region, Gimblett/Mere Road district; hand picked 14 March 1987; tank fermented; aged 8 months in year-old 500-litre French Nevers oak puncheons.
Winemaker: Alan Limmer
Best drinking: 1995–98

Ripe, green-gold colour, still looking fresh and young. The bouquet is full of fragrant, toasty bottle age characters with traces of fresh oak and subtle grapefruit fruit. An attractive palate, given interest by the nuances of bottle age and pleasure by the lovely ripe grapefruit flavours that maintain their presence right through the moderate finish. It still has plenty of vigour and appeal, in spite of the touch of coarse oak that interferes at the end, and should last a few good years yet.

1988

12.5% alc/vol; 100% Chardonnay, Mendoza clone; Hawke's Bay region, Gimblett/Mere Road district; hand picked 5 March 1988; tank fermented; 5% malolactic fermentation; aged one year in 50/50 new/reconditioned 500-litre French Nevers oak puncheons.
Winemaker: Alan Limmer
Best drinking: 1995–96

Light, brassy gold wine, with a mature toasty-oaky bouquet that shows an underlying aroma of fat fruit. Nice citrus-grapefruit flavours, still very sweet at the heart of the wine, giving depth to the pleasant texture and long, delicate, flowery finish. A mature, attractive wine, rather rustic in approach, but very satisfying and not lacking in either flavour or warmth.

1989

13.9% alc/vol; 100% Chardonnay, Mendoza clone; Hawke's Bay region, Gimblett/Mere Road district; hand picked 4 March 1989; tank fermented and transferred to barrels; 15% malolactic fermentation; aged one year in 50/50 new/used 500-litre French Nevers oak puncheons.
Winemaker: Alan Limmer
Best drinking: 1995–2000

The waft of sweet grapefruit fruit aromas on the nose of this lightly coloured, green-gold wine is enhanced by those of toast and vanilla. Lovely, fresh, sweet fruit flavours are also firmly grapefruit in character, and are similarly seasoned with pleasing oak and the complexities of bottle-developed characters that recall shortbread. A big, warm wine with vigour and great depth of flavour, tuned up with a freshness of acidity and the evolving subtleties of bottle age, it has such resilience and breadth that it tastes as if it will last for years.

1990

13.5% alc/vol; 100% Chardonnay, Mendoza clone; Hawke's Bay region, Gimblett/Mere Road district; hand picked 17 March 1990; tank fermented and transferred to barrels; aged one year in 50/50 new/used 500-litre French Nevers oak puncheons.
Winemaker: Alan Limmer
Best drinking: 1995–99

Light straw-coloured, clear wine, with a very mellow, lightly toasted bouquet and attractively warm, very soft and supple palate, again with those grapefruit flavours but this time with a punch of alcohol at the very end and an uncomfortable finishing astringency. Pleasing, slightly coarse, nicely flavoured.

1991

13.5% alc/vol; 100% Chardonnay, Mendoza clone; Hawke's Bay region, Gimblett/Mere Road district; hand picked 14 March 1991; tank fermented and transferred to barrels; 15% malolactic fermentation; aged one year in 50/50 new/used 500-litre French Nevers oak puncheons.
Winemaker: Alan Limmer
Best drinking: 1996–2003

Ripe straw in colour, with a tinge of green, this wine is immediately demanding on the nose with mildly spicy oak aromas and an urgent, firm grapefruit character that has intensity and a real presence. In spite of this tough approach the wine is never lean, but strong and full of sweet fruit 'feel', very deep flavour and a warm lingering finish that gives an overall impression of assertiveness without being abrasive. This is not wine for the faint-hearted, or those who like a jolly, fruity dimension to their Chardonnays, but its strength lies in aristocratic power clearly based on deep, strong fruit flavour and confident winemaking, suggesting that it will gradually fine down and gain in elegance as it gets older. A wine with real presence.

1992

13.5% alc/vol; 100% Chardonnay, Mendoza clone; Hawke's Bay region, Mere Road 80%, Moteo 20%; hand picked 28 March 1992, 10 April (Moteo district);
20% malolactic fermentation; 100% barrel fermented, 50/50 new/used 500-litre French Nevers oak puncheons; aged one year in 50/50 new/used puncheons.
Winemaker: Alan Limmer
Best drinking: 1997–2003

Pale straw, very light and a touch green to look at, it smells big and rich, with a battery of creamy rich, butter, nut and oak aromas all squeezed into one glass. The creamy aroma hints at cream custard, and this character is more apparent in the texture in the mouth, where the creaminess balances the concentrated, ripe grapefruit flavours and spiced oak emerging from a broad, spreading palate packed with flavour and warmth. A powerful presence that is matched by neatly grainy abrasiveness and fresh acidity all the way through to the end, which is long indeed. A very youthful, assertive wine that needs years to settle down and deliver some subtlety from its depths of flavour and obvious vigour.

1993

13.5% alc/vol; 100% Chardonnay, Mendoza clone; Hawke's Bay region, Gimblett/Mere Road district; hand picked 9 April 1993; 100% barrel fermented, 50/50 new/used 500-litre French Nevers oak puncheons; 30% malolactic fermentation; aged 5 months on lees in new/used puncheons.
Winemaker: Alan Limmer
Best drinking: 1998–2005

Pale, sandy-straw wine, with a fresh but subdued bouquet that is currently showing fine banana and oak aromas and a quiet, general richness faintly reminiscent of cream custard. The palate is big and creamy, with a huge kickback of sweet grapefruit, busting to get out of the youthful density and tight oak currently hemming it in. It is simply alive with promise, a Chardonnay demanding to be bottle aged for at least five years. It has everything it needs to evolve into a quite spectacular wine, particularly a sense of balance between its component parts that have strong alcohol, acid and creamy-nutty flavour components to complement its great weight of fruit. It is already showing an integration, if not yet a complete harmony, that makes particular isolation of individual characteristics difficult, the sign of a very fine wine that is more than just the sum of its parts.

TE MATA ESTATE ELSTON CHARDONNAY

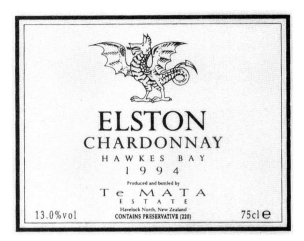

Te Mata's Elston Chardonnay has always had to struggle for attention in the shadow of the company's outstanding red wines, but it has never been less than one of the very finest New Zealand Chardonnays, combining power and elegance with the inimitable fruit intensity and character of high-quality Hawke's Bay-grown chardonnay. A sensitively crafted style, with winemaking skill in support of fruit rather than a blockbuster riding on oak, it is one of the most powerful and deeply flavoured Chardonnays and has a record for aging gracefully, without losing its characteristic vigour.

1984

13% alc/vol; 100% Chardonnay, Mendoza clone; 100% Hawke's Bay region, Elston vineyard; 100% hand harvested 2–3 April 1984; 100% tank fermented; aged in used 500-litre barrels; 100% malolactic fermentation.
Winemaker: Mike Bennett
Best drinking: 1995

Very pretty wine, fresh and yellow, with a faint sandy-lemon hue. The bouquet is lifted, fine and very attractive, a delicate pattern of warm toast, peach-like fragrances and creamy nut kernels, all tenderly held in an effortless frame of vinosity. The palate, too, is fine

with beautifully wrought patterns of flavour and texture, at once creamy and fresh, with the shortbread and toast complexities of bottle maturity, some quite delightful, peachy fruit, and a supporting structure that is warm and virile, without being intrusive. Although it is starting to dry out at the end, this is quite beautiful, fragrant wine that is a pleasure to sip and savour.

1985

13% alc/vol; 100% Chardonnay, Mendoza clone; 100% Hawke's Bay region, Elston Vineyard; 100% hand harvested 22–23 March 1985; mostly tank fermented, small proportion barrel fermented; no malolactic fermentation; aged in 50/50 new/used oak barriques for 7 months on lees.
Winemaker: Peter Cowley
Best drinking: 1995

Plump to look at, lemon-yellow and glossy with a bouquet that starts with the inimitable fragrance of expensive French oak and leads on to some succulent grapefruit aromas and traces of yeasty richness, with shortbread bottle maturity nuances finishing off the trail of complexities. Fresh and mellow at once, it is very finely textured, supple and warm with grapefruit flavours and lively oak. It tails off somewhat at the end to a soft, gentle finish with a faint tingle of citrus. Neat, tidy wine with delightful oak and a very nice feeling in the mouth.

1986

14% alc/vol; 100% Chardonnay, Mendoza clone; 100% Hawke's Bay region, Elston Vineyard; 100% hand harvested 25–27 March 1986; mostly tank fermented, small proportion barrel fermented; no malolactic fermentation; aged in 50/50 new/used French oak barriques for 7 months on lees.
Winemaker: Peter Cowley
Best drinking: 1995–96

Clear yellow wine, with a hint of hay about its colour and spice to its bouquet, which is light and very complex with touches of orange peel, shortbread and toast. The palate is open and honest, its orange-grapefruit flavours and oak nuances married with well-modulated grainy texture and warm alcohol that give it a muscly air of toughness. Brave, sturdy, cleverly crafted right through to its hearty finish, its strength is its dominating characteristic, but it is in no way a rough or even a rustic wine, maintaining a sophisticated poise throughout.

1987

14% alc/vol; 100% Chardonnay, Mendoza clone; 100% Hawke's Bay region, Elston Vineyard; 100% hand harvested 17–20 March 1987; barrel fermented from 14 brix; aged in new and used French oak barriques.
Winemaker: Peter Cowley
Best drinking: 1995–2000

This wine makes a brilliant first impression. Its bright colour offers the hues of mellow hay or straw burnished with the glow of new brass, and its most beautiful bouquet is a spectacle of cleverly woven fragrances — creamy hazelnuts, mealy yeast, vanilla, toast and a whiff of smoke — all clinging to the lush perfume of ripe grapefruit with its hints of succulence and citric tang. The expectations of this special introduction are satisfied by a suitably spectacular palate full of big, sweet, ripe grapefruit flavours that immediately wash your mouth, and last without fading to the final fragrant lilt of the finish, delivering their succulence without ever appearing overbearing, or detracting from the dextrous filigrees of subtle flavour the winemaker has contributed with shafts of fine oak and numerous other details. For all their energy, these flavours are matched by balancing power, the sinuous, almost animal strength of a winework where force is always subservient to grace. Unquestionably great wine that deserves all its international accolades, it refuses to lie down, lingering on in the mouth, the glass and ultimately in the memory long after the final swallow. It has all the structural imperatives of acid, fruit, alcohol and phenolics to keep scientists happy, and enough sensuality to satisfy the most passionate hedonist.

1988

12.5% alc/vol; 100% Chardonnay, Mendoza clone; 100% Hawke's Bay region, Elston Vineyard; 100% hand harvested 10–15 March 1988; partially barrel fermented; aged in new and used French oak barriques.
Winemaker: Peter Cowley

Copperish, brassy yellow, with a deep, mellow bouquet that is showing orange peel, with a suggestion of dusty old sideboards and other furniture. Aromatic, clean, light and orangy, it is a pleasant drink with an austere, light finish. Past its best.

1989

13.5% alc/vol; 100% Chardonnay, Mendoza clone; 100% Hawke's Bay region, Elston Vineyard; 100% hand harvested 24 February–3 March 1989; 100% barrel fermented in new and used French oak barriques; 25–30% malolactic fermentation; aged in new and used French oak barriques.
Winemaker: Peter Cowley
Best drinking: 1995–2000

Light, bright straw colour, with a fragrant bouquet that has an abundance of succulent grapefruit, seasoned with smoky, charred oak and a quite charming creaminess that faintly suggests nougat. Very, very fine wine, so easy and balanced it almost slips by unnoticed, the sweet grapefruit flavours deep and even to the point of perfect subtlety, but opening up treasures of flavour to the inquisitive taster. In spite of this subtlety, there is plenty of vigour here, with warmth and quiet power, but most of all this wine is about feel, a texture that is soft and fresh, with creamy suppleness harmonised with aromatic, woody astringencies, and lingering, luscious warmth. Big, impressive, elegant wine.

1990

12.5% alc/vol; 100% Chardonnay, Mendoza clone; 100% Hawke's Bay region, Elston Vineyard; 100% hand harvested 20 March–3 April 1990; 100% barrel fermented in new and used French oak barriques; 50% malolactic fermentation; aged in new and used French oak barriques.
Winemaker: Peter Cowley
Best drinking: 1995–99

Light, happy yellow colour, with a fresh grapefruit, oak, cream cheese and nuts nose that is delightfully fragrant. Very fresh, sweet with fruit and a depth of flavour to match, this is substantial but very pretty wine, its sweet grapefruit creaminess charming to the end of a long, lingering palate. Oak seems to have taken a role subservient to the fruit, while the texture and weight of the yeast components have added to its charm. Warm and lovely.

1991

13% alc/vol; 100% Chardonnay, Mendoza clone; 100% Hawke's Bay region, Elston Vineyard; 100% hand harvested 21–26 March 1991; 100% barrel fermented in new and used French oak barriques; 50% malolactic fermentation; aged in new and used French oak barriques.

Winemaker: Peter Cowley
Best drinking: 1995–2001

Light straw, with a tinge of yellow, bright and pretty to look at. The bouquet, with a gentle, almost savoury cast and a distinct grapefruit fragrance touched by oatmeal and smoky oak, is very fine, with an almost silvery texture. All the component flavours and structural pieces of the palate are also well melded into a fine, restrained pattern that is clean and fresh but given resonance by the underlying deep fruit presence. There is delightful oak seasoning throughout, and the fruit asserts its presence with a final touch of sweetness on the finish, but although all the various winemaking components can be sought and found, it is the integrated finesse of the wine that is its paramount characteristic, a holistic balance and clarity which speak of true class.

1992

13.5% alc/vol; 100% Chardonnay, Mendoza clone; 100% Hawke's Bay region, Elston Vineyard; 100% hand harvested 24 March–3 April 1992; 100% barrel fermented in new and used French oak barriques; 50% malolactic fermentation; aged in new and used French oak barriques.
Winemaker: Peter Cowley
Best drinking: 1996–2001

Creamy, with sweet oak and grapefruit on nose and palate, this straw-coloured wine is juicy, clean, long and sweetly attractive, with some nice nutty characteristics and an overall sense of proportion. A sonata in oak and Chardonnay fruit, it is quiet but not shy, with a distinct feel of gracious, expensive quality, even if it is less majestic than its predecessors.

1993

13.5% alc/vol; 100% Chardonnay, Mendoza clone; 100% Hawke's Bay region, Elston Vineyard; 100% hand harvested 14–20 April 1993; 100% barrel fermented in new and used French oak barriques; 45% malolactic fermentation; aged in new and used French oak barriques.
Winemaker: Peter Cowley
Best drinking: 1996–98

Very attractive, light, fresh yellow-straw colour, and a delicious nose of cream cheese and lime juice bordered by sweet, fine oak. The palate also has a fresh, limy perspective, and a *crème anglaise* texture that fits well with the slight nuttiness and suggestion of camembert cheese flavour. Still tight and very young, this wine has a piercing character which, when allied to its air of finesse and determined fragrance, suggests a long life and some delicacies to come. It has, like all the Elstons, an inimitable grace that defies long, complicated descriptions because aromas and flavours blend so effortlessly that the total effect is one of elegance. Tasting, you are aware of the structural soundness of the wines, but their parts seem to confirm what you already know.

THE MILLTON VINEYARD CLOS DE STE. ANNE CHARDONNAY

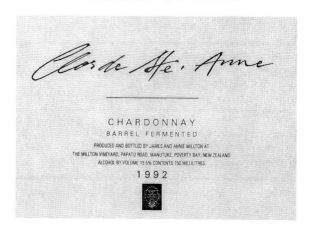

Millton's top Chardonnay label, the Clos de Ste. Anne Chardonnay, is a development of the earlier barrel-fermented wine, named after one of the proprietors, Annie Millton. A superbly harmonious, complex style noted for its 'creamy' texture, it is made only in better vintages and is rarely seen, but widely respected.

1986

BARREL FERMENTED
CHARDONNAY

13.5% alc/vol; 100% Chardonnay; Gisborne region;
100% barrel fermented.
Winemaker: James Millton
Best drinking: 1995

Light gold colour, with creamy, nutty, vanilla aromas among the sweetness on the nose, and a hearty dollop of toast. Taut and quite lively in the mouth, with freshness and a complex range of flavours that linger rather well. Big, still vigorous, but with the moderating influence of bottle age characteristics to give it some supporting mellowness, it is not quite fine but remains pleasantly satisfying.

1987

13.5% alc/vol; 100% Chardonnay; Gisborne region;
100% barrel fermented.
Winemaker: James Millton
Best drinking: 1995–96

Light gold colour, with a soft bouquet suggestive of old furniture and toast. The palate is moderately creamy rolled oats in taste and texture, with a touch of nuts and green-edged fruit that turns the finish just a shade sour. There are some orange peel nuances among the slightly peachy fruit flavours, all subtle and retaining their clean, acid edge, making a wine that has a feeling of life to it, but is somehow subdued.

1989

13.5% alc/vol; 100% Chardonnay; Gisborne region;
100% barrel fermented.
Winemaker: James Millton
Best drinking: 1995–97

Light, yellow gold-colour with a lovely, plump bouquet that is alive with a host of fragrances, including vanilla and toasty oak, subtle spices, rolled oats and more than a dash of marmalade. The palate, too, is deliciously complex, with some plump fruit and a harmony of flavour nuances that combine everything from more marmalade to nuts and figs, all held together by a svelte, silky texture enhanced by freshness and warm generosity that never slip to coarseness. Very fine, harmonious wine that is invitingly complex, sparkling with a kaleidoscope of flavours and fragrances that linger on well after the last swallow.

1992

13.5% alc/vol; 100% Chardonnay; Gisborne region; 100%
barrel fermented.
Winemaker: James Millton
Best drinking: 1996–2001

Light to look at, with a superbly fragrant lemon peel and vanilla cream nose that is fine, delicious and precise. Very naive on the palate, with a hearty measure of oak, but as it progresses a wonderful filigree of delicate flavours cascade down from the bouquet through the creamy texture, strong alcohol and fresh acidity. Beautifully supple, with a heart of concentrated, suggestively tropical fruit and delicious, fleshy flavours washed with creamy texture, this wine is a harmonious, coy, succulent beauty, still in its infancy but promising a glittering future.

VAVASOUR RESERVE CHARDONNAY

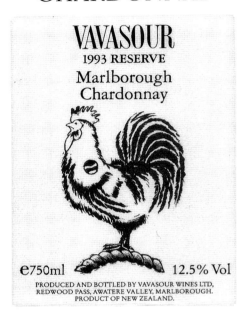

The Vavasour winery is very new, even in terms of New Zealand's youthful fine wine industry, and the commitment of its owners to grapes grown in the entirely untested Awatere Valley of Marlborough makes the appearance of this wine in such company quite an achievement. Winemaker Glenn Thomas is no newcomer to premium Chardonnay making, however, having already established his credentials at Corbans where his impetus started the highly rated Private Bin Chardonnay line. In spite of difficult vintages in 1992 and 1993, he has done enough with the Reserve wines at Vavasour to create for the new company a justifiable reputation for fine Chardonnay. They are wines of graceful character, and latterly fine texture, with heart and the complex patterns of assured winemaking.

1990

12.7% alc/vol; 100% Chardonnay, Mendoza clone; hand picked 26 March 1990; 100% barrel fermented in French oak barriques; 10% malolactic; aged for 10 months in oak.
Winemaker: Glenn Thomas
Best drinking: 1995–97

Light, polished yellow-gold with a touch of green. Fresh oak and fragrant lime blossom fruit, with neatly integrated details on the nose, the palate also offers a tempering of lime-like fruit, with sweet characters, oak, general lightness and a slightly abrasive texture that holds right through the finish to the very end, sustaining its flavours. The oak is a trifle aggressive, adding to the impression of austerity this wine gives, but a pleasant, suitably complex bottle.

1991

13.5% alc/vol; 100% Chardonnay, Mendoza clone; hand picked 10 April 1991; 100% barrel fermented in French oak barriques; 20% malolactic; aged for 9 months in oak.
Winemaker: Glenn Thomas
Best drinking: 1995–98

Light, green-hued pale gold colour, with a fascinating bouquet of oak and creamy, mealy, lime-tinged sweetness that has a fragrant clarity. Oodles of sweet fruit, but cool, fresh, tingly, with an underlying richness and moderately suave texture furred up by a bit of oak. Limy right through, warm, and giving an overall impression of ripeness within a cool package, this is a well-balanced, neatly textured, suave wine with an air of sophistication.

1992

13% alc/vol; 100% Chardonnay, Mendoza clone; hand picked 8 April 1992; 100% barrel fermented in French oak barriques; 90% malolactic; aged for 9 months in oak.
Winemaker: Glenn Thomas
Best drinking: 1996–2002

Aromatic vanilla, oak and concentrated fruit bouquet with a slight cream cheese dimension and an element of kumquat freshness. Rich, plump and sweet with fruit on the palate, and nicely soft, spicy oak characters, it has excellent momentum, the flavour and weight flowing through the wine without diminishing, supported by a silky-creamy texture that is light but sound. A wine with all the bits, it seems narrow, focused in its youth, an understated Chardonnay with an edge of clarity like a good soprano voice. Under control, but not lacking in warmth or promise, or that touch of class that is good breeding.

1993
MARLBOROUGH CHARDONNAY

12.5% alc/vol; 100% Chardonnay, Mendoza clone; hand picked 11 May 1993; whole bunch pressed; 100% barrel fermented in French oak barriques; 90% malolactic; aged for 8 months in oak.
Winemaker: Glenn Thomas
Best drinking: 1996–2001

Pale, greenish, bright, with a creamy, mellow yeast and mealy nose that is ripe and evocative, with light, fine fruit aromas bordering on lime juice, and the sweetly musty sharpness of camembert cheese. Flavours of limes and mandarins come through on the palate too, among the creamy, lactic sweetness and rich tints of oatmeal, giving taste to a beautifully fine, lithe-textured, mouth-filling wine that is very classy indeed. Not a big wine at all, but a very smart one, with a lovely touch of sweetness and delicately rich texture that leave a very attractive impression of meticulous, fine Chardonnay.

VIDAL RESERVE CHARDONNAY

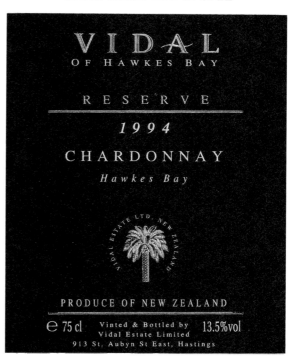

An illustrious record in wine competitions marks this wine as one of the country's prestige labels. In the form of the 1989 Gimblett Road wine, it has provided one of the great early New Zealand Chardonnays, a wine that did much to attract attention to the suitability of the stony land west of Hastings for growing wine of the highest quality.

1989
GIMBLETT ROAD CHARDONNAY

13.5% alc/vol; 100% Chardonnay; Hawke's Bay region, Gimblett Road district; harvested 3 March 1989; 100% barrel fermented in new 225-litre French Nevers oak barriques; partial malolactic fermentation; aged 10 months on light lees in French barriques.
Winemaker: Kate Marris (Radburnd)
Best drinking: 1995–2000

Ripe, lemon-straw in colour and very fragrant, this is

beautiful wine from the first noseful to the last, lingering taste. The bouquet is wonderfully complex, a filigree of intricate aromatic patterns that recall fresh ground oatmeal, nuts, citrus blossom, oak, grapefruit and butterscotch among its many nuances. In the mouth it feels alive, a supple, vibrantly textured wine with flavours to match its complex bouquet; more creamy nut kernels, hints of meal, fine grapefruit, vanilla cream custard and warm toast all held together by a freshness of acidity, a firm grip of oak and warm alcohol. Quite superb, this wine is skilfully crafted to give elegance and fine textures, with nothing over-done, yet offers an abundance of tempting flavours as deep and substantial as they are delicately tuned. It is a subtle touch that lingers on and on, delivering a complete, even inspiring Chardonnay that is already showing the benefit of bottle age mellowness and complexity, but should still be impressing enthusiasts at 10 years of age.

1989

HAWKE'S BAY CHARDONNAY

*13% alc/vol; 100% Chardonnay; Hawke's Bay region;
harvested 14 and 22 March 1989; 100% barrel fermented
in new 225-litre French Nevers oak barriques; partial
malolactic fermentation; aged 10 months in French
barriques with extended yeast lees.
Winemaker: Kate Marris (Radburnd)
Best drinking: 1995–99*

Great to look at with its ripe, bright yellow-gold colour, this wine also delivers a mouth-watering bouquet of fresh, toasty oak and sweet, creaming soda fruit. Very nice right through, with a suave, silky texture implying creaminess, neat acid freshness and a healthy measure of toasty oak that matches the bouquet. Well-crafted, pleasurable, lovely-feeling wine, with a tidy finish and charming, juicy fruit characters kept in balance by the oak, it suffers in comparison with its contemporary, having more accent on texture, but less complex flavour patterns. A very fine bottle, however, firmly based on delicious fruit and classy oak.

1990

*12.5% alc/vol; 100% Chardonnay, Hawke's Bay region;
harvested 10 April 1990; 100% barrel fermented in new
225-litre French Nevers oak barriques, partial malolactic*

*fermentation, aged 10 months in French barriques with
extended lees contact.
Winemaker: Kate Marris (Radburnd)
Best drinking: 1995–96*

The bouquet of this fresh, lemon-gold-hued wine is very buttery and nutty, with lashings of oak and a good whiff of rolled oats mealiness mingled with the fragrance of limes. Firm oak on the palate, too, but it feels very slick and smooth through the middle where the soft fruit gains some sort of dominance over the oak. A moderately light wine, with very clever oak treatment giving it an edge the fruit does not have, but pleasing nevertheless.

1991

*13% alc/vol; 100% Chardonnay; Hawke's Bay region;
100% barrel fermented in new 225-litre French oak
barriques; 15% malolactic fermentation; aged 9 months in
French barriques with partial lees contact.
Winemaker: Elise Montgomery
Best drinking: 1995–99*

Bright and fresh, its greenish lemon-gold colour is most attractive. The bouquet is rich with the expensive aroma of French oak, faintly enhanced by a dash of citrus blossom fragrance and a hint of caramel sweetness. Fresh and limy flavours compete with nut kernels, rolled oats and toasty oak in a very compact, tightly knit wine that appears to need a bit more bottle age to help it mellow out. Still fresh in taste and feel.

1992

*13% alc/vol; 100% Chardonnay, Hawke's Bay region;
100% barrel fermented in new 225-litre French oak
barriques; 12% malolactic fermentation; aged 9 months in
French barriques with partial lees contact.
Winemaker: Elise Montgomery
Best drinking: 1996–2000*

Ripe, lemon-gold colour. French oak and a ripe, intense fruit nose suggesting limes and grapefruit set up a wine which is racy in style, with jazzy fruit flavours that have an edge of intensity and depth, underlaid with a sophisticated, creamy texture shot with oak grip and toasty oak flavour nuances. Well-made wine, still very young, with a long, long finish that is quite complex and fresh, promising more bottle age development to come. In the light of earlier vintages, very much a thoroughbred.

VILLA MARIA BARRIQUE FERMENTED RESERVE CHARDONNAY

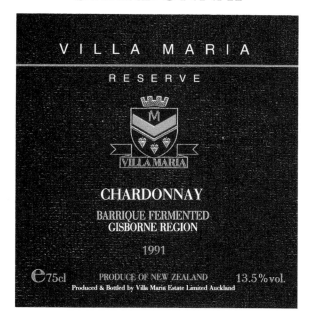

Villa Maria's Barrique Fermented Reserve Chardonnay is one of the most successful wines in New Zealand competitions, having won numerous gold medals and trophies since it was first introduced with the 1986 vintage. Its big, rich, complex style, ripe with winemaking intrusions and fine oak, has a large following among New Zealand's Chardonnay aficionados, making this arguably the most respected of this much-acclaimed company's reserve label wines.

1986

100% Chardonnay; 100% barrel fermentation in French 225-litre barriques.
Winemaker: Kym Milne
Best drinking: 1995–96

Deeply coloured wine, still tinged with green. There is a solid oakiness on both the nose and palate, but this is moderated somewhat by nut kernel creaminess and a just fading sweetness of fruit. Still very much alive at eight years of age, with a lively freshness of acidity, slightly at odds with the gentle subtlety of bottle age, but keeping the energy levels up.

1987

100% Chardonnay; 100% barrel fermentation in French 225-litre barriques.
Winemaker: Kym Milne

Bright and golden, the glow of this wine promises richness, but the bouquet and palate are less than generous. A faded wine, still showing traces of time spent in close company with expensive French oak, but it slides quickly to nothing at the finish.

1989

13% alc/vol; 100% Chardonnay, Mendoza clone; Gisborne region; harvested 9–18 March 1989; 100% barrel fermentation; 9 months in 225-litre Nevers and Vosges oak; 10% malolactic fermentation.
Winemaker: Kym Milne
Best drinking: 1995–97

More big, rich colour promising a generous, warm personality that the bouquet, all fruit wrapped in slick oak and creamy nut kernel-oatmeal nuances, confirms. A nice touch of intensity on the palate, some toasty hints of maturity and lashings of all those tropical fruit characters wine writers like so much—papaya, passionfruit, melons, sweet and jolly like a can of fruit salad. This is no simple party piece, however, as a warm body of alcohol harmonises with the oak to give entrancing complexity and plenty of weight to back it up. Fat and comely, it is pleasure garden stuff packed with succulent expectation. Sadly, it is over rather too quickly after such a build-up.

1990

12.5% alc/vol; 100% Chardonnay, Mendoza clone; Hawke's Bay and Gisborne regions; harvested 23 March 1990; 100% barrel fermentation; 8 months in 225-litre French oak, 66% new, 34% one year old; 15% malolactic fermentation.
Winemaker: Kym Milne
Best drinking: 1995–96

Rich, golden green colour, deep and bright. The open, florid bouquet is embellished with jungly fruit aromas, chunky oak and butterscotch, leading into a soft, tender wine that is most attractive. Lingering lightly in the mouth, it leaves behind a pleasant memory of warmth and succulence that makes for a very satisfying drink.

1991

13.5% alc/vol; 100% Chardonnay, Mendoza clone; Gisborne region; harvested 14 March and 4 April 1991; 100% barrel fermentation; 8 months in 225-litre French oak, new and one year old; 30% malolactic fermentation.
Winemaker: Kym Milne
Best drinking: 1995–2001

Pretty, bright green-gold in colour, with a bouquet that is a sophisticated harmony of sweet, fine oak, milky ripeness, and plump, juicy fruit, that is a particularly elegant wine, still very young and slightly abrasive. Very suave to taste, it has oak-spiced elements of cream and a silky tone that combine with subtle intensity of flavour, acid and underlying energy to leave an impression of considerable depth and strength. A poised wine, less assertive than earlier vintages, less obviously fruit absorbed and juicy, but holding much promise for the future.

1992

14% alc/vol; 100% Chardonnay, Mendoza clone; Gisborne region; harvested 27 March–9 April 1992; 100% barrel fermentation; 8 months in 225-litre French oak, new and one year old; 30% malolactic fermentation.
Winemaker: Kym Milne
Best drinking: 1996–2002

Pretty, bright, green-tinged, light golden wine. The bouquet is a mealy complexity of lanolin and vanilla-like oak, soft, with hints of fruit that are reminiscent of ripe grapefruit. Big wine, still tasting very young and a bit hollow in the middle where the oak makes its virile presence felt, but finishes as strongly as it starts, with a heart of intense flavour that lingers nicely and leaves a positive impression of complexity and smart winemaking. Certainly one for the future.

1993

13% alc/vol; 100% Chardonnay, Mendoza clone; Ihumatao district, South Auckland region; harvested March 1993; 100% barrel fermentation; aged 7 months in 225-litre French oak, 70% new and 30% one year old; 15% malolactic fermentation.
Winemaker: Kym Milne
Best drinking: 1997–2004

Light gold with green lights, this is a pretty young thing, all lime juice, oak and minerals on the nose, and a palate that is very supple, plump with concentrated fruit, citrus flavour and a bundle of fresh oak. Fresh with acid, it implies richness in the future, has the length of flavour expected of quality wine, and a very fine texture that provides a touch of class in its moderation of the considerable warmth hovering at the finish. A solid wine that appears to be heading for a reasonable life which will expand on its complexity and provide for greater subtlety.

CHENIN BLANC

ALTHOUGH CHENIN BLANC WAS POPULAR DURING THE DEVELOPMENTAL period of New Zealand table wine, with Corbans making some notable examples from grapes grown in Tolaga Bay during the late 1970s, this interest has not converted into a healthy fine wine family of Chenin Blanc wines.

This is due primarily to Chenin Blanc's propensity to overcrop and suffer botrytis, which lost it favour with winemakers who were not prepared to put their efforts into a variety that was consistently in poor condition, and producing lightly flavoured, high acid wines. As most Chenin Blanc was being grown by non-winemaking growers, the solution of improved viticulture and careful site selection was not seriously attempted, and Chenin Blanc has slipped into the position of an also-ran variety.

Some wineries, however, notably Collards and the Millton Vineyard, have put an effort into Chenin Blanc, and have made wines that at least show that the variety does have a fine wine potential in this country. Given better vineyard locations, where neither vigour nor botrytis are a problem, it could become a serious fine wine variety for late harvest, naturally sweet wines; aromatic, dry wines; and even moderate quality sparkling wines.

Chenin Blanc has been in New Zealand since at least late last century, although its original importation is unrecorded. In recent times, however, new clones have been introduced from California (UCD1) in 1964, South Africa in 1972, Australia in 1982 (also known as the Delegat's clone) and from South Africa (Stell 68/1/19) in 1985.

Production is continuing to drop, with Chenin Blanc making up less than 3 per cent of the national vineyard.

COLLARDS DRY CHENIN BLANC

COLLARDS

1994

CHENIN BLANC
Hawke's Bay

12% Vol   BOTTLED BY COLLARD BROTHERS LTD
WINEMAKERS AT HENDERSON, AUCKLAND   750ml
PRODUCE OF NEW ZEALAND

Collards have been the pre-eminent Chenin Blanc producers in New Zealand since the early 1980s, with wines that have always been treated as well-made, low-priced dry whites which serve as a good alternative to Chardonnay and Sauvignon Blanc. Because of this low status, they have rarely been treated with the respect their careful making and bottle-aging potential has deserved; even the winery has no stock of older wines at all, and bottles more than five years old are extremely rare in private cellars.

They are wines that do repay bottle age, however, and stand as excellent examples of what can be done, and is yet to be done, with this very promising variety in New Zealand conditions.

1991

12% alc/vol; 100% Chenin Blanc; 50% Hawke's Bay region, 50% Te Kauwhata district, Waikato region; harvested 7 April 1991 in Hawke's Bay, 4–5 April in Te Kauwhata; stainless steel fermentation; briefly aged in used French oak barrels.

Winemaker: Bruce Collard
Best drinking: 1995–2002

A mild, sandy-lemon colour, with a honeyed, earthy bouquet, fresh-edged yet mellow in character, some herbal edges and a nice hint of spice. Soft yet fresh-edged palate, honeyed and waxy, almost loose in its easy way, but it does not lack life or length, setting up a lovely spread of juicy feeling and flavour around the mouth, finishing brisk, clean, with fading herbal notes. Nice wine with interesting flavours and an attractive blend of mellowness and brisk clarity.

1992

12.5% alc/vol; 100% Chenin Blanc; 50% Hawke's Bay region, 50% Te Kauwhata district, Waikato region; harvested 15 April 1992 in Hawke's Bay, 23–24 April in Te Kauwhata; stainless steel fermentation; briefly aged in used French oak barrels.
Winemaker: Bruce Collard
Best drinking: 1995–2001

The herbal character of this wine, especially the bouquet, is reminiscent of the famous Green Chartreuse liqueur. Bright lemon-yellow in appearance, it has a herbal nose lit up with waxy, honeysuckle aspects, a deeper, earthy note and a growing mellowness that hints at richness. The palate is full of nice subtleties that complement the herbal, earthy flavours, with hints of wax and honeysuckle again, mixed with sweet and juicy fruitiness and a mealy, balancing texture. Quite brisk and flavourful. Delicious.

1993

12.5% alc/vol; 100% Chenin Blanc; 70% Hawke's Bay region, 30% Te Kauwhata district, Waikato region; harvested 28 April 1993 in Hawke's Bay, 19 April in Te Kauwhata; stainless steel fermentation; briefly aged in used French oak barrels.
Winemaker: Bruce Collard
Best drinking: 1996–2002

Light lemon-yellow, with moderate depth of colour, and a full, fresh, ripe gooseberry and aromatic hay and honeysuckle bouquet, classically balanced by the darker tone of earthiness. A wholesome, very attractive wine, with easy texture, plump fruit weight, waxy, herbal notes and an echo of earth, it is enlivened and balanced by an almost prickly vigour that feels like edgy youth. Brisk at the finish, it is a nice drink now, but feels as though it needs to relax a little before the full benefit of its more mellow features can come into play.

1994

12% alc/vol; 100% Chenin Blanc; 90% Hawke's Bay region, 10% Te Kauwhata district, Waikato region; harvested 20–21 April 1994 in Hawke's Bay, 11 April in Te Kauwhata; stainless steel fermentation; briefly aged in used French oak barrels.
Winemaker: Bruce Collard
Best drinking: 1997–2005

Almost glowing with freshness, this young wine has a bouquet of good clay fringed with the fragrance of wax and honeysuckle, and is similarly fresh and fulsome on the palate, with blossom-like flavours and a hard green edge of herbs to complement its ripe gooseberry fruit. Sweetness of fruit spreads through the mouth, lightly concentrated, mellow in character, a counterpoint to the piquant finish left by the wine's youthful vigour and fresh acid. Heading for a fine future.

GISBORNE
CHENIN BLANC DRY
BARREL FERMENTED
1994

GROWN AND BOTTLED
ON THE PROPERTY
THE MILLTON VINEYARD
MANUTUKE GISBORNE

75cl℮

CERTIFIED ORGANICALLY GROWN PRODUCE OF NEW ZEALAND 13.0% VOL

THE MILLTON VINEYARD CHENIN BLANC

Given more lavish treatment than the Collards wine, this often botrytised Chenin Blanc has for a decade been one of the most exotic New Zealand wines, keeping the Chenin flag flying while others have neglected the variety. Complex, sometimes sweetish, sometimes dry, it makes full use of botrytis whenever possible to concentrate its flavours, working to meld an intricately patterned palate.

1984
MAY HARVEST

100% Chenin Blanc; Gisborne region.
Winemaker: James Millton
Best drinking: 1995–2000?

Polished, light yellow-gold with an unusual bouquet

that is remarkably like ripe, sweet pumpkin and lemon, clear and complex. The palate is lovely and sweet, supple, fresh and clean but without intensity, or the complexity the bouquet implies. Light, clear, high-toned, sweetly lemon-scented wine, it is a refreshing experience, if slightly simple. Tastes as if it could stay in this condition forever.

1984
DRY

100% Chenin Blanc; Gisborne region.
Winemaker: James Millton
Best drinking: 1995

A wine with a very pretty, light green-gold colour, and a spicy, waxy, ripe lemon essence bouquet that is lifted and tempered by fragrances of herbs and honey. The silky, wax-riddled palate is fresh and clear, with a moderate length and a finish that is just starting to dry out at the very end, but it compensates for this fading off with a lovely array of delicate flavour subtleties. Very attractive wine, perhaps lacking in texture and more mouth-filling qualities, but an intriguing, pleasurable glassful.

1985
DRY BARREL FERMENTED

11.5% alc/vol; 100% Chenin Blanc; Gisborne region; 100% barrel fermented in French oak.
Winemaker: James Millton

Young, plump, light green-gold wine with a big, fat,

oaky nose that promises more than the palate delivers. Too lean to be a special treat, it has some creamy depths that would have been a boon for either of the 1984s, but the oak is intrusive now the flavours have faded away. Still has a fresh tang of acid to keep it alive, but the soul has gone.

1986

12% alc/vol; 100% Chenin Blanc; Gisborne region; 100% barrel fermented in French oak; partial malolactic.
Winemaker: James Millton
Best drinking: 1995–96

A cleverly made Fair Isle jumper of flavours, this fresh, moderate-weight wine holds a bundle of interest for wine drinkers keen on the intricacies of taste. Freshly green-gold in defiance of its age, it has a bouquet with the petrol-tainted ring of aged Australian Riesling but, in spite of this tendency to shout, the overall impression is of mealiness, oak and toast, with a wash of creaminess throughout. Cream, too, on the palate, where its soft mellowness tugs against the fresh vigour of still keen acidity, a squabble that neither character manages to win, but that is at times unsettling. All those little flavour subtleties keep dipping in and out of these pools of cream and acid, keeping up the drinker's interest right to the last whisper of a slightly astringent, clarion clear finish. Fascinating wine.

1988
BARREL FERMENTED

11.7% alc/vol; 100% Chenin Blanc; Gisborne region; 100% barrel fermented in French oak.
Winemaker: James Millton

This wine starts beautifully, with a lovely layered bouquet of herbs and apricots to match its polished, light gold colour. The pleasantly sweet palate is rather too light for such promise, however, a lemon-hearted, gentle thing with delicate orange peel and subtle apricots around the fringes, and strains of oak and toast throughout. Fresh from beginning to end, it seems to have faded into the shadows.

1989

13% alc/vol; 100% Chenin Blanc; Gisborne region; 100% barrel fermented in French oak.
Winemaker: James Millton
Best drinking: 1995–2003

Bright-eyed and strong, this lovely wine is an excellent example of what Chenin Blanc can do in the right conditions. Its bouquet beautifully lined with aromas of honeyed cream and softly floral hints of honeysuckle and sweetly spiced oak, it offers quite a come on, which the palate delivers with easy grace. Fresh and tremendously long, its lemon honey, beeswax and creamy oak flavours are alternately softened by sugar plump sweetness, and clarified by acidity in waves of harmony that are by turn succulent and refreshing. Big wine, it has an enchanting purity of character and warmth and deliciously worked flavours that imply this enchantment will evolve much further into intricacy before it fades. Not quite elegant, it is comely wine with a deep well of satisfaction.

1990
DRY BARREL FERMENTED

13% alc/vol; 100% Chenin Blanc; Gisborne region; 100% barrel fermented in French oak.
Winemaker: James Millton
Best drinking: 1995–96

A polished golden wine, with fresh orange peel aromas and a complex range of fragrances bound by freshness and the mellow tones of oak. The flavours are immediately fine, orange-tinged, oaky, with a trace of oatmeal and nuts, and the clarity of acid, but after such an impressive beginning they fade somewhat, and the finish is much lighter and softer than the wine appears to be at first taste. Pretty wine, with a nice nose and some attractive flavours.

1991
BARREL FERMENTED

11.3% alc/vol; 100% Chenin Blanc; Gisborne region; 100% barrel fermented in used French oak; aged 8 months in used French oak.
Winemaker: James Millton
Best drinking: 1996–98

Ripe-smelling, orange-fresh and crisp bouquet, with waxy, honeyed tinges and a gentle spice of oak. A lovely, even, silky palate refreshed by acidity, its flavours still understated yet deep, it seems like a sleeper that is yet to open out and reveal itself. Very light, in spite of its ripe bouquet and feel, but the slightly grainy feel of oak astringency and fresh acidity give it life, and hold the flavours right to the end. Lively, interesting, neatly made wine that should look even better after another year or two in bottle.

1992
DRY BARREL FERMENTED

12% alc/vol; 100% Chenin Blanc; Gisborne region; 100% barrel fermented in used French oak; aged 8 months in used French oak.
Winemaker: James Millton
Best drinking: 1997–2000

Glossy, green-gold wine, with a mellow, oaky nose that has traces of earth and herbs. Fresh and very immature on the palate, its flavours tightly held, with oatmeal and oak apparent, and a distant fruit succulence that is slightly concentrated and touched with lemon. It feels good, with a close-grained texture, sweetness of fruit and an easy gloss, but the mass of very subtle flavours need more time to show themselves.

1993

12% alc/vol; 100% Chenin Blanc; Gisborne region; 100% barrel fermented in used French oak; aged 8 months in used French oak.
Winemaker: James Millton
Best drinking: 1997–2001

Ripe-looking, light golden-coloured wine with a fragrant, waxy-honeyed bouquet that has a nice pat of clay-like earthiness to balance its fresh, light-toned clarity. The lovely, fresh, lemon and honey-wax palate is deeply flavoured and meticulously clean, with a flurry of oatmeal and oak, and some creamy, nut kernel richness among herbal tones. Young and moderately light, its flavours tightly packed and very fresh feeling, this wine is already long and is shaping a finely balanced finish that will be very fine once its youthful vigour fades, and the brisk herbals mellow.

GEWÜRZTRAMINER

Gewürztraminer, under its now less-common name of traminer, has been present in New Zealand vineyards since at least the end of the 19th century, but there is no record of its performance as a winemaking grape from that time.

It was not until Matawhero made its now legendary 1976 Gewürztraminer that the variety became a serious contender for fine wine status, and during the early table wine years it was often touted as the variety on which New Zealand would build its international reputation. Collards and Villa Maria also made wines that added to industry excitement over the potential of a wine with the sort of dramatic aroma and flavour that instantly appealed to drinkers.

That this potential has not been realised is partly due to Gewürztraminer's poor performance in the vineyard, where it can lose a significant proportion of its potential crop should flowering conditions be less than perfect. Add to this its susceptibility to botrytis and other mildews, and it becomes an economic risk for winegrowers, one that is too high for them to sustain, given more reliable and higher returns from other varieties.

Less than acceptable winemaking practice also limited Gewürztraminer's progress. At Matawhero the brilliance of the early vintages gave way to a less than consistent performance, and other winemakers were too ready to use Gewürztraminer's flamboyance to enhance the character of lesser wines. Producers also tended to make Gewürztraminer into a moderately sweet, soft, and gently floral 'commercial' wine, a style that is at odds with Gewürztraminer's natural high flavour and low acidity. 'Commercial' came to mean flabby and slight, as well as sweet, and never provided the sort of returns needed to reward growers of a difficult variety.

Leading the way back has been the uncompromising Neil McCallum, who has made Gewürztraminer at its flourishing best, full of spice and roses, and with a hearty charge of alcohol to balance these otherwise excessive characters. Robard & Butler, too, have never stepped away from the essence of Gewürztraminer, and now the ranks of true Gewürz makers are steadily swelling as winemakers realise that it does make high-quality wines under New Zealand conditions.

Other than the very early importation, which seems almost to have vanished, shortly after the end of the Second World War the Department of

Agriculture imported from France a clone known as Roter Traminer. It was unsuccessful, but the clone known as UCD1, imported from California a few years later, was the basis for the first successful Gewürztraminer wines. This was added to in 1976 when W. Irwin of Matawhero imported the UCD4 clone from California. Subsequently there have been a number of other introductions of various clones, so that there are now more than 12 in vineyards around the country.

After a number of years when the area has been steadily reducing, interest is again being shown in Gewürztraminer, and there have been new plantings, especially in the Wairarapa. It remains a minority grape, however, making up approximately 2 per cent of the total vineyard area.

DRY RIVER GEWÜRZTRAMINER

Dry River have emerged in recent years as the pre-eminent Gewürztraminer makers in New Zealand, concentrating on dry, powerful, deeply flavoured wines that never compromise spice for prettiness. Proprietor Neil McCallum's efforts indicate that the early optimism held for this variety in New Zealand was not misplaced, in spite of its slip in popularity and easy abuse by cheap wine producers.

1984

12.5% alc/vol; 100% Gewürztraminer, clone UCD5;
Martinborough district, Wairarapa region; hand picked
11 April 1984.
Winemaker: Neil McCallum
Best drinking: 1995

A clear, toasty, delicate bouquet sets up this pretty, slightly tired wine that still has a tracery of delicate spice, perfume and subtle roses. Still warm, but drying out at the end.

1986

12% alc/vol; 100% Gewürztraminer, clone UCD5;
Martinborough district, Wairarapa region; hand picked.
Winemaker: Neil McCallum
Best drinking: 1995

Pale straw wine, clear, with a sparkle of tartrate crystals. The bouquet is mellow, fully mature and fading, but there are some nice flavours still, just a trace of cloves and a hint of cinnamon among the shortbread. Finishing dry, it seems past its best, but is still an intriguing glassful.

1987

13.2% alc/vol; 100% Gewürztraminer, clone UCD5;
Martinborough district, Wairarapa region; hand picked
9 April 1987.
Winemaker: Neil McCallum
Best drinking: 1995–96

Pretty, glowing yellow-straw wine, bright and clear with a bouquet to match, one that offers aromas of rose petals, cloves and cinnamon, hints of lime and a growing toastiness. Fragrant but mellow, from bouquet to palate, there is a lift of floral perfume that drifts across the tender flavours of mellow spice, fading lychee fruit, mandarins and mild biscuits. There is still an element of intensity, though, which tempers the astringency in its tail, and the tapered, dry finish. A wine in parts, it starts prettily, builds to a climax of flavour and astringency, and then fades to a delicate farewell. Very nice.

1988

13.5% alc/vol; 100% Gewürztraminer, clone UCD5;
Martinborough district, Wairarapa region; hand picked
10 March 1988.
Winemaker: Neil McCallum
Best drinking: 1995

Light, yellow-straw with a mellow, toasted, spicy bouquet that is delicate but not lacking in substance. Nice flavour, tender, with an edge of freshness and a slowly accumulating bitter-astringent texture that gives carry to the finish without disturbing the wine's equilibrium. Typically for Dry River, it is a surprisingly elegant Gewürztraminer; certainly it has no rough edges, just an unusual fresh quality to its sweet fruit feel, and a vagueness that seems like an echo of earlier vigour.

1989

13.5% alc/vol; 100% Gewürztraminer, clone UCD5;
Martinborough district, Wairarapa region; hand picked
12 March 1989.
Winemaker: Neil McCallum
Best drinking: 1995–97

Cream custard and toast nose, gently spiced with nutmeg and cinnamon. A fine, highly strung wine with a lovely, suave palate, delicately but precisely flavoured with ripe fruit in the heady papaya-lychees category, glossy with cream custard texture and a lingering, slightly astringent finish of raisin-like intensity, all larded with bottle age toast characters. Very attractive, concentrated, mature wine tasting at its peak, with enough strength to last a while yet.

1990

12.9% alc/vol; 100% Gewürztraminer, clone UCD5;
Martinborough district, Wairarapa region; hand picked
31 March 1990.
Winemaker: Neil McCallum
Best drinking: 1995–96

Light straw in colour, with a pretty, light, dusty fragrance that has heart but remains very delicate. Fragrant right through, though without any easily identifiable characters, this wine is more about texture than flavour, for it is soft and creamy, with mid-palate sweetness, and a fine, lingering finish that hints at mild spice and perfume, but seems to keep its suave texture to the very end. Balance is maintained by an almost subtle astringency. Very fine, elegant, tender.

1991

13.9% alc/vol; 100% Gewürztraminer, clone UCD5;
Martinborough district, Wairarapa region; hand picked
30 March 1991.
Winemaker: Neil McCallum
Best drinking: 1997–?

Very pale straw, lean, with a light, vaguely spicy fragrance. Although it has a nice palate, pleasant, with pretty, fruit-like flavours and a robe of sweetness and light, rich texture, the finish is fiery, setting flavours alight and bringing what seems to be a slumbering giant back to life. Very reserved for a wine made from this variety, it has depth and energy in abundance, but no striking aroma or flavour characteristics, and appears big enough to last another decade at least.

1992

13.9% alc/vol; 100% Gewürztraminer, clone UCD5;
Martinborough district, Wairarapa region; hand picked
5 May 1992.
Winemaker: Neil McCallum
Best drinking: 1995–2003

The big aromatic-fragrant bouquet of this wine wells steadily up from the glass, laden with rose petals, lanolin-like richness, concentrated, juicy lychee fruit and a dusting of ginger and cloves. The palate is equally impressive, packed with deep flavours so concentrated that raisins spring to mind, although it is never sticky or simple, and backed by hearty power and fine, close texture just roughed up by a portion of astringency. Grand stuff awash with the sweetness of ripe fruit, yet completely dry, it has MGM scale but the class and resonance of Shakespeare, and already possesses little asides of complexity, flavour seedlings that will flourish as the wine ages. For all its abundance, it maintains its elegance throughout, the lingering flavours never obstructed by alcohol or bitterness, and neither the spice nor the roses taking over from the other. Simply superb.

1994

14% alc/vol; 100% Gewürztraminer, clone UCD5;
Martinborough district, Wairarapa region; hand picked
10 April 1994.
Winemaker: Neil McCallum
Best drinking: 1997–2007

Very pale, clear, bright wine with a young, fresh, slightly yeasty nose that is alive with a spicy, floral fragrance reminiscent of Margaret Merril roses. Very fine in spite of its youth, close packed with ripeness and intensity, its characters begin to emerge from the depth of concentrated, sweet fruit that is the palate. Rose petals appear with lychees and mandarins, and a rainbow of spices: nutmeg, cinnamon, cardamom, cloves and even a speck of aniseed. Nothing loud, but all there and supported by the structural essentials of Gewürztraminer: vigorous alcohol, softness and the balancing texture of astringency. This will be very fine wine indeed when it grows up, perhaps the finest yet from this producer. Watching it grow will be a wonderful experience, or a number of wonderful experiences for those lucky enough to have more than one bottle in their cellar.

MARTINBOROUGH VINEYARD GEWÜRZTRAMINER

14% VOL 750ml

PRODUCED AND BOTTLED BY MARTINBOROUGH VINEYARD LTD, PRINCESS STREET, MARTINBOROUGH, NEW ZEALAND.

PRODUCE OF NEW ZEALAND

This winery's reputation for Pinot Noir and Chardonnay has kept attention away from its very good Gewürztraminers, perfumy, fruity wines with lovely balance that have gained an extra dimension of spice and power in recent vintages. As a duo with Dry River's Gewürztraminer, they make a point about the future for this variety in Wairarapa, especially as a seriously strong-flavoured style, rather than a frivolity.

1984

13% alc/vol; 100% Gewürztraminer; Martinborough district, Wairarapa region; hand picked 7 April 1984.
Winemaker: Russell Schultz

Light brassy colour that suggests oxidation, confirmed on the nose. Soft, mild, very toasty and rough about the edges. Not quite dead yet, but well past its best.

1985

10.5% alc/vol; 100% Gewürztraminer; Martinborough district, Wairarapa region; hand picked 18 March 1985.
Winemaker: Larry McKenna

Pale brassy gold. Toast and spice and creaming soda on the nose, this is well gone now.

1986

12% alc/vol; 100% Gewürztraminer; Martinborough district, Wairarapa region; hand picked 26 March 1986.
Winemaker: Larry McKenna

Light, yellow-brass colour, with a herbaceous, canned peas character on the nose, and a fresh, simple, polite palate that is past its best.

1987

11.8% alc/vol; 100% Gewürztraminer; Martinborough district, Wairarapa region; hand picked 30 March 1987.
Winemaker: Larry McKenna
Best drinking: 1995–96

Light, brassy yellow to look at, with a sweet, aromatic, toasty bouquet that has depth and freshness as well as characters of lychees and rose petals among its array of fragrances. A complex, quietly flavoured wine still, it has real depth on the palate, length and a most appealing fresh, fragrant air. In spite of its bouquet, the rest of the wine is never overstated and, if it were not for the light weight and too gentle finish, it could be called elegant. A lovely drink.

1988

12.3% alc/vol; 100% Gewürztraminer; Martinborough district, Wairarapa region; hand picked 20 April 1988.
Winemaker: Larry McKenna
Best drinking: 1995

Pale, brassy colour, with a light nose and palate, and a touch of bitterness at the finish. Not bad, simply lacking in character.

1989

12.6% alc/vol; 100% Gewürztraminer; Martinborough district, Wairarapa region; hand picked 5 March 1989.
Winemaker: Larry McKenna
Best drinking: 1995

Light, clear colour that is reminiscent of new brass, with a touch of green. The bouquet is very aromatic, toasty, shot with splashes of ginger and rose petals and with an overall character of freshness that is also a feature of the palate. An abundant, lively wine, with lychee flavours predominating, but it has a lean aspect that takes the gloss off a little, leaving the flavours without a corresponding balance of texture or richness. Soft, and neatly astringent at the very end, it remains a most attractive bottle.

1990

11.5% alc/vol; 100% Gewürztraminer; Martinborough district, Wairarapa region; hand picked 22 March 1990.
Winemaker: Larry McKenna
Best drinking: 1995–96

Clear, green-tinged, pale brass-coloured wine, with a meaty, lightly spicy, floral bouquet that is notable for its clarifying freshness. Fresh, clean and crisp in the mouth, with a tracery of citrus and mild spice, this is a very attractive wine, tidied up at the end by a twist of astringency and lingering hints of spice and orange peel.

1991

LATE HARVEST

14% alc/vol; 100% Gewürztraminer; Martinborough district, Wairarapa region.
Winemaker: Larry McKenna
Best drinking: 1996–2000

Beautiful wine from its glimmering, pale brass colour to the lingering ginger-embellished flavours at the finish, its sweetness never cloys, nor do its ebullient flavours quite override its elegance. The bouquet is quiet but very deep and vaguely spicy, suggesting that there is more yet to come from its sweetness and intensity. Very dense, warm, deep, laced with ripe lychees and ginger, it has a heart of intensity and a long, very drawn out assemblage of flavours that endorse its soft, sweet nature, but never compromise the wine's clarity and youthful freshness. It is still incredibly youthful and the wonderful textural balance

between astringency, sweetness and fresh acidity, matched by a hearty measure of alcohol, promise a bright future for this wine.

1991

14% alc/vol; 100% Gewürztraminer; Martinborough district, Wairarapa region; hand picked 3 April 1991.
Winemaker: Larry McKenna
Best drinking: 1996–2000

Very fragrant, fresh, vinous wine that is not obviously Gewürztraminer, but is pretty and floral, with a fine texture and remarkable depth on the nose. The palate, too, is fine textured, fragrant and tastes as if it were made yesterday, with layers of as yet imprecise flavour building like waves to a very long finish. Powerful, intense wine with shafts of spice and rose petals calling through its depths, and a lovely rich texture that is still tingling with youth. A beauty that has momentum, superb balance and real presence.

1992

13.5% alc/vol; 100% Gewürztraminer; Martinborough district, Wairarapa region; hand picked 2 April 1992.
Winemaker: Larry McKenna
Best drinking: 1996–1999

Light, burnished brass colour, and a flattish nose that is saved by an intriguing edge of ginger-rich spice. Earthy yet fresh on the palate, with a thread of concentration and good depth of flavour, it builds with vigour and rich, fine texture to a fresh, slightly astringent finish that leaves a good impression of flavour, spice and clarity. Suitably warm, almost generous, its hints of honey and raisins add more layers of interest to this fascinating wine.

1993

13% alc/vol; 100% Gewürztraminer; Martinborough district, Wairarapa region; hand picked 15 April 1993.
Winemaker: Larry McKenna
Best drinking: 1995–2000

Light straw, with a lovely florid bouquet that hums rose petals and lychees, and is faintly tweaked by a touch of five spice powder character. Fresh, quite zingy wine, yet supple, with real intensity at its heart that recalls concentrated lychee flavours, building a flavour momentum to leave a powerful impression of taste and weight, tempered by freshness and a twist of astringency. A lithe, fine Gewürztraminer that is flexing its muscles impressively but, for all its power, is never out of rhythm with its finer points.

1994

14% alc/vol; 100% Gewürztraminer; Martinborough district, Wairarapa region.
Winemaker: Larry McKenna
Best drinking: 1997–2002

Clear, bright wine, pale lemon-straw in colour, with a bright, pungently fragrant bouquet that suggests powder, and a floral, gingery spice. Fat and implying sweetness with its rush of fruit in the mouth, this is a big, ripe wine, strong, deeply flavoured and carefully textured, with a pervasive, grainy astringency that begins in the middle and works to moderate the impressive power and richness of the palate. Positive, forthright stuff, with lingering powdery flavours and plenty of vigour, it is still bristling with youth, but should, with maturity, emerge as one of the great New Zealand Gewürztraminers.

ROBARD & BUTLER GEWÜRZTRAMINER

Robard & Butler have produced consistently attractive, floral wines that are characteristically rose-like in character, gently spicy and soft. Regular medal winners in local wine competitions, they have also performed well outside the show ring to be one of the most widely respected New Zealand Gewürztraminer labels.

1988
MATAWHERO GEWÜRZTRAMINER

13.1% alc/vol; 100% Gewürztraminer; Matawhero district, Gisborne region.
Winemaker: Simon Waghorn
Best drinking: 1995–96

Golden wine with a collar of bubbles at the rim, it has a lactic, oily, rich bouquet, tinged with cinnamon and the ghosts of roses. Fat, with a lovely rich, liqueur texture, it is beautifully balanced on the palate, soft, but not lacking life, with a flavour that has gentle richness, the mellow tones of bottle-aged fruit and a gorgeous floral lift that lingers along the softly spiced finish. Lovely wine, charming and pretty without being twee, it has life yet, although drying out at the end.

1990

12.5% alc/vol; 100% Gewürztraminer; blend of Gisborne and Marlborough fruit.
Best drinking: 1995

Pale golden wine with a mildly fruity aroma tinged faintly with floral hints. The palate is pretty, floral, with pudgy fruit flavours and a twist of bitterness at the finish, and an unexpected, lingering flavour of cloves and rose petals. Never assertive, it has a quiet presence that is nicely persuasive.

1991

13.5% alc/vol; 100% Gewürztraminer;
Marlborough region.
Winemaker: Alan McCorkindale
Best drinking: 1996–1997

The forceful, rosé petal aroma is full without being blowsy, but is somewhat at odds with the light, green-gold appearance of this wine. Vinous, and pleasantly flavoured with very pretty rose petal and clove flavours, characters that lift the finish nicely, but are never as bold as the bouquet implies. A warm, strong wine that is still youthful, and although not as assertively Gewürztraminer as its weight would suggest, there are indications that the fruit character and spice will grow with more bottle age.

1992

12% alc/vol; 100% Gewürztraminer; Marlborough region.
Winemaker: Alan McCorkindale
Best drinking: 1995–1996

Light, polished yellow wine, with very sweet, fragrant, rose-like aromas. A pretty mouthful, dryish, with a crisp, almost sharp finish, it is a light wine compared with earlier vintages, but pleasant enough.

PINOT GRIS

PINOT GRIS WAS PROBABLY BROUGHT TO NEW ZEALAND LATE LAST CENTURY by the Marist Brothers at Mission Vineyards in Hawke's Bay. It was recommended by government viticulturist Romeo Bragato at the turn of the century for its productivity, and for the quality of white wine it produced, but generally it seems to have failed to inspire early winemakers.

As an introduction to the fine winemaking era, it was given some attention by Cooks (NZ) Wine Company, who made a fairly bland single varietal Pinot Gris wine during the 1970s, and both Mission and Brookfields have continued with it in some form or other. Generally, however, it has not captured the imagination of either winemakers or consumers until recently, when the efforts of Dry River in Martinborough have illustrated how well it can perform, especially in the cooler conditions of the South Island wine regions. This has led to an increase in plantings of Pinot Gris by over 60 per cent since 1989, but even with this burst today less than 1 per cent of the total vineyard area in New Zealand is planted in Pinot Gris.

The small-berried clone in Dry River's Martinborough vineyard was secured from Mission, where it is believed to be the original Pinot Gris imported from pre-phylloxera stock in Alsace in 1886. Subsequently, other clones have been introduced from Switzerland in 1962 and 1978, and from Germany (called Rulander) in 1982. These all have larger berries, and are heavier producers of grapes, and of typically lighter flavoured, lighter bodied wines.

DRY RIVER PINOT GRIS

PINOT GRIS

1994

DRY RIVER

Dry River Estate

№ 2942

BOTTLED BY DRY RIVER WINES LTD, PURUATANGA RD, MARTINBOROUGH
PRODUCE OF NEW ZEALAND
℮ 750ml   CONTAINS PRESERVATIVE (220)   13.5% VOL

The pioneers with Pinot Gris as a truly fine wine, Dry River alone have proven that it deserves serious attention with their long line of big, well-flavoured, fine-textured wines that exhibit the classic, fragrant richness of the variety. They also mature particularly well, developing, with bottle age, viscosity and richness, as well as with greatly enhanced flavour complexity, while retaining their freshness and substance.

1986

*12% alc/vol; 100% Pinot Gris, ex Mission clone;
Martinborough district, Wairarapa region; stainless
steel fermentation.
Winemaker: Neil McCallum
Best drinking: 1995–96*

Clear, light yellow-straw colour, with a very fresh, toasty, quince-like fruit bouquet. It has a nicely sweet fruit presence on the palate, with some bitterish astringency balancing a lovely, even flow of slightly thick fruit flavours that have been eased by the mellowing, mildly toasty effects of bottle age. Although it is just starting to dry out at the end, the flavours are still deep and fine, retaining all the elusive viscosity that is a feature of Pinot Gris, with the prettiness of maturity and a gentle, lingering persistence. Neatly balanced between aromatic freshness and ripe, oily depths, it is light yet immensely satisfying.

1987

*13% alc/vol; 100% Pinot Gris, ex Mission clone;
Martinborough district, Wairarapa region; stainless steel
fermentation; hand harvested 8 April 1987.
Winemaker: Neil McCallum
Best drinking: 1995–98*

A ripe, glossy-looking wine, the colour of light yellow gold, it has a ripely aromatic honey-wax bouquet, lined with toast and the unmistakeable mellow citrus tones of marmalade. Suave almost to the point of lightness, it has an upfront freshness that quietly disputes the warm depths and silky texture lying behind resonant flavours of marmalade and succulent, fat fruit which are simultaneously ripe and delicately elusive. Very stylish wine, primarily because of its slick texture, it just rolls on and on, never losing its gloss, finesse or that cargo of flavour, lingering on and on in a vaguely fragrant breeze of subtlety.

1988

*14.2% alc/vol; 100% Pinot Gris, ex Mission clone;
Martinborough district, Wairarapa region; stainless steel
fermentation; hand harvested 15 March 1988.
Winemaker: Neil McCallum
Best drinking: 1996–2003*

An enigmatic wine that is infinitely better than any of its parts suggest. From the sweet depths of its flat, damp bouquet, to its almost incognito finish that is all lithe textures and grace, it is impressively deep, supple, wine with a perplexing, tender thickness which is its finest characteristic. It compounds its mystery with a paradox of sullen flavour and tempting freshness that completes an ugly duckling display which verges on being glamorous, but is still only promise.

The flavours seem to be packed so closely together you never quite get a look at them, being fully aware only of their texture and the swelling warmth that lies behind. Big and very deep, it promises richness and abundance of flavour nuances given more time in bottle, but it is already fine wine, with a long, textural finish and real presence.

1989

13.8% alc/vol; 100% Pinot Gris, ex Mission clone;
Martinborough district, Wairarapa region; stainless steel
fermentation; hand harvested 20 March 1989.
Winemaker: Neil McCallum
Best drinking: 1995–2002

A real beauty, it comes on pretty with its bright, yellow-straw colour and forthright melon and quince bouquet, spiced for added interest with fresh highlights, aromatic toasty bits and an appealing, sensual earthiness. This sensuality is complemented by a stroking feeling in the mouth that has the texture of *crème anglaise*, a delicious touch of satin smoothness, deliriously light and glossy, larded with succulence, concentration and finely traced fruit flavours. There is warmth, too, a charge that is just beneath the surface where it stays until you feel the glow of its presence. It is part of a superb complement of rich, gracefully balanced parts held by that lovely texture. Quite superb wine, a feeling as much as a taste.

1990

13.5% alc/vol; 100% Pinot Gris, ex Mission clone;
Martinborough district, Wairarapa region; stainless steel
fermentation; hand harvested 12 April 1990.
Winemaker: Neil McCallum
Best drinking: 1995–96

Fresh, yellow-straw wine, with a light, toasty bouquet that puts the accent firmly on delicacy rather than strength, it is transformed into a bigger, chunkier thing by the palate. Pleasant, with warm alcohol and some pretty fruit flavours, it is solid rather than fine, with a nervy edge but a lack of crispness and clarity that leaves the alcohol to ruffle its calm without check.

1991

13.8% alc/vol; 100% Pinot Gris, ex Mission clone;
Martinborough district, Wairarapa region; stainless steel
fermentation; hand harvested 1 May 1991.
Winemaker: Neil McCallum
Best drinking: 1995–2006

Clear, light straw in appearance, it has a mealy, solid bouquet with slight abrasion for interest and just a hint of toastiness among fruit aromas that are typically elusive but obviously present. The palate, too, is loaded with similarly elusive ripe, sweet, fruit flavours that are fine yet solid, enlivened by fresh acid, and cladding the warm alcohol in a silky covering. This wine leaves a lasting impression of sweetness and depth that hangs around right to the end of the very long, beautifully balanced, flavoury finish, giving a delightful sense of satisfaction. Packed with potential, it may taste nice now, but is destined to be wonderful.

1992

13.2% alc/vol; 100% Pinot Gris, ex Mission clone;
Martinborough district, Wairarapa region; stainless steel
fermentation; hand harvested 29 April 1992.
Winemaker: Neil McCallum
Best drinking: 1997–2004

Very light, bright, straw-coloured wine that is powerfully youthful, with a full load of concentrated fruit and energy. The bouquet has wafts of perfumed fruitiness, like some exotic fruit salad, and a vaguely oaty, solid wholesomeness that would impress vegetarians. In the mouth it is slick, ripe and easy, with amazing strength and length framed by a refreshing concentration. Still close, deep wine that is just beginning to unravel its best parts, it has the balance and length of something very smart indeed.

1993

13% alc/vol; 100% Pinot Gris, ex Mission clone;
Martinborough district, Wairarapa region; stainless steel
fermentation; hand harvested 29 April 1993.
Winemaker: Neil McCallum
Best drinking: 1998–2003

Pale, glossy straw-coloured wine, with a ripe, earthy, dry straw nose that has considerable depth but no apparent fragrance. It does have hints of fruit peel and even apples in the mouth, with excellent viscosity that gives a chewy thickness, assets complemented by a gentle furriness of mild astringency. Solid and deep, it is all wine, not a fruit bowl, its vinous character overwhelming everything else. Still very youthful, there is promise in its impressive length and the flickering of fruit flavours amid the mouthful of texture and depth.

RIESLING

RIESLING HAS ALWAYS HAD A STRONG PRESENCE IN THE NEW ZEALAND WINE industry. It was one of the earliest varieties planted, on the basis of the inherited British wine-drinking tradition that included Hock and Mosel among its favoured wines, and was one of the first to make a comeback when the fine wines movement took its first progressive steps in the early 1960s. Then it was overshadowed by the enthusiasm shown by many winemakers and grape growers for Müller Thurgau, which was often erroneously labelled Riesling or Riesling Sylvaner, with true Riesling being tagged 'Rhine' Riesling.

The resulting confusion, compounded by the often overly sweet, light, innocuous nature of most Müller Thurgau wines, has detracted from Riesling's once impeccable image, a situation that has not been helped by the declining standard of German wines, and misleading German labelling. So Riesling currently has a low status among fine wine drinkers, despite consistently fine Riesling wines from a number of producers in most regions. It represents the best value of all New Zealand's fine wines, but this, in turn, has seen it neglected by many winemakers, to the point where it is often made without the attention and respect that fine wines deserve. There is also a tendency to overcrop Riesling to suit returns from low-priced wines, producing light flavours and short lifespans.

In spite of its reputation as a cool-climate variety, some very good wines have been made from Gisborne-grown fruit, and Hawke's Bay has also proved to be a successful growing region. Marlborough and Nelson, however, have consistently been the most successful Riesling regions, producing wines that are typically fragrant, deeply flavoured and very fresh in character. When carefully grown, handled with respect and given the full attention of winemakers, Rieslings are among the finest of New Zealand's fine wines.

The origins of the oldest Riesling vines in the country are uncertain, but stock has been imported from Germany, Australia, California and South Africa at regular intervals since 1962, and the selection of clones is among the most extensive of all classic varieties in New Zealand.

COOPERS CREEK RIESLING

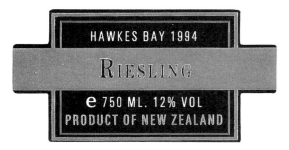

The reputation enjoyed by these wines has been accumulated over years of competition success, and is confirmed by their appeal and lively drinkability when young. They have yet to show any great ability to age, however, and youthfulness is perhaps their greatest charm.

1984
RHINE RIESLING
100% Riesling.
Winemaker: Randy Weaver

The clear, deep yellow colour of this wine is its best feature, for it has faded into a disgruntled retirement.

1985
100% Riesling.
Winemaker: Randy Weaver

Very pale wine, in colour and in character, but its faint bouquet and distant flavour have just enough biscuity bottle age to be at least interesting.

1986
12% alc/vol; 100% Riesling; Hawke's Bay region.
Winemaker: Randy Weaver

Golden colour, with a touch of brown, but the rest of the wine is well over the hill.

1988
11.5% alc/vol; 100% Riesling; Hawke's Bay region.
Winemaker: Randy Weaver

Attractively yellow, it has an idiosyncratic bouquet that is edged with honey and dry, dusty aromas. There is also honey on the palate, and some mellow bottle age, but this wine is now fading fast and, although pleasant enough, is devoid of highlights.

1989
HAWKE'S BAY
11% alc/vol; 100% Riesling; Hawke's Bay region.
Winemaker: Kim Crawford
Best drinking: 1995

Light colour, bright and touched with yellow-green. An attractive, very toasty bouquet, with some fragrant moments of floral fruit and lime blossom introduces this light, slightly frail but pretty wine. There are nice toast and fruit flavours, delicate, almost intricate in parts, and a real gentleness throughout, but this all fades very quickly at the finish, leaving an impression of emptiness.

1990
12% alc/vol; 100% Riesling; Hawke's Bay region.
Winemaker: Kim Crawford
Best drinking: 1995

Ripe in colour, which is yellow and plump-looking, but, in spite of some nice bottle age aromas and some pineapple-like fruit, this is a rather lean wine. Touches of citrus peel aromas and flavour add interest and, although light, the fruit flavours persist at the finish, in their shadowy way.

1991

12% alc/vol; 100% Riesling; Hawke's Bay region.
Winemaker: Kim Crawford
Best drinking: 1995

Toasty, biscuity bottle age and some juicy apricot and citrus characters are at the heart of the charm of this light, yellow wine. The bouquet is also embellished with floral touches and a delicate freshness, and the palate has lime marmalade to add to the toast. Very fresh, it has a lovely sense of clarity, and a long, delicately flavoured finish that leaves an echo of the marmalady toast. Light, pretty, clean-tasting wine.

1992

12% alc/vol; 100% Riesling; Hawke's Bay region.
Winemaker: Kim Crawford
Best drinking: 1995–96

Plump, juicy, smelly wine with suggestions of mellow, ripe fruit and flowers showing the first signs of bottle age. The taste has a tension to it, a crispness and clarity that are relieved only partially by juicy fruit flavours and a soft, floral touch, but which extend the finish into a lovely, lingering delicacy of flavour and nicely burred astringency. Healthy, fresh wine, never assertive or simple, it is a very satisfying drink.

1993

12% alc/vol; 100% Riesling; Hawke's Bay region.
Winemaker: Kim Crawford
Best drinking: 1995–99

Very pale-looking wine, with a delicate, fragrant floral bouquet that also shows warmer fruit subtleties. Supple in the mouth, with deep, moderately intense mid-palate flavours that are lime-tinged, it is a very appealing wine, offering a mouth-watering invitation to have another glass. Not quite dry, its youthful fruit is its most charming asset, and it appears to have flavour in reserve, suggesting a tasty future that the long, clear finish affirms. This does not detract from its succulent, fresh drinkability right now.

1994

12% alc/vol; 100% Riesling; Hawke's Bay region.
Winemaker: Kim Crawford
Best drinking: 1996–2001

A very lively wine, its lime-blossom fragrance almost tingling with uplifting freshness, and the young, sweet-edged flavours alive with delicate fruit and citrus tastes. Very young, but with promising depth and intensity, it also has a vibrant, lengthy finish that is as beautifully marked with delicate flavours as the rest of the wine. Crisp, dry and vigorous, it retains a Riesling finesse that gives it an air of class which is more than youthfulness and ripe fruit.

DRY RIVER RIESLING

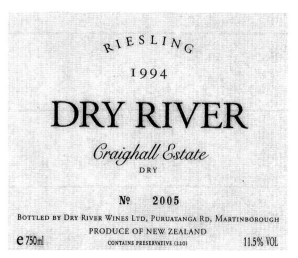

Winemaker Neil McCallum makes Riesling with such elegance and purity of flavour that this is one of the most sought after in the country. The residual sugar varies according to the vintage conditions each year, dependent for this sweetness on a certain amount of botrytis infestation of the crop, but the style is essentially dry. The vines planted in the Craighall Estate Vineyard in Martinborough are clone Gm 239 Riesling, originating in Geisenheim, Germany, and sourced from Te Kauwhata.

1988

*11% alc/vol; 100% Riesling; Framingham Vineyard,
Marlborough region; hand picked 5 May 1988.
Winemaker: Neil McCallum
Best drinking: 1995–98*

Light-coloured, yellow-straw wine with a fragrant, fruit
and gunpowder nose that is light in character. The
palate is fresh and deeply flavoured with intense fruit,
hinting at pineapple, and enhanced by nuances of
toasty bottle age. Particularly charming wine, its
intensity of flavour working as a co-ordinating thread
between the various subtleties and delicate sweetness,
an intensity that lingers at the finish with conclusive
clarity. Very stylish from beginning to end.

1989

*10.5% alc/vol; 100% Riesling; Craighall Estate Vineyard,
Martinborough district, Wairarapa region; hand picked
22 March 1989.
Winemaker: Neil McCallum
Best drinking: 1995–97*

Light, sandy, straw-coloured wine with a slightly
lanolin bouquet lined with floral fragrances and a
sweet dab of fruit among the toasty bottle age aromas.
All the subtleties of fruit flavour, toast and freshness
cling to a moderately intense core, making for a
satisfying, juicy wine that is quite delicious, but lacking
the classy edge of its companions from other vintages.
Light, fruit salady and friendly.

1990

*10% alc/vol; 100% Riesling; Craighall Estate Vineyard,
Martinborough district, Wairarapa region; hand picked
13 May 1990.
Winemaker: Neil McCallum
Best drinking: 1995–98*

There are sweet biscuits, flowers, toast and ripe fruit
in the bouquet of this light, straw-coloured wine,
creating a very good first impression of complexity and
charm. The palate is also pretty, complex and finely
tuned, a tracery of delicate, pretty fruit flavours and
bottle age embellishments, the finish clean, lingering
enough to sustain the edge of class that this wine
conveys. Overall, crisp clarity and grace complement
the cosmopolitan complexity with a tone of
refinement.

1991

*11.8% alc/vol; 100% Riesling, 60% affected by Botrytis
cinerea; Craighall Estate Vineyard, Martinborough district,
Wairarapa region.
Winemaker: Neil McCallum.
Best drinking: 1999–2010*

Plumper colour, yellowish straw in hue, with an
aromatic-fruity-fragrant bouquet that manages to be
both fat and fine at once, with faint suggestions of
mushrooms among the limes and flashes of apricot. A
big, creamy, intense mouthful, remarkably supple yet
fresh, it has a great physical presence to complement
the almost ethereal qualities of fragrance and
concentrated lightness. Classic stuff, with apricots and
lychees and every other sort of fruit as well as traces of
soft spice woven around a heart of clarity, elegance and
a lingering intensity that fades only gradually, as does
its tender sweetness, to a mouth-watering, dry finish.
It leaves the impression that it could last a generation
without losing any of its beauty, class or clarity.

1992

*11.8% alc/vol; 100% Riesling, 40% affected by Botrytis
cinerea; Craighall Estate Vineyard, Martinborough district,
Wairarapa region.
Winemaker: Neil McCallum
Best drinking: 2000–2012*

The colour of yellow straw and as bright as morning,
this is a particularly fragrant wine, with wafts of spring
flowers lined with honeyed mandarin peel, and a heart
of juicy, sweet fruit. Following such a gorgeous
introduction, the palate is no surprise, but a mouthful
of pure pleasure, intense, slightly limy, apricot and
nectarine fruit, deep, lively and enriched with a
creaminess. It is a succession of counterpoints: fresh
and sweet, lively fruit and tender cream, clarity and
complexity. Very long, its juicy flavours enhanced by
mellow sweetness, it has the effortless balance that is
the essence of elegance. Still youthful, it should be
dazzling with more bottle age.

1993

11.8% alc/vol; 100% Riesling; Craighall Estate Vineyard, Martinborough district, Wairarapa region; hand picked 15 May 1993.
Winemaker: Neil McCallum
Best drinking: 1999–2010

Light, sandy straw wine, with a mellow fragrance, delicately floral and hinting at intense fruit, but managing a quiet reserve. Pleasant in the mouth, cool, with a juicy heart and a very tidy tension that underpins its clarity, its vague intensity, all of which is brightened immeasurably by a long, piercing acidity. The finish is enhanced by a pinch of astringency that complements the fruit and flowers theme, but the youthfulness of this wine comes across as a succession of characteristics rather than an integrated whole. One to wait for.

1994

11% alc/vol; 100% Riesling; Craighall Estate Vineyard, Martinborough district, Wairarapa region; hand picked 8 May 1994.
Winemaker: Neil McCallum
Best drinking: 2000–2015

Light, sandy, straw-coloured wine, it has a fresh, juicy bouquet that is prettily decorated with floral fragrances and an intriguing hint of raisin-like concentration. Although it is still yeasty, youthful, the concentrated pineapple tang reveals an abundance of vigorous acid and fruit to complement its very apparent depth, clarity and austerity. Warm, lingering, with a core of succulence, this is potentially a superb bottle of Riesling that has elegance in its genes.

GIESEN ESTATE CANTERBURY RIESLING

Giesen, who look to their German background and Canterbury-grown grapes to make fine-quality Rieslings, are the only Canterbury-based producers to show any track record with this

Still Life with Crayfish by C. Jansen

GIESEN
Canterbury
Riesling Extra Dry

Vintage
1994

Produced and bottled by GIESEN WINE ESTATE, Christchurch
PRODUCT OF NEW ZEALAND

variety, in spite of the high hopes of local wine-growers. The style varies from dry to moderately sweet, and although the range is limited to just three vintages, they represent the culmination of a decade of work.

1989
DRY RESERVE

12% alc/vol; 100% Riesling; Burnham district, Canterbury region; picked 24 April 1989.
Winemaker: Marcel Giesen
Best drinking: 1995–99

Light, softly golden-coloured wine, beautifully ripe, toasty, creamy, and fruit-filled, its fragrance tinged with light notes of honey and mandarin peel. Taut, clean wine, a little softer than the bouquet suggests, with nice mandarin characters in the middle, and a long, delicate, complex finish that maintains the slightly creamy, dusty texture of the wine, and ends on a note of fresh clarity. Very good, just off dry, attractively weighted wine, tasting in very good form right now.

1990
LATE HARVEST RESERVE

*10.6% alc/vol; 100% Riesling; Burnham district,
Canterbury region; picked 10–11 May 1990.
Winemaker: Marcel Giesen
Best drinking: 1995–96*

Brassy, shiny gold, very smart-looking wine with a fresh, fragrant, but light bouquet showing a trace of orange peel and herbs among the sweet, mildly fruity aromas. Sweetness on the palate is complemented by light, complex flavours, and a glossy texture, balanced with mild astringency. Good, vigorous mouth feel fends off a tendency to lightness and there are some lovely flavours here making this a most attractive sipper.

1991
EXTRA DRY

*10.5% alc/vol; 100% Riesling; Burnham district,
Canterbury region; picked 29 April 1991.
Winemaker: Marcel Giesen
Best drinking: 1996–2005*

Bright and flashy in the glass, with a greenish cast, this is fragrant, hard-edged, limy wine, clean and crisp with a strong undercurrent of fruit. Light in style, clear and bright, with a very long, fragrant finish, it has depth to its delicacy, a firm stance, and long-term promise that is enhanced by a furry touch of astringency at the finish. For all its dryness, it is the flavour of this wine that impresses.

THE MILLTON VINEYARD RIESLING OPOU VINEYARD

Grown under a biodynamic regime, this Riesling has proved that the variety can succeed as far north as the Gisborne region. It was the first of the Millton wines to attract attention, and one of the first Rieslings to gain widespread

support as a fashionable 'boutique' wine in the era of Chardonnay, Sauvignon Blanc and Cabernet Sauvignon. The winemaker has always made a feature of the botrytis that frequently affects these wines, harmonising his winemaking to the phenomenon, rather than spraying vigorously to eliminate it.

1987
BOTRYTIS CINEREA RHINE RIESLING MEDIUM OPOU VINEYARD

*100% Riesling; Opou Vineyard, Manutuke district,
Gisborne region; hand picked.
Winemaker: James Millton
Best drinking: 1995–97*

A very pretty-looking wine, the colour of light, polished, copper-tinged gold, it has lovely apricot aromas of botrytis interwoven in fine, lace-like intricacy with the fruit-and-flowers fragrance of Riesling and a softly mellow trim of shortbread sweetness. The palate has a light, lanolin silkiness supporting the apricot, nutty, ripe Riesling flavours giving an impression of subtle richness and supple texture that is succulent, sweet-seeming, but quite dry. Long, ethereal wine, its flavour purposeful, it has a faintly bitter finish that creates extra interest rather than detracts, and a kernel of concentration that balances the dry finish and holds the drinker's attention. Lovely wine, soft and not as fine as Riesling aficionados would expect, but its flavour and harmony are of the highest quality. Simply delicious.

1988

100% Riesling; Opou Vineyard, Manutuke district,
Gisborne region; hand picked.
Winemaker: James Millton

Bright, clear gold, big and clumsy wine, with a strong orange peel and damp dust nose. Fresh, quite simple, short and rather watery.

1989

100% Riesling; Opou Vineyard, Manutuke district,
Gisborne region; hand picked.
Winemaker: James Millton
Best drinking: 1995–2001

There is something of Australian Riesling petrol about this big wine. That, and a heartiness of flavour enhanced by some apricot-orange peel intensity, make this bold wine, from its golden colour to the dry, slightly austere finish. The bouquet has simple fruit characters among the others, and there is a suggestion of sweetness on the palate, a softness of sugar that moderates the wine's coarser tendencies while it supports the deep, solid fruit flavours. Never quite supple, this is still an appealing wine, its fruit flavours matching its muscle, making for a harmony that is intriguing for Riesling.

1990

100% Riesling; Opou Vineyard, Manutuke district,
Gisborne region; hand picked.
Winemaker: James Millton
Best drinking: 1995

Lightish gold in colour, this wine has a flatness in spite of its honeyed, waxy bouquet and apricot-orange peel flavours, a light, watery quality that undermines its complexity and fruit. A pleasant enough drink.

1991

100% Riesling; Opou Vineyard, Manutuke district,
Gisborne region; hand picked.
Winemaker: James Millton
Best drinking: 1996–2003

Delicious wine, its bouquet packed with aromas of honeyed apricots and peaches, concentrated and very fragrant, with a whiff of minerals, and just as succulent flavours of fresh, ripe fruit. Rather than warm fuzzies, however, there is real clarity here; the fruit and orange peel are quite precise, as are the lingering floral fragrances that permeate the wine. Long and just short of elegant, this is fine wine in spite of its overweight flavour tendencies, an almost casual harmony making up for finesse and giving grace to the easy juiciness of it all.

1992

100% Riesling; Opou Vineyard, Manutuke district,
Gisborne region; hand picked.
Winemaker: James Millton
Best drinking: 1995–98

Light yellow-gold, this chunky little thing has a furry quality about it, from its aromatic bouquet to the dry, fleshy finish, a soft burr that gives a gravelly texture to fresh, ripe, muscat-like Riesling ripeness. Mellow, clean, tasty wine, its pervasive softness given just a touch of juiciness by ripe fruit, it seems compact, in spite of its lingering, flavourful finish.

1993

100% Riesling; Opou Vineyard, Manutuke district,
Gisborne region; hand picked.
Winemaker: James Millton
Best drinking: 1996–2005

The dominant feature of this wine is its spectacular fragrance, all ripe fruit and flowers with a tang of nettles and enlivening clarity. It is so fresh, supple, delicious with apricot intensity and mandarin oranges throughout, and a long, furry, beautifully textured finish that lasts and lasts. For all its youth, it has real substance, with moderate fruit intensity, depth and fine, long flavour, decorated with citrus spangles and juicy succulence. It is a delicious glass now, but promises more complexity, harmony and finesse in the future.

GROVE MILL MARLBOROUGH RIESLING

From the first vintage produced by this small, Marlborough company, Riesling has been one of the best of their range, a regular medal winner, and a wine that has consolidated Marlborough's reputation as a premium Riesling winegrowing region.

1988

12.5% alc/vol; 100% Riesling; Marlborough region.
Winemaker: David Pearce

A pale, greenish wine, with a mature, toasty bouquet, hints of oiliness and faded muscat aromas. Light and simple wine, past its best.

1989

13% alc/vol; 100% Riesling; Marlborough region.
Winemaker: David Pearce
Best drinking: 1995–97

Mellow-hued, light and greenish gold, this wine has a fine fragrance, at once toasty and blossom-like. The very attractive palate endorses this impression, laced as it is with delicate flavour subtleties, warmth and an easy sweetness that lingers on at the end with a vague note of orange peel. Pleasing, pretty stuff.

1990

10% alc/vol; 100% Riesling; Marlborough region.
Winemaker: David Pearce
Best drinking: 1995–96

Pale, sandy-coloured wine, very fragrant, blossom-like with hints of fresh beans and a vibrant, edgy quality. Fresh, clean and beautifully balanced palate right to the end, with a tracery of sugar in support, but a long, dry finish. Pretty, lively wine, very neat and tidy, with the flavour just fading away in the face of the dry finish.

1991

12.5% alc/vol; 100% Riesling; Marlborough region.
Winemaker: David Pearce
Best drinking: 1996–2010

Fragrant, floral and ripe, the bouquet of this wine is deep and particularly inviting, its juiciness shot with apple and mandarin nuances. This lovely fragrance is complemented by a perfect mouthful, just starting to show the savoury-biscuit touches of bottle age, but otherwise juicy and still tingling with a youthfulness that bathes flavours of stone fruit, mandarin and light treacle in shimmering exuberance. The whole wine is a neatly balanced blend of sweetness, depth, weight and clarity, holding its poise through to the finish, and leaving a warm, soft glow of fruit behind. Delicious, almost strokable wine, it has a sensuous intensity as well as lovely balance, textural qualities that make it more than just good wine.

1992

12% alc/vol; 100% Riesling; Marlborough region.
Winemaker: David Pearce
Best drinking: 1996–2006

Pale, sandy straw with touches of green, and a fresh, appley fragrance that has overtones of blossom. Certainly pretty wine, with an intensity that grabs your attention, tidy sweetness, depth and refreshing clarity, all in support of rolling, tumbling fruit flavours that have a passing similarity to muscat and other soft, rich fruits. It dries out somewhat at the end, but the lingering grapey flavour keeps it pleasant. Altogether a most toothsome wine, its appley tone showing just a flicker of mandarin now and then, but always fresh and crisp.

1993

11% alc/vol; 100% Riesling; Marlborough region.
Winemaker: David Pearce
Best drinking: 1999–2012

Pale straw-coloured wine, fresh to look and to smell, its bouquet lively with forthright fragrance that suggests apple blossom. Concentrated, fresh and long-flavoured, with excellent clarity and an abundance of fruit—grapes, apples, kumquats, even a touch of fresh limes—all embedded in a concentrated background of intensity. The freshness and intense nature of this wine make it almost fierce, certainly piercing, but very long and fragrant right to the end, but there is a trace of mellowing sweetness to keep the acidity in check and moderate the hard edges of concentrated fruit. With the softening influence of bottle age it could turn into a dazzling wine.

1994

11% alc/vol; 100% Riesling; Marlborough region.
Winemaker: David Pearce
Best drinking: 2000–2014

Very pale, youthful-looking wine, tinged green, with a frothy bouquet of rich, flamboyant beauty, ripe and juicy with the tang of minerals. Super fruit flavour, generous, ripe and very juicy, with enough depth and a fine balance of sugar and acid to help it grow, with more maturity, into an especially good bottle. Although it is very young, it already seems to lack only experience, making for delightful fresh drinking with puppy fat filling in where sensuous elegance will come with time. One for the cellar.

MARTINBOROUGH VINEYARD RIESLING

Although not a wine that this famous Pinot Noir and Chardonnay producer is particularly noted for, Riesling is invariably one of the company's most successful wines, bearing the mark of professional, skilful winemaking and fine-quality fruit.

1984
RHINE RIESLING

13% alc/vol; 100% Riesling; Martinborough district,
Wairarapa region; hand picked late April 1984.
Winemaker: Russell Schultz
Best drinking: 1995

Pale, coppery yellow-gold, almost tanned. Juicy, plump, lychee nose detailed with toast and a lime-like freshness. Big and forcefully fragrant, with all the extra advantages of bottle age nuances complementing its essency fruit. Has dried out somewhat, and astringency at the finish roughens it up, but it is difficult not to be impressed by the power of fruit flavour this wine undoubtedly had, and its longevity if it had had more refined winemaking.

1986

RHINE RIESLING

11.8% alc/vol; 100% Riesling; Martinborough district,
Wairarapa region; hand picked 25 April 1986.
Winemaker: Larry McKenna
Best drinking: 1995

Light, straw-yellow wine, with a flat, almost earthy aroma that is enhanced by toasty, bottle age overtones and a vaguely lime freshness. The flavour is somewhat faded, but hearty acid is keeping everything together: bottle age tone, pleasant fruit and a nice finish that is showing signs of drying out.

1987

11% alc/vol; 100% Riesling; Martinborough district,
Wairarapa region; hand picked 27 April 1987.
Winemaker: Larry McKenna
Best drinking: 1995–2005

Ripe-looking wine, golden yellow and glossy, with a surprisingly fruity nose that smells much younger than the vintage date suggests it should. The bouquet is ripe and toasty, with layers of complex subtleties, fragrances, to grace the lively fruit. The palate is awash with sweet fruit and freshness, kept in check by marvellous clarity and depth of flavour that hangs on to the very end of a long, lingering finish which whispers away. Over this is laid a delicate and quite enchanting pattern of bottle age and other intricacies Delightfully poised wine, ripe with bouquet and flavour, youthful without being young, the epitome of Riesling drinkability and charm, modulated by a dash of astringency at the finish that perfectly frames its final flavour impression, balances its gentle sweetness. Simply lovely.

1988

11% alc/vol; 100% Riesling; Martinborough district,
Wairarapa region; hand picked 27 April 1988.
Winemaker: Larry McKenna
Best drinking: 1995–2002

Bright, clear, light straw, deliciously plump and toasty on the nose, with wafts of fragrance and a pervasive delicacy that runs right through. It feels beautiful in your mouth, and is full of aged fruit and sweet juiciness that steadily builds towards the end, where it fades gently to give way to gentle astringency and dryness. Fresh, very alive wine, the charm of its delicacy given

substance by the mouth-filling quality of its flavour. Most impressive, attractive, persuasive wine that would charm a tax collector, it still has plenty of life in it yet.

1989

12.2% alc/vol; 100% Riesling; Martinborough district,
Wairarapa region; hand picked 27 March 1989.
Winemaker: Larry McKenna
Best drinking: 1995–96

Polished, light, bright, clear, straw-coloured wine, with a toasty, mealy, mature bouquet that is soft and a little short of fruit and intensity. The palate is clear and true, with traces of quite pretty, delicate fruit and a twist of astringency that comes with a subtle surge of flavour right at the finish. Fresh-feeling and reasonably weighty wine, but, lacking the fruit to match this weight, it comes across as rather sullen, without charm or flair.

1990

9.5% alc/vol; 100% Riesling; Martinborough district,
Wairarapa region; hand picked 4 April 1990.
Winemaker: Larry McKenna
Best drinking: 1995

Very youthful wine, light and moderately stylish, it has a waxy, delicately fragrant bouquet, with hints of toast and concentrated peach jelly. There is none of this concentration in the mouth, however, the lightness kept company by a vaguely tough edge. A pleasant drink.

1991

11% alc/vol; 100% Riesling; Martinborough district,
Wairarapa region; hand picked 21 April 1991.
Winemaker: Larry McKenna
Best drinking: 1995–2005

Delicious, poised wine, with the gracious beauty of classic Riesling right from the first sniff of its lilting, softly fragrant bouquet to the last traces of delicate flavour. There are also glimmers of orange peel in the bouquet, which offers a quiet introduction to a climax of flavour as the wine hits your palate. Big, ripe, sensuously beautiful flavours seem to tumble out, touched with lightness and sweet clarity, and never anything but deep, penetrating essences of summer and stone fruits, traces of marmalade and posies of spring flowers. The fruit flavours, the succulence, would be powerful if they were not so finely balanced, so graceful, and the twist of astringency at the end helps to sustain these into a lingering, effortless finish. Very classy wine indeed, slick and generous without being either too clean or too blowsy.

1992

11% alc/vol; 100% Riesling; Martinborough district,
Wairarapa region; hand picked 8 May 1992.
Winemaker: Larry McKenna
Best drinking: 1995–97

Pale, lemon-straw-coloured wine that looks as delicate as its bouquet suggests, but the flavours are quite fat and juicy, mouth-wateringly attractive. Clear, pretty, very drinkable wine with some nicely floral and fruity Riesling characteristics.

1993

10% alc/vol; 100% Riesling; Martinborough district,
Wairarapa region; hand picked 14 May 1993.
Winemaker: Larry McKenna
Best drinking: 1998–2005

The bouquet of this light, straw-coloured wine has the intriguing fragrance of perfumed tropical fruit, of babaco, melons and even limes, with a hint of wax for extra interest. The palate, too, is tropically exotic with layers of lime-edged, intense fruit characters that hold on until the very end of a long, lacy finish. Smart stuff, youthful, elegant and succulent, all its joys wrapped up in precious fruit that is scrubbed to freshness with keen acidity. Pure pleasure.

MONTANA MARLBOROUGH RIESLING

This is the pioneer Riesling of the fine wine movement in New Zealand, the wine that proved New Zealand could grow and make high-quality Riesling in Marlborough, wine of distinctly finer quality than that produced from Müller Thurgau. Machine harvested and processed in stainless steel, this is not the most carefully made of wines, but it is produced with precision, and has proved the longevity of New Zealand Riesling wine, as well as confirming the viability of Riesling grapes.

1982

10.5% alc/vol; 100% Riesling; Marlborough region.
Best drinking: 1995

Light, greeny gold with the distinctive aroma of wine biscuits dominating its bouquet, the mellow signs of bottle age. Gentle, round and fresh, it is quite sweet, light on flavour, and beginning to fade a little at the finish, but among the bottle age toast there remains the very pleasurable shadow of juicy fruit flavour. Delightful wine.

1983

11.5% alc/vol; 100% Riesling; Marlborough region.
Best drinking: 1995–98

Light, fresh, green-gold in colour, a very pretty and lively wine with a floral, toasty bouquet that is lifted and clean, with hints of exotic fruit, almost cape gooseberry in character. Has sweet, fresh, ripe flavours, and moderate weight making it a most delicious wine, fine and neatly balanced, showing the benefit of bottle age in its mellow toastiness. Plump and juicy in the middle, still holding onto its clarity, it does fade off slightly at the end, but still holds your attention with its delicious purity and warmly complex shading. Lovely stuff.

1984

11.5% alc/vol; 100% Riesling; Marlborough region.
Best drinking: 1995

Bright, clean, golden wine, with a slight whiff of sulphur. Clean and simple, nice enough, and certainly still alive, but the slightly astringent finish does detract from its charm.

1985

12% alc/vol; 100% Riesling; Marlborough region.
Best drinking: 1995

Light golden colour, with an appealing dash of fruit intensity in the bouquet keeping company with aromas of toast and sweet biscuits. With faintly creamy character among the slightly green fruit flavours, it is rather clunky, lacking in freshness and finesse, but a nice enough drink.

1986

11.5% alc/vol; 100% Riesling; Marlborough region.
Best drinking: 1995

Moderate golden colour, with just a hint of copper about it, and an almost herbaceous edge to the bouquet. Characteristic aged aromas and flavours add complexity to the chunky, ripe fruit palate, which is mildly rich and solid, still very pleasant drinking. The finish has fruit flavour among the astringency and light, soft sweetness.

1987

12% alc/vol; 100% Riesling; Marlborough region.
Best drinking: 1995–99

Ripe, green-gold wine, it has an inviting bouquet full of richness and abundant aromas of apricot-peach fruit, trimmed with intensity and a fresh note of acidity. This gives substance to its fragrant character, turning prettiness to beauty. The palate, too, is lovely — easy, clean and sweetly sensuous, laden with ripe flavours and dried fruit complexities, a flicker of mandarin peel and a long, trailing finish. Not big wine, but filled to its edges with excellent fruit, enhanced by beautiful balance and interesting bottle age characteristics.

1988

12% alc/vol; 100% Riesling; Marlborough region.
Best drinking: 1996–2002

Light gold with green touches, clear and bright. Very pretty, delicate, floral bouquet underpinned by ripe stone fruit characters and a bit of bracing lime juice. Nicely palatable, pretty and sweet with fruit enough to complement the touch of sugar, and a perfect spice of age. Long, delicious, mild, with sufficient succulence still to keep its juicy edge, and pervasively floral right through, it is sunny and delightful wine.

1989

12.5% alc/vol; 100% Riesling; Marlborough region.
Best drinking: 1995–2005

Light gold, freshly fragrant, with a slightly citric aroma and plump, succulent fruit smells. Very tempting. Fat, ripe flavours continue the appeal. So Riesling in character that you can almost taste fresh grapes, it is a wine made interesting by the first touches of bottle age and slightly rough astringency, lively with acid, and a satisfyingly long, easy, finish. Excellent wine, with enough flavour and life to compensate for a slight coarseness, it makes for delicious drinking now, but also holds much promise for improvement with more age.

1990

11.5% alc/vol; 100% Riesling; Marlborough region.
Best drinking: 1995

Pale, lemony yellow colour. Very light wine, softly fragrant, fresh, but rather nondescript. Simple, short, clean.

1991

12% alc/vol; 100% Riesling; Marlborough region.
Best drinking: 1998–2015

Pale, lemon-yellow, clear, bright-looking wine with an equally bright bouquet. Fresh, floral and sweet on the nose, with elements of citrus among the flowers and ripe, grapey fruit, it is also fresh and lively in the mouth, with grapey characters again a feature, hinting at muscat, mildly sweet, clean, fresh and lingering. Still extremely young, but in excellent shape for a long and illustrious future. Very tempting stuff.

1992

12% alc/vol; 100% Riesling; Marlborough region.
Best drinking: 2000–2018

Pale lemon-straw colour, looking as young as it smells, fresh, clean and zingy with life. There is a element of intensity on both the bouquet and palate that balances the lively acidity, and the flavours are youthfully grapey, fresh, fat, ripe. A very pleasant, almost perfumed young wine, packed with Riesling character and lingering well, it is another with a bright future.

1993

12% alc/vol; 100% Riesling; Marlborough region.
Best drinking: 1996–2003

Very pale, lemon-straw wine, with an intensely youthful, grapey bouquet, and a mouthful of fresh, juicy, grape flavour that already shows depth and an element of substance. Very fresh, clean, and moderately lengthy, it should become another pleasant, drinkable wine.

NEUDORF MOUTERE RIESLING

Neudorf have only recently joined the ranks of fine Riesling producers, but they have done so with such spectacular success that the Neudorf name has quickly become as much a sign of Riesling quality as it has of Chardonnay. These are classic, northern South Island wines, elegant and racy, delightfully fragrant, with zesty clarity.

1990
RHINE RIESLING

11% alc/vol; Moutere district, Nelson region; hand picked 23 and 25 April 1990.
Winemaker: Tim Finn
Best drinking: 1995–2000

Light, pleasantly attractive, straw-coloured wine, its bouquet fragrantly floral, sparkling with notes of spring flowers, honey and mandarin. Always delicately beautiful, it has a structural firmness than supports its intricate lacework of aroma and flavour, abetted by some juicy fruit textures and a fresh, clean acidity. As the first signs of bottle age are creeping in, it is developing into a real sophisticate, deep and carefully lithe, bordered with zesty pineapple flavours that hang on even into the long, dry, crisp finish. The epitome of balance, the impression of delicacy it leaves is a lingering one, but it is delicacy with substance.

1991

11.5% alc/vol; Moutere district, Nelson region; hand picked
3 May 1991.
Winemaker: Tim Finn
Best drinking: 1998–2016

Deliciously pretty wine, with spangles of floral fragrance against a ground of soft, easy bouquet, tinged with concentration. The palate continues the concentration theme, laying a base of moderate fruit intensity on which the rest of the wine is built, a flavoury, mildly juicy foundation against which nuances of lime, suave stone fruit and light succulence exude their charm. Packaged with freshness, this is particularly delicious wine, mouth-wateringly so, its lingering delights inviting a return after each sip, its fruit enhanced by clarity and grace.

1992

12% alc/vol; Moutere district, Nelson region; hand picked
11 May 1992.
Winemaker: Tim Finn
Best drinking: 1997–2007

Light straw-coloured wine, touched with a hint of lemon. The mellow fragrance of the bouquet, with hints of citrus blossom and a muscat-like fruit richness, is restrained by a creamy note, but so far shows no signs of bottle maturity. The palate has a brilliant balance of fruit and acid, with flavour intensity, depth and a clever twist of astringency maintaining interest right at the finish, holding the flavours so that their momentum carries into the aftertaste. Heart and soul Riesling, delivering floral beauty with a flash of flavour and a lingering buzz of clarity, it is as much about style as it is about flavour and crafted structure.

1993

12% alc/vol; Moutere district, Nelson region; hand picked
14 and 18 May 1993.
Winemaker: Tim Finn
Best drinking: 1999–2012

Light, bright, lemon-straw in colour, this wine is falling down fragrant, with waves of floral and grape characters welling up from some depth within it, delivering an impression of ripeness and juicy invitation. The palate is fresh, beautifully shaded with fruit flavours that hint at mandarin, apple and clear, lime-like freshness. This tracery of flavours lingers on at the end, and the wine's dryness never reduces its juicy appeal or limits the flavour momentum. Trimmed with intensity and founded on fresh clarity, it has the form of a thoroughbred, all elegance and class.

1994

12% alc/vol; Moutere district, Nelson region; hand picked
13 and 18 May 1994.
Winemaker: Tim Finn
Best drinking: 2000–2016

Pale, lemony straw wine, with a fabulous bouquet of grapey, floral aromas that have not yet developed any detailed subtlety, but are succulently impressive. The fresh touch of fruit is light and clear on the palate, deep with clarity like spring water and yet as freshly delicate as morning blossom, woven with mandarin and honey. Exquisite, finely wrought wine, intricately balanced, it may still be a very young beauty but such is its depth, flavour and delicious balance that it promises to become quite ravishing with time.

NGATARAWA HAWKE'S BAY RIESLING

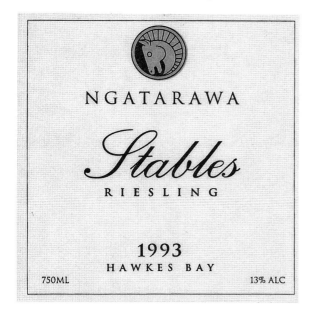

Popular wine mythology suggests that Hawke's Bay is not the place to grow top-class Riesling, but Ngatarawa's efforts of more than a decade make a strong case against such beliefs. Alwyn Corban is already acknowledged as a master of sweet Riesling, and these drier styles confirm his Riesling reputation, and show that it is possible to make top-class Rieslings in the North Island.

1984
RHINE RIESLING DRY

11% alc/vol; 100% Riesling; Hawkes Bay region.
Winemaker: Alwyn Corban
Best drinking: 1995

Polished, brassy colour, light and pretty. The bouquet is fresh, strongly toasty, with delicate fruit fragrances. The palate, too, is very delicate, the fruit almost completely gone, leaving a clear freshness behind to mingle with the toasty, shortbread, bottle-aged characters.

1985
RHINE RIESLING DRY

11% alc/vol; 100% Riesling; Hawke's Bay region.
Winemaker: Alwyn Corban
Best drinking: 1996

Light, pale, very clear-looking wine, with a vaguely essency, concentrated character beneath its toasty aromatics, honey and delicate floral notes. A gently complex wine, still fresh, with traces of delicate fruit and toast in its soft palate, it has a remarkably long finish, spiced with a dash of astringency. Quietly satisfying, it has a clever balance of age, fruit, flowers and texture, bound with just enough alcohol and acidity.

1986
HARVEST RIESLING

10% alc/vol; 100% Riesling; Hawke's Bay region.
Winemaker: Alwyn Corban.

Some nice fruit here, but this has submitted to aldehyde with time. Interesting, but not entirely pleasurable.

1987

11% alc/vol; 100% Riesling; Hawke's Bay region.
Winemaker: Alwyn Corban
Best drinking: 1995–99

Beautiful wine, a clamour of flavour colours and complexity, but all of good character, like a crowd at a smart garden party. Light, lemon-gold, it glitters in the glass, and sparkles, too, on the nose, with an elegant spectacle of floral, toast and honey nuances all finely, delicately balanced to gracefulness. It drinks like sunshine mouthwash, its delicate textures and myriad flavours leaving a bright, gently fading memory of mandarins and flowers. The grace of its bouquet is a predominant theme right through, with the delicate fruit, flowers and mellow toasty flavours expertly dovetailed with fine textural details of acid, mild astringency and alcohol. Dry, effortless, light, exquisite.

1988
LATE HARVEST

11% alc/vol; 100% Riesling; Hawke's Bay region.
Winemaker: Alwyn Corban
Best drinking: 1995–97

Ripe and waxy, the charming floral character of the bouquet is enhanced with tints of honey and mandarin-kumquat fruit, giving an impression of fine perfumed fragrance. Pure, clear, wonderfully balanced wine with an intriguing earthy quality underlying the shortbread and toast, the honeyed, faintly concentrated fruit, its soft sweetness gracefully matched by a refreshing acidity. A stand-out bottle, with flavour substance and real momentum, it has all the advantages of fruit energy and a touch of botrytis, tempered by the sweet-savoury complexities of bottle age. In spite of its flavoury substance, it also has elegance, an easy mixture of finesse and poise that lifts it above the mere technical details of its structure. Quite superb, but it is unlikely to get any better beyond this point.

1989

12% alc/vol; 100% Riesling; Hawke's Bay region.
Winemaker: Alwyn Corban
Best drinking: 1995–2000

Fullish colour, with a floral, beeswax-tinged bouquet that has attractive kumquat characters. Flavoury, with sweet, ripe fruit flavours in spite of its dryness, and a pleasant, mellow character just lifted by a parting twist of astringency and a growing presence of bottle age biscuits. Chunky Riesling, warm and inviting.

1990

STABLES RIESLING LATE HARVEST

11% alc/vol; 100% Riesling; Hawke's Bay region.
Winemaker: Alwyn Corban
Best drinking: 1995–2000

Sandy-coloured wine, tinged with green, it has a fine, fresh bouquet, sweetish, fragrant and appley, with a pinch of citrus peel. With a nice, slick palate, fresh flavoured with lively acid, pleasantly decorated with sweetness, it is notably perfumed from beginning to end, making a flighty, pretty glass of delight, its flavours even-tempered enough to keep the overall enthusiasm in check.

1991

STABLES LATE HARVEST RIESLING SELECTION

11% alc/vol; 100% Riesling; Hawke's Bay region.
Winemaker: Alwyn Corban
Best drinking: 1996–2007

Light, moderately coloured with yellow and green hues, this wine demands attention from the first sniff, which reveals an exciting bouquet shot with honey wax and camphor wood, with bunches of flowers and a clear edge of intensity. The palate, too, makes you sit up and take notice, so deeply laden is it with lime-fringed, intense fruit, hints of apricots and a graceful, lithe tension that gives the whole wine a racy feel. Fruit intensity tends to dominate the palate, but the finish is still rather delicate and softly trailing, giving an appearance of shortness. This could change with more bottle age to moderate the intense freshness with some mellowing complexities, calming the heart to match the gentleness of the finish. Impressive, very youthful wine, brassy but fine in texture and breeding.

1992

12.5% alc/vol; 100% Riesling; Hawke's Bay region.
Winemaker: Alwyn Corban
Best drinking: 1996–2003

Light, fresh, green-hued wine, it has a very structured bouquet of acid and formal fruit aromas, with some milky, nut-cream complexities and a touch of apples. The palate is more masculine than expected, but a charming sweetness undermines the fierce fruit intensity and warm alcohol somewhat, making a lively if less than fragrant wine. Good, staunch Riesling that is still well in its angular, dense youth.

1993

12.5% alc/vol; 100% Riesling; Hawke's Bay region.
Winemaker: Alwyn Corban
Best drinking: 1997–2010

A wonderfully fresh wine, its straw colour still tinged with green, its bouquet a lively jumble of floral fragrances and ripe fruit aromas, with just a hint of creaminess. This enthusiasm is matched by an equally ebullient mouthful, with floral and mandarin flavours, and a suitable intensity presented in cool style. In spite of this, and the hearty, intense substance of the wine, it is quite ravishing already, with sensual, sinuous texture and an immensely long finish. A most promising aristocrat.

ROBARD & BUTLER AMBERLEY RHINE RIESLING

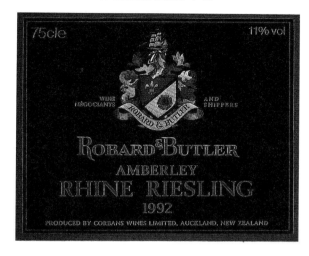

When first released, this wine showed that the potential of North Canterbury was being realised, at least in Riesling. The fact that this has not been followed up by other producers has not undermined the respect that Amberley Rhine Riesling has gathered with its regularly classy performances.

1986

13% alc/vol; 100% Riesling; North Canterbury district, Canterbury region.
Winemaker: Glenn Thomas
Best drinking: 1995–98

Light, golden yellow with hints of green and a fat, ripe, citrus and spring flowers bouquet, matched with a good dollop of toasty bottle age. Has a surprising measure of sweetness, both fruit weight sweetness and that of residual sugar, but this is beautifully supported by nice citrus and fat melon flavours. Clear, attractive and lingering, it is well constructed with warm alcohol, mild acid and very harmonious flavours, still very much alive even if the intensity is showing signs of fading. Smart wine, beautifully crafted, deliciously graceful, it lacks only some energy, some grainy texture, for balance.

1988

12.6% alc/vol; 100% Riesling; North Canterbury district, Canterbury region.
Winemaker: Glenn Thomas
Best drinking: 1995–2000

Pretty gold, tinged with green, this wine has a particularly succulent bouquet, plump with ripe fruit aromas, tinged with toast, juicy and inviting. This is followed by a mouthful of ripe, clear, juicy flavour, fresh-edged with clarity, sustained by depth and some mild tannin grip. Mouth-freshening wine, full of positive life, with traces of honey arriving just in time for the mellow, lingering finish, where they keep company with an undercurrent of citrus-limes. Very appealing wine, at the boundary of exuberance, just falling short on elegance.

1989

11.5% alc/vol; 100% Riesling; North Canterbury district, Canterbury region.
Winemaker: Alan McCorkindale
Best drinking: 1995–2009

Light, golden-coloured wine, with a deep, ripe, clear fragrance that has the character of mature, rich, slightly perfumed ripe fruit. Very attractive palate, freshly fruit flavoured. Long, drying and very deep, it is in total a superb wine, firm but beautiful, with each of its parts delicious enough almost to stand alone: the perfumed, fragrant, fruit-laden bouquet, a real mouthful of clean fruit flavour trimmed with toast and an uplift of fragrance at the end, all underpinned with a tracery of citrus. Fine, texturally suave, full of life and future, but a wonderful drink now, it is a superb combination of energy and grace.

1990

12% alc/vol; 100% Riesling; North Canterbury district, Canterbury region.
Winemaker: Alan McCorkindale
Best drinking: 1995–97

Light, golden yellow wine, shot with green, its clear, softly tender floral aromas a perfect introduction to its softly pretty palate. Quietly flavoured, with hints of honey, neatly styled, but lacking in verve and depth, it is very suppable, but not quite memorable. Nice wine, easy drinking.

1991

12.5% alc/vol; 100% Riesling; North Canterbury district, Canterbury region.
Winemaker: Alan McCorkindale
Best drinking: 1997–2015

Pretty, green-yellow, clear and bright. The bouquet is honeyed and floral, with a fragrance that is delightfully fine, almost ethereal. Ripe flavours all through the fresh palate complement the fresh liveliness of this wine, maintaining a flavour substance beneath its inclination to fragrance and lightness. Pervasively fine, it leaves an impression of elegant style, all components of which are fine-grained, almost, but never quite, delicate. Long, slender and graceful, it is classically elegant Riesling with the advantage of fine fruit clarity. Lovely.

1992

11% alc/vol; 100% Riesling; North Canterbury district, Canterbury region.
Winemaker: Alan McCorkindale
Best drinking: 1995–2000

Ripe, fresh, light yellow colour. Vaguely fragrant, with pineapple-citrus aromas and flavour deeply inlaid with crisp acidity, this wine has energy, with floral tones to match the intense fruit. It seems drier than it is, but is yet to unfold enough of its fruit character for a sound judgement to be made on its real character. Quite light for all of its seeming vibrancy.

SEIFRIED ESTATE RIESLING

Along with Montana, Seifried is one of the Riesling pioneers in New Zealand, and although this Nelson producer makes a wide-ranging selection of Riesling styles, in German fashion, it can always be relied on to show New Zealand Riesling in a positive light.

1979

WEINGUT SEIFRIED RHINE RIESLING

100% Riesling; Upper Moutere district, Nelson region.
Winemaker: Herman Seifried.

Old, oxidised and well past its best.

1981

10.5% alc/vol; 100% Riesling; Upper Moutere district, Nelson region.
Winemaker: Herman Seifried
Best drinking: 1995

Polished, brassy gold with some green lights. Toasty, bottle-aged nose, with floral textures and a silky character that borders on richness. Nice on the palate, supple, fresh, slightly coarse, but very interesting, with a petrol cast and some lovely waxy, fine-grained fruit. Suave in texture, this is a beautiful old bottle of Riesling, showing neat harmony of its many complex parts. Drying out at the finish, it leaves a mellow echo of fruit behind, gracefully fading.

1983

RHINE RIESLING LATE VINTAGE

10.5% alc/vol; 100% Riesling; Upper Moutere district, Nelson region.
Winemaker: Herman Seifried
Best drinking: 1995

A beautiful, deep, golden wine with a slightly dusty, dry cellar nose, trimmed with old honey and hints of toast. Remarkably fresh on the palate, structurally sound, but the fruit has not held on for long enough to give the palate any substance. Pretty, though, with a delicate tracery of flavour that just slides away at the end.

1985
RHINE RIESLING BEERENAUSLESE STYLE

*9.5% alc/vol; 100% Riesling; Upper Moutere district,
Nelson region.
Winemaker: Herman Seifried
Best drinking: 1999*

Richly coloured, like polished, deep, brassy gold, with a golden syrup nose, gently spicy, waxy and sweet. The palate is also sweet, fine and fresh, with citrus-mandarin flavours, a trace of juiciness and as clean as a whistle with piercing fresh acidity. Very young-seeming, clean, wonderfully light, fresh wine with a crisp edge like ice, and lingering, golden syrup flavours. Not rich, but gracefully sweet, lingering, pleasing.

1986
RHINE RIESLING

*12% alc/vol; 100% Riesling; 50% Upper Moutere,
50% Redwood Valley districts, Nelson region.
Winemaker: Herman Seifried
Best drinking: 1995*

Pretty, full, yellow colour, waxy and aromatic, slightly toasty, with a lifted floral-fruit fragrance. Light and fresh on the palate, with a creamy note and an element of coarseness that makes it stumble slightly. Good, honest wine, showing the mellowing benefit of some bottle age, but lacking finesse. Nice enough.

1988
RHINE RIESLING

*12% alc/vol; 100% Riesling; 50% Upper Moutere,
50% Redwood Valley districts, Nelson region.
Winemaker: Herman Seifried
Best drinking: 1995–97*

Pretty yellow wine, clean and hard-edged on the nose, but clean and fresh-tasting, with some ginger flavour characters that suggest Gewürztraminer rather than Riesling. Has a nice age-induced mellow trim, adding a little complexity to a nice glass of wine.

1988
RHINE RIESLING BEERENAUSLESE STYLE

*9.5% alc/vol; 100% Riesling; 50% Upper Moutere district,
Nelson region.
Winemaker: Herman Seifried
Best drinking: 1995–2005*

Burnished, brassy copper-gold, this wine looks rich and valuable, and there is an expensive concentration of intense aromas on the nose, which is otherwise appley, with a dash of toffee and an interesting light touch. Very sweet, fresh-edged and golden syrup-like, tinged with kumquat and apple flavours, and fiercely intense, it is saved from overkill by a fresh, crisply clean finish. Like its colour, a brassy wine, loud and piercing, but scrumptious for all that.

1990
RHINE RIESLING

*12.2% alc/vol; 100% Riesling; Upper Moutere district,
Nelson region.
Winemaker: Herman Seifried
Best drinking: 1995–96*

A real softy, this wine has pretty, yellow-green colour, light, fluffy fragrance, and traces of mandarin peel and sweetness in its palate. Pleasant, easy wine with nice fruit flavours and a soft finish, it is lovely drinking now.

1991
RHINE RIESLING LATE HARVEST

*9.5% alc/vol; 100% Riesling; Redwood Valley district,
Nelson region.
Winemaker: Herman Seifried
Best drinking: 1997–2006*

Freshly polished, light golden colour, with a fine honey and apple nose, taut like a high note on a violin, seductively sweet rather than luxuriously so, but enough to be wickedly tempting. The palate confirms this appeal, fresh and succulent, it is full of the flavours of clover honey, ripe, juicy apricots and peaches, toffee, apples and flowers for luck. Very light, easy and scintillatingly fresh, its intensity making the jumble of flavours linger on and on, it is a very tidy, entrancing little wine.

1991
RHINE RIESLING RESERVE DRY

12.5% alc/vol; 100% Riesling; Upper Moutere district,
Nelson region.
Winemaker: Herman Seifried
Best drinking: 1995–99

Finely textured, with clean, floral notes and good weight, its dryness adding an interesting austerity to the charm of Riesling flowers and fruit. Nicely, deeply flavoured, verging on elegant, but still rustic to the point of being hearty, it seems more a healthy, dry wine for the table than an aristocrat. Well-made wine, with life and pleasure in abundance.

1993
RHINE RIESLING RESERVE DRY

12% alc/vol; 100% Riesling; Redwood Valley district,
Nelson region.
Winemaker: Herman Seifried
Best drinking: 1996–2003

Clean, light yellow-green wine, with a fragrant, muscat and sweets nose lifted by floral notes. Weighty, full, vigorous, with the dry finish coming as something of a surprise after the luscious flavours and their hints of ginger and spring flowers. A tasty, easy style, clean as spring water, its flavours linger nicely, leaving an testing invitation to the next sip. Nevertheless it feels as if it could last a long time and gain considerably from the experience.

1994

13% alc/vol; 100% Riesling; Upper Moutere district,
Nelson region.
Winemaker: Herman Seifried
Best drinking: 1998–2009

Green-tinged, pale and sandy, with a faint bubble, this wine is gorgeously fragrant, all flowers and lime-perfumed froth. The palate at first appears light, but it grows in substance and depth, always clean, fresh-edged, but weighted with sweet, plump, ripe fruit and flowers, tinged with lime, apples and mandarin, it becomes quite generous, before finishing dry and flavoury. Remarkably ripe and deep for such a young wine, it is already showing a fine texture to match its depth and length. It should become a class act with some bottle age.

STONELEIGH VINEYARD RHINE RIESLING

Stoneleigh, grown in the company's Marlborough vineyards, is one of Corban's impressive range of Rieslings. It has consistently been a very attractive, fruity style, a regular award winner in competitions and one of the most highly respected Rieslings in the country.

1986

12.5% alc/vol; 100% Riesling; Raupara Road district,
Marlborough region; picked 2 May 1986.
Winemaker: Glenn Thomas
Best drinking: 1995–97

This is a charming older wine, with an abundance of interesting bottle age characters matched by a persistent freshness. A jolly, light yellowish golden colour, it has a bouquet that is abundantly toasty, with a fine subtlety of matured fruit aromas. A lingering shot of juicy, pretty fruit flavour is an important part of the charm, woven among the toast and shortbread flavours of age, and brightened by a hearty cut of acid. As the flavours slip away at the finish, this acid takes on a more dominant role, but the memory of fruit and complexity is enough to maintain the poise of this fading beauty.

1988

11.5% alc/vol; 100% Riesling; Raupara Road district, Marlborough region; picked 26 April 1988.
Winemaker: Glenn Thomas

Nicely touched with gold, this is a toasty, mature wine, quite delicate and full of fascinating complexities. Light, attractively sweet and fresh on the palate, it has a nice filigree of flavours and subtleties, but the juice has gone. Its faded beauty still has some charm, even if it is only a reminder of how attractive this wine once was.

1989

11% alc/vol; 100% Riesling; Raupara Road district, Marlborough region; picked 4 April 1989.
Winemaker: Alan McCorkindale
Best drinking: 1995

Its light, yellow-golden colour has a pretty, polished look, which is also true for the rest of the wine. The frilly, floral, fragrant bouquet, nicely trimmed with toasty biscuits, is followed by an equally pretty, fresh, fragrant palate, light, with a touch of juice. All this appealing front quickly fades, however, to a light astringent finish, leaving the impression that this wine is all facade.

1990

10.5% alc/vol; 100% Riesling; Raupara Road district, Marlborough region; picked 28 April 1990.
Winemaker: Alan McCorkindale
Best drinking: 1995

Soft, yellow-straw wine, clear and bright, with a lightly fragrant bouquet that is already showing considerable toasty bottle age character, along with an unusual dustiness. The very delicate, lightly flavoured palate, quite pretty in a soft, lacy way, fades quickly.

1991

12.5% alc/vol; 100% Riesling; Raupara Road district, Marlborough region; picked 24 April 1991.
Winemaker: Alan McCorkindale
Best drinking: 1995–2001

This very moreish wine is delightfully fragrant, with a trace of shortbread among its clean, freshly floral aromas. The palate, too, is eminently sippable, alive with floral and fruit flavours and the mellow edge of sweet biscuits. It is delicate, but with depth, good weight and nicely sustained length, and just enough sweetness to bind the whole into a graceful, gently impressive wine.

1992

12% alc/vol; 100% Riesling; Raupara Road district, Marlborough region; picked 11–14 May 1992.
Winemaker: Alan McCorkindale
Best drinking: 1995–97

Fresh, light, straw-coloured wine, its bouquet distantly floral and perfumed with the lavender-like scent of soap. It seems sweeter than it really is, with a heart of fruit intensity but floral flavours and an edge of greenness. Nice wine, with a lingering, fresh, green-tinged finish, it is very quiet at present but should open up with more time in bottle.

1993

11.5% alc/vol; 100% Riesling; Raupara Road district, Marlborough region.
Winemaker: Alan McCorkindale
Best drinking: 1996–2001

Very lightly coloured, just hinting at straw, this fragrantly citrus wine is angular and fruity fresh. Limes and other citrus note abound, from the blossom-like fragrance right through to the finish, with an attractive moment of sweetness in the middle, which thickens its palate and turns it away from sharpness. Very clean, crisp and well made to the point of finesse, if you don't let its liveliness dominate, it is full of promise.

SAUVIGNON BLANC

SAUVIGNON BLANC HAS BEEN THE IDEAL VEHICLE FOR NEW ZEALAND character in wine, that unique aromatic presence and clarity of flavour which is the outstanding feature of produce grown in this country. Sauvignon Blanc's natural zest and high acidity have delineated these characteristics with such precision that the wines are almost a caricature of New Zealand flavour and, as such, have made an immediate impression on wine critics and consumers for whom New Zealand was formerly a distant, sheep- and butter-growing enclave of the British Empire, if it was known at all.

For all this, Sauvignon Blanc was a relative latecomer to the revived wine industry in New Zealand, arriving at the earliest only in the 1960s, and not planted for serious winemaking use until Ross Spence at Matua Valley adopted it in the early 1970s. The wine he made was impressive enough to influence Peter Hubscher, Montana's winemaker, who allocated substantial numbers to his company's vast new vineyard project in Marlborough.

As is so often the case in the new world, the marriage of Sauvignon Blanc and Marlborough that has had such a profound influence on the New Zealand fine wine industry was a matter of individual intuition and luck, but it is luck that winemakers have seized and capitalised on with intelligence and energy.

One of the advantages of Sauvignon Blanc in the early stages of fine wine development was its ability to perform on the basis of its fruit quality alone, without any need for sophisticated or refined winemaking craft. Even when machine harvested and processed in the minimal conditions of large, stainless steel-dominated wineries such as Montana's, the results are exciting.

These conditions are easy to replicate, and new wine producers have done so, following the example set by Montana, and producing fruit-dominated wines that have enough character to thrive on international fine wine markets. Now most New Zealand wineries produce at least one example of the stainless steel, Marlborough style.

Other winemakers, generally in other regions, have evolved more subtle ways of handling Sauvignon Blanc, both in the vineyard and in the winery. These have involved the use of oak, often in extreme ways, as well as the introduction of related grape varieties such as Semillon.

The evolution of the now varied styles of New Zealand Sauvignon Blancs has only been successful, however, when winemakers have paid attention to the particular character of the variety under New Zealand conditions. The best wines continue to be those that use this special vitality and flavour as a feature, rather than subdue it under a mess of winemaking baggage.

Most of the current production of Sauvignon Blanc in New Zealand is based on the clone originally used by Matua Valley and Montana, although a number of new selections are currently under trial in various regions.

CLOUDY BAY
SAUVIGNON BLANC

New Zealand's glamour wine in most international markets, Cloudy Bay has set standards of subtlety and complexity for other winemakers to achieve if they want to match the Marlborough winery. Part of its class arises from the fact that it has been able to achieve this without loss of the fruit intensity, clarity and vigour which are the region's inimitable marks of character. Ten years of high quality, sophisticated winemaking without so much as a stumble, in spite of fluctuating vintages, is an impressive performance for any winery, in any country.

1985

90–85% Sauvignon Blanc, 10–15% Semillon; 100% Marlborough; 10% barrel fermentation; aged in oak barrels, on lees for 3 months.
Winemaker: Kevin Judd
Best drinking: 1995–96

A wine with pretty, golden straw colours and a dusty, toasty, very cosmopolitan nose complemented by a grain of lively fruit aromas that still appear youthful. The very suave, silky, even glossy-textured palate has more of the nice, bright fruit embedded in it, stacked up with toast and round wine biscuits in fine layers. No longer a big, energetic wine, but still with life and a complex, savoury character that is quite intriguing, it is drying out at the end, fading gracefully.

1986

90–85% Sauvignon Blanc, 10–15% Semillon; 100% Marlborough; 10% barrel fermentation; aged in oak barrels, on lees for 3 months.
Winemaker: Kevin Judd
Best drinking: 1995

Bright, clear, yellow straw-coloured wine, tinged with green, it has a full, fragrant bouquet ripe with the toasty nuances of bottle age, and still crowded with a slurry of ripe, time-mellowed fruit. Maturity gives it a certain complex substance, along with tones of compost, but underneath it lacks the weight of flavour this implies. In spite of a rather fierce finish, again more warmth than substance, it seems to be throwing in the towel.

1987

90–85% Sauvignon Blanc, 10–15% Semillon; 100% Marlborough; 10% barrel fermentation; aged in oak barrels, on lees for 3 months.
Winemaker: Kevin Judd
Best drinking: 1995

Young-looking wine for its age, it also smells plump enough, sweet enough, to be young, but the toastiness gives it away. Quite fresh and delicate to taste, its palate seems soft, tender, with a complex wash of gentle flavour nuances, but it lacks the pleasing texture of earlier vintages. Hung about with hints of limes, it is good in parts.

1988

*90–85% Sauvignon Blanc, 10–15% Semillon; 100%
Marlborough; 10% barrel fermentation; aged in oak
barrels, on lees for 3 months.
Winemaker: Kevin Judd
Best drinking: 1995–97*

Light and pretty, its yellow straw colour as bright as
ever, this wine has a most enchanting nose, fragrant
and toasty with a heart that intimates richness and
mellow summers. Quite meaty-mealy, almost chewy,
for a wine with such fresh notes in it, it has a deep heart
of sweetness that appears endless, and provides a lovely
backdrop for the abundant elements of toast and
concentrated fruit which, although mature, still has
energy. A big, richly mellow wine that covers its short
finish with a generous palate.

1989

*100% Sauvignon Blanc; 100% Marlborough; 10% barrel
fermentation; aged in oak barrels, on lees for 3 months.
Winemaker: Kevin Judd
Best drinking: 1995–99*

Full of life and the resonant tones that bottle age
provides, this is a superb bottle of wine, a masterful
example of winemaking art that on its own almost
justifies Cloudy Bay's reputation. Bright, and the
colour of ripe hay, it has a bouquet which is just
showing fragrant toast highlights among the more
chunky aromas of maturing fruit and that quality of
effervescence without bubbles that is Marlborough
Sauvignon Blanc. There are green herbs here, red
capsicum, nettles, aromatic notes that just keep
popping out from a cloud of fragrance and ripening
complexity. The palate is equally demonstrative and
interesting, a fresh, clear wave of flavours, lively, but
bound by a texture that is vaguely nut-like, hinting at
richness, present yet never obvious. The nettly, herbal
fruit flavours are at hand right through, lively, well-
behaved characters that stay to the very end of a long,
long finish that carries almost every subtlety into
memory. Super stuff. It will not get any better, but it
will be good for a long time yet.

1990

*13.3% alc/vol; 100% Sauvignon Blanc; 100%
Marlborough; picked 2–29 April 1990; 20% barrel
fermentation; aged in oak barrels, on lees for 3 months.*

*Winemaker: Kevin Judd
Best drinking: 1995–97*

Mellowing straw-coloured wine, bright and clear with
a bouquet of ripe hay and toast, light and fragrant to
the end. The palate, too, seems light on flavour, but it
has a milk-soft texture that moderates this somewhat.
A bit fresh and jumbled, it lacks cohesion in the
middle, but still manages to finish fine, with lingering
traces of flavour that are better than the palate leads
you to expect.

1991

*12.9% alc/vol; 96–90% Sauvignon Blanc, 4–10%
Semillon; 100% Marlborough; Sauvignon Blanc harvested
10–21 April 1991; 10% barrel fermentation; aged in oak
barrels, on lees for 3 months.
Winemaker: Kevin Judd
Best drinking: 1995–2001*

A light, bright, sandy-straw wine, its bouquet filled with
ripe fruit aromas, the first toasty fragrances, and a note
that suggests minerals, all very neatly balanced, fine
yet lively in Cloudy Bay style. The palate feels light,
but the flavours and slight mealy texture have great
depth and build a layered complexity, developing from
a swelling throatful of flavour that keeps delivering
taste messages back to your mouth. These concentrated fruit notes of ripe straw, limes, jungly
passionfruit and papaya are precisely matched by a
balancing astringency that builds towards the end
where it adds to the strength of finish. Neat, well-knit,
very smart wine that is as good as you could expect
lively Sauvignon Blanc to be.

1992

*13.3% alc/vol; 96–90% Sauvignon Blanc, 4–10%
Semillon; 100% Marlborough; Sauvignon Blanc harvested
21 April–13 May 1992; 10% barrel fermentation; aged in
oak barrels, on lees for 3 months.
Winemaker: Kevin Judd
Best drinking: 1995–97*

Light, sandy, straw-coloured wine, with an unusual
smell reminiscent of warm stones and minerals, but
backed by vibrant, concentrated, herbaceous-edged
fruit aromas and nuances of ripe hay. Fresh in taste,
with mildly sweet fruit and a subtle seam of softness
running through, a softness that has a vaguely mealy

texture and flavour. Citric in parts, it also has the fresh tension of lime juice, but without its concentrated flavour, and there is an astringent presence that grows towards the finish to give it a dry, lingering quality. Interesting wine with a well-made feel, but without the persuasive presence of ripe fruit.

1993

13% alc/vol; 96–90% Sauvignon Blanc, 4–10% Semillon; 100% Marlborough; Sauvignon Blanc harvested 22 April– 20 May 1993; 10% barrel fermentation; aged in oak barrels, on lees for 3 months.
Winemaker: Kevin Judd
Best drinking: 1995–98

Very light in colour, a pale, green-tinged, sandy straw, this wine has a mineraly, canned peas and cut grass bouquet, and a palate with a light, herbaceous-edged flavour. Its freshness and mild fruit sweetness are pleasant, its astringency neatly balanced, but rather austere. It is a nice wine, if not a succulent one, well crafted and satisfying enough.

1994

13.6% alc/vol; 96–90% Sauvignon Blanc, 4–10% Semillon; 100% Marlborough; Sauvignon Blanc harvested 19 April–9 May 1994; 10% barrel fermentation; aged in oak barrels, on lees for 3 months.
Winemaker: Kevin Judd
Best drinking: 1995–2004

This is very smart wine, with a bright, green-tinged, pale straw colour, and a bouquet alive with fresh gooseberries and clear, mellow fruit tones that hint at passionfruit. The palate, tight and very focused on fine, ripe, energetic fruit, is concentrated and very deeply flavoured, but with the succulence of youth. Perhaps most impressive, however, is its texture, a suave, effortless feeling of light creaminess that spreads right across your palate, complementing the obvious weight and concentration of fruit flavours to perfection. Superbly finished with astringency and subtlety to match its lively freshness, this is top-class stuff.

COLLARDS ROTHESAY SAUVIGNON BLANC

Conservatively fruit-based Sauvignon Blancs, the Rothesay wines are always finely crafted, a clever balance of features provided each year by the vineyard. They also have an intriguing flavour dimension, a character that hovers between those of herbaceous nettles and tropical fruit, with a dash of smokiness or minerals thrown in. This provides an interesting flavour composite that gives the wines a certain tension, spicing their purity and fresh fruit succulence.

1987

12.5% alc/vol; 100% Sauvignon Blanc; Rothesay Vineyard, Waimauku district, Auckland region; harvested 31 March– 7 April 1987.
Winemaker: Bruce Collard
Best drinking: 1995–96

Bright, lemon-yellow wine, clear and fresh, with an aromatic, sweet, ripely mature bouquet with hints of shortbread, a background of hay-like aromas and great momentum. Full of sweet fruit from the first tongue touch, plump, juicy and still finishing brisk, its flavours suggest figs and kumquats, with flickerings of orange peel and nettles. It finishes neat and suave, with the savoury, toasty edges of bottle maturity showing up, but still fresh and full of life. Lovely older wine.

1988

11.5% alc/vol; 100% Sauvignon Blanc; Rothesay Vineyard,
Waimauku district, Auckland region; harvested
30 March–5 April 1988.
Winemaker: Bruce Collard
Best drinking: 1995

Bright, fresh, yellow wine with a smoky bouquet, mellow, clean and fresh-smelling, perhaps an antipodean rendition of the mythic gunflint character of Pouilly. A light palate, nice and easy with a flavour presence rather than something definable, spreading out around the mouth, and leaving a brisk, orange peel-tinged farewell. Nice wine, not momentous, but with life and a subtle charm.

1989

12% alc/vol; 100% Sauvignon Blanc; Rothesay Vineyard,
Waimauku district, Auckland region; harvested
28–29 March 1989.
Winemaker: Bruce Collard
Best drinking: 1995–99

This wine has a beautiful bouquet of aromatic, summer cut grass, hints of beeswax and sweet, tropical fruit that just blossoms gently without rushing up your nose. There is a vague earthiness, too, that warms the palate as well as the bouquet, adding comfort to the delicate sweetness of ripe fruit and other effortlessly easy flavours that swirl around, enchanting the drinker. A lovely wine that has become gracefully calm with bottle age, it leaves at the end of its neat finish a memory of youthful vigour, and does so without even a minor assault on your mouth's sensitivities.

1990

12% alc/vol; 100% Sauvignon Blanc; Rothesay Vineyard,
Waimauku district, Auckland region; harvested
22–23 March 1990.
Winemaker: Bruce Collard
Best drinking: 1995–96

A straw colour, tinted yellow, this wine has mellow fruit aromas lined with sweetness, flavours reminiscent of nettles and orange peel. Fresh, with a tracery of sweet fruit right through it, this lightly flavoured wine is a very pleasant, easy-going thing with a dry finish that leaves just a hint of smoke behind.

1992

12.5% alc/vol; 100% Sauvignon Blanc; Rothesay Vineyard,
Waimauku district, Auckland region; harvested 15, 16,
22 April 1992.
Winemaker: Bruce Collard
Best drinking: 1995–99

A rich, lively-smelling, yellow-straw-coloured wine, its bouquet has peas and asparagus aromas lined with more tropical notes. A lightly concentrated, fresh, sweetly suave wine, easy to drink, with neat nectarine characters at its heart, moderate depth of flavour and a tidy finish that departs with a flick of furry astringency and a tingle of freshness which is most appealing. It delivers its quality with such ease that it seems quite simple if you choose to ignore the lovely fruit textures and flavour in the palate, but it is made quality, a product of fine winemaking which keeps everything in balance.

1993

13.5% alc/vol; 100% Sauvignon Blanc; Rothesay Vineyard,
Waimauku district, Auckland region; harvested 8, 11,
13 April 1993.
Winemaker: Bruce Collard
Best drinking: 1995–2003

The fresh, light beans nose is quite reserved, but the palate is more forthcoming, full, ripe and deep, almost rich with sweet fruit textures and flavour characters of nettles and mellow, juicy tropical tones. Has clarity and freshness to match its depth, and a big, warm heart that should keep the palate going for a long time, matching fruit sweetness with vigour. A finely poised wine, beautifully crafted and showing the wonderful advantages of ripe fruit in its juicy succulence and suave suppleness.

1994

12.5% alc/vol; 100% Sauvignon Blanc; Rothesay Vineyard,
Waimauku district, Auckland region; harvested
12, 18 April 1994.
Winemaker: Bruce Collard
Best drinking: 1996–2003

Light, sandy, straw-coloured wine, fragrant and ripe, its slightly brisk bouquet revealing hints of passionfruit and new-mown hay. The palate is full to the brim with ripe-sweet fruit, but this quickly passes in the fizz of energy that takes over, a fierce liveliness which jangles all the way to the deep heart of the wine. This obscures somewhat the soft textures and juiciness of the fruit, but spicy and herbal flavours do return at the end of a long finish, completing the wine with a satisfying tastiness.

CORBANS PRIVATE BIN FUMÉ BLANC

An oaked Sauvignon Blanc style that gained early prominence, this has maintained a reputation for interesting, oaky wines with an appealing fruit freshness.

1985

12.5% alc/vol; 100% Sauvignon Blanc; Marlborough region; harvested 17 April 1985; fermented and aged 3 months in 500-litre French Nevers oak puncheons.
Best drinking: 1995

Fresh, moderate gold, bright and clear, with a toasty, soft, vegetable-tinged, oak-riddled nose. This is mellow wine, its oak always a close companion, with interesting asides such as a hint of milky sweetness and a modicum of canned peas character. A nice, easy-paced old timer that has lost its verve.

1986

12% alc/vol; 100% Sauvignon Blanc; Marlborough region; harvested 5 May 1986; fermented in German oak 500-litre puncheons and French oak 225-litre barriques; aged in oak 9 months.
Winemaker: Glenn Thomas
Best drinking: 1995–1997?

Nice, ripe, golden-coloured wine, still with a trace of bubbles, its nose is very much one of canned peas-matured herbaceousness with lashings of oak that seem to heighten, rather than moderate, this thick character. In spite of this, there is an air of restraint in the palate, with hints of depth behind the oaky, peasy facade. An almost alluring, reluctant wine, it seems to be waiting for something, such as the flavour intensity that arrives at the very end, to make it complete. Could it need more age?

1987

12.7% alc/vol; 100% Sauvignon Blanc; Marlborough region; harvested 27 April 1987; fermented and aged 2.5 months in 225-litre French Nevers oak barriques.
Winemaker: Glenn Thomas
Best drinking: 1995–97

A fresh, lively wine full of enthusiasm, with a backdrop of vegetal characters that verge on redcurrants, and a hearty band of oak, it looks fresh in its green-tipped, light gold livery, and smells as fresh as it looks. The freshness of flavour, in spite of some hints of asparagus, is surprising, almost juicy in its youthfulness, and there is plenty of sweet flavour to keep it lively to the very end. Very attractive wine that keeps its keen fruit above the oak and light toastiness, only slipping to complete mellowness at the very end.

1988

12.5% alc/vol; 100% Sauvignon Blanc; Marlborough region; harvested 25 April 1988; fermented and aged 8 months in French and Californian oak.
Winemaker: Glenn Thomas
Best drinking: 1995

A most interesting bouquet character that is like honey and raspberries flickers through tones of herb-aceousness, dried fruit and sweet oak, making the nose seem big in spite of its edge of freshness. Good weight and complexity on the palate, but it fades away somewhat after the bold first impression, and appears to be drying out at the end. A nice drink.

1989

12% alc/vol; 100% Sauvignon Blanc; Marlborough region; harvested 10 April 1989; fermented and aged in 225-litre French oak barriques.
Winemaker: Alan McCorkindale
Best drinking: 1995–1998

A lightly polished straw colour that looks very pretty introduces a wine which is afloat with oaky aromas and flavour. Sweet from palate to finish, it impresses with its plump fruit characters and a nice flavour balance that restrains the oak. An easy, pleasing wine, it is quite fine for Fumé Blanc, with moderate weight and fewer of the thick fruit flavours that can bog these wines down. It retains a fresh liveliness in spite of its age, and leaves a good impression with a gently tailing finish.

1991

12% alc/vol; 100% Sauvignon Blanc; Marlborough region; harvested 22 April 1991; fermented and aged 6 months in 225-litre French oak barriques.
Winemaker: Alan McCorkindale
Best drinking: 1995–97

Straw-tinged, gold-coloured wine, it is bright and clear with some very oaky characters keeping company with ripe, redcurrant-like fruit aromas and persimmon flavour. In spite of its attractive fruit, its oak is currently a burden to this fresh, eager wine that never feels quite big enough to carry such a collection of flavours, although the fruit certainly is delicious. Acid is a little intrusive at the very end, but on the whole the good points outweigh the difficulties, for it is an attractive wine.

1992

11.5% alc/vol; 100% Sauvignon Blanc; Marlborough region; harvested 25 April 1992; fermented and aged 6 months in 225-litre French oak barriques.
Winemaker: Alan McCorkindale
Best drinking: 1995–96

This wine smells like fruit soda, with a background of pungent herbaceousness and a very zesty air. The blend of oak and herbaceous fruit in the mouth is almost canned peas before its time, but it does not disturb the lively, fruit sweet palate with its zingy finish. Clean and vigorous, its blend of oak and fruit complexities make for an interesting wine.

HUNTER'S SAUVIGNON BLANC

It was Hunter's who made the British notice Marlborough as a Sauvignon Blanc-growing region of real promise, and they have always been at the forefront of New Zealand's Sauvignon Blanc makers with very stylish renditions of ripe Marlborough Sauvignon Blanc. Subtle, refined, they are as delicate as Sauvignon Blanc can be, often making suggestions where others make bold statements.

1986

11.7% alc/vol; 100% Sauvignon Blanc; Marlborough region; harvested 24 April 1986.
Winemaker: Almuth Lorenz
Best drinking: 1995

Straw-coloured wine, tinged with lemon-yellow, bright, clear and as fresh as its bouquet, which is clean, light, with whiffs of toast and a vague hint of lanolin. There is no suggestion of peas on nose or palate, and there is a real frisky quality in the mouth that endorses the fresh bouquet, as well as a slight complementary oiliness and an enigmatic shadow of flavour. It is excellently poised between fresh-edged friskiness and that vague oiliness, and although the lack of any real flavour presence detracts from an otherwise neatly fashioned wine, its shadowy quality continues to fascinate.

1987

12.3% alc/vol; 100% Sauvignon Blanc; Marlborough region; harvested 24 April 1987.
Winemaker: John Belsham
Best drinking: 1995

Moderately deep, youthful, bright wine, fined down, and with that shadowed quality of its predecessor. Slight peas characters whisper across the palate, and there is a well-shaped weight in the mouth, rounded, gently balancing the still lively freshness. Delicate, fine-grained at the finish, this is a nice wine, well crafted and still holding its structure, if not all its flavours.

1988

12% alc/vol; 100% Sauvignon Blanc; Marlborough region; harvested 28 April 1988.
Winemaker: John Belsham
Best drinking: 1995–96

Clean, fresh, green-edged wine, its bouquet alive with scents of fresh nettles and just-made toast. Flavoury and still sweet with fruit, it has slightly peasy flavours among the ripe gooseberries and juicy, fresh texture. Most appealing wine, with attractive details of flavour for decoration, and mouth-watering, fresh-edged fruit still sending out its inviting messages. Toast runs right through, but never takes over, and the finish lingers beautifully with more of those delicately intricate flavours. A lovely drink.

1989

13% alc/vol; 100% Sauvignon Blanc; Marlborough region; harvested 30 March 1989.
Winemaker: John Belsham
Best drinking: 1995

Glittering, green-edged colour freshness does not compensate for a rather meek bouquet that has toast and some strange dusty characters, but only vague suggestions of fruit. The palate is similarly imprecise, but it does have a lovely feeling to it, with ripe fruit sweetness, weight and a fine-grained liveliness that just

goes on and on. The elusive aromas and flavours are its only disappointment, for this is another shadowy Sauvignon performance.

1990

12.5% alc/vol; 100% Sauvignon Blanc; Marlborough region; harvested 9 April 1990.
Winemaker: John Belsham
Best drinking: 1995–96

Light-looking wine, with yellow touches. Very fine and pleasant from start to finish, it has a slightly smoky, gunflint bouquet, with hedge-like herbaceous notes and a subtle mellowness that seems to be the first signs of bottle age. Light fruit flavours, mildly herbal, with a trace of sweetness and substance, all finely balanced with warmth and gently flavoured length that lingers beautifully. An easy, stylish wine that feels as elegant as it tastes.

1991

12% alc/vol; 100% Sauvignon Blanc; Marlborough region; harvested 9 April 1991.
Winemaker: Gary Duke
Best drinking: 1995–97

Green-touched, clean-looking wine with nettle, passionfruit and gooseberry aromas that are lifted by lemon-scented freshness in a mellow, complex bouquet full of flickering aromatic highlights. Immediately sweet and round fruit fills the mouth, glowing with ripeness, tumbling in a cascade of ripe passionfruit, goosberries and lemon citrus flavours that rides on and on with vigour and style. A very fine wine indeed, the flavour hanging on to a furry freshness of acid and tannin at the end but, in spite of its liveliness it has an endearing, mellow tone that invites you back for more. A superb example of balance, this wine has a graceful quality that makes it perfectly self-contained.

1992

12.5% alc/vol; 100% Sauvignon Blanc; Marlborough region; harvested 5 May 1992.
Winemaker: Gary Duke
Best drinking: 1995–97

Light, bright and yellow-tinged wine, with a similarly light, fresh bouquet that has a fragrant, citrus character. Clean, simple and appealing, it is sunshine bright with pleasing fruit tones that hint at citrus and concentrated, almost tropical ripeness. Fragrant even in the mouth, it is a very pretty wine, subtle, long and fine, again very self-contained, with more hard-edged freshness and concentration, but less definable flavour. It feels rather than tastes very good, if the freshness would only step aside a little.

1993

12% alc/vol; 100% Sauvignon Blanc; Marlborough region; harvested 19 May 1993.
Winemaker: Gary Duke
Best drinking: 1995–1999

Green-tinged, fresh, light and bright, all the points of lively Sauvignon matched by a pushy bouquet that is an aromatic confusion of papaya and other tropical fruit, with a good measure of gooseberries. Quite a fruit salad, and so is the palate, which has a creamy, lightly soft texture with hints of buttermilk among the concentrated blend of fruit flavours, with a very crisp, piercing stab of acid that matches the sweet fruit all the way through. Good now, it should be better when bottle age mellows the acid somewhat, and releases a few more flavour nuances to reduce the present clamour with a note or two of subtlety.

1994

12.5% alc/vol; 100% Sauvignon Blanc; Marlborough region; harvested from 18 April–4 May 1994.
Winemaker: Gary Duke
Best drinking: 1996–2003

Pale, clear, green-tinged, very youthful-looking wine that still has a yeasty fresh bouquet, with keen, juicy fruit all over it. There is heaps of fruit in the palate, too, a sweet abundance that is too young and stroppy to be anything other than an glossy feeling among the jangles of brisk acid and youthful exuberance. Ripeness, intensity and excellent length point to a wine with a big future.

HUNTER'S OAK AGED SAUVIGNON BLANC

Among the Marlborough labels, this wine is matched only by Cloudy Bay for consistency and elegance. Like its partner, it has a strain of delicacy and finesse running through it, which is invariably matched with very clever oak handling that contributes a degree of richness and breadth to the palate. Invariably a top-class wine, it provides an eloquent argument against those who say Sauvignon Blanc cannot produce wines of the highest quality.

1986
FUMÉ

11.7% alc/vol; 100% Sauvignon Blanc; Marlborough region; harvested 24 April 1986; 100% barrel fermented in new 225-litre French Nevers oak barriques; aged 8 weeks in new French Nevers oak barriques.
Winemaker: Almuth Lorenz

Lemony yellow, glossy-looking wine with a fading, oxidised nose, but it is not yet dull, retaining a kernel of life that keeps it in the drinkable class.

1987
FUMÉ

*12.3% alc/vol; 90% Sauvignon Blanc, 10% Semillon;
Marlborough region; Sauvignon Blanc harvested 15 April
1987; 20% barrel fermentation; a blend of oak aged and
unwooded Sauvignon Blanc.*
Winemaker: John Belsham
Best drinking: 1995–96

Another richly yellow wine, this time with a mellow, light bouquet that is passing pleasant. The bouquet is even better, tense and moderately fresh in character, with some lively citrus flavours and a pleasing, permeating warmth that makes a nice foil to the freshness. Easy, charming wine, with a tracery of toastiness and delicate nuances, and a long, subtle finish.

1989

*12.5% alc/vol; 100% Sauvignon Blanc; Marlborough
region; harvested 26 March 1989; 25% barrel fermented;
aged 6 months in French oak barrels.*
Winemaker: John Belsham
Best drinking: 1995–97

This delicate, fine and vaguely fresh bouquet has some lovely toasty details that add finesse to a juiciness of sweet fruit. Fruit, too, makes its presence felt on the palate, where its ripeness gives the wine real momentum, and serves to underscore the tracery of toast and subtle oak details, all of which are kept sharply clear by a pervasive freshness of tone. Very fine, long, gracefully elegant wine, its details are so delicately worked that it invites concentration, and rewards with some lovely nuances and flavour fretworks that would elude guzzlers.

1990

*12.5% alc/vol; 100% Sauvignon Blanc; Marlborough
region; harvested 26 April 1990; some barrel fermented;
aged 8 months in French oak barrels.*
Winemaker: John Belsham
Best drinking: 1995

Light, bright, yellow-hued to the eyes, and very attractive to the nose with its grainy, sawdusty, mildly spicy aromas and flutter of sweet fragrance. Although the fruit is almost too delicate here, oak provides a dimension and range of flavours that are pleasing, although they do not quite compensate for the finesse

of balancing fruit. Mild wine, attractively crafted and good company.

1991

*12.5% alc/vol; 100% Sauvignon Blanc; Marlborough
region; harvested 11 April 1991; some barrel fermented;
aged 8 months in French oak barrels.*
Winemaker: Gary Duke
Best drinking: 1995–2000

To look at, this wine is a light concoction of tints — yellow, green and straw — with a perfumed bouquet full of the fragrance of passionfruit and fine spice. Not overt, but quite definite, with its fruit restrained by the oak and a mild mealiness. The palate has real weight, and is packed with fruit that is all jungly and tropical, finely wrought with oak details and a subtle creamy texture to keep it in check and yet add to its brisk beauty. A resonantly flavoured, warm, deep wine with a cool style and excellent momentum that has the flavour subtleties still bright and fresh at the very end, its elegance alone makes it a star.

1992

*13% alc/vol; 100% Sauvignon Blanc; Marlborough region;
harvested 4 May 1992; some barrel fermented.*
Winemaker: Gary Duke
Best drinking: 1995–2002

Fresh-looking, youthful wine with a concentrated, cordial-like aroma at the heart of the bouquet, seasoned with mellow, charming oak. Very sweet on the front palate, and a bit herbaceous in the background, around its solid heart it also has lashings of intense tropical and citrus highlights that hint at essence in their fierceness, but finish effortlessly light. Added to this is a carefully detailed frame of fine oak and barrel-made flavours and textures, from dry to mildly creamy-mealy tones that balance and check each aspect that the fruit has provided. A keen, lively wine, yet masterfully fine and elegant, it is a superb example of winemaking craft.

1993

*12% alc/vol; 100% Sauvignon Blanc; Marlborough region;
harvested 18 May 1993; 40% barrel fermented in new and
used French oak barrels, followed by aging on yeast lees for
6 months; 60% stainless steel fermented, aged in new and
used French oak for 7 months.*

Winemaker: Gary Duke
Best drinking: 1996–2002

Light, yellowish straw in colour, with a bouquet that is as intricately ornate as a Rococo ceiling, fine fruit aromas detailed with a filigree of oak and held in a cloud of graceful ease, this is as exciting as an introduction to Sauvignon Blanc gets. The sweetly concentrated passionfruit flavours are shot with other tropical suggestions, have a clarity of freshness, and have a collar of finely textured oak, complete with mealy-creamy nuances, for company. Not big wine, but extremely beautiful, and so finely made it is quite glittering. What will it do with the extra subtleties of bottle age?

KUMEU RIVER SAUVIGNON

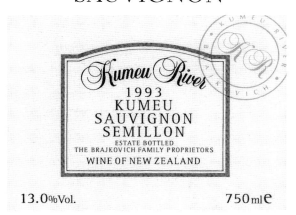

Kumeu River have always followed a completely different Sauvignon Blanc path from other New Zealand winemakers. Using only Kumeu-grown fruit, they have had a different range of flavours to deal with, and have sought complexity and palate texture rather than the fresh, fruit-based energy that has made Marlborough's reputation. Use of oak and barrel fermentation has given the wines immediate complexity in their youth and, without the conflicting character of herbaceousness this treatment has provided depth and richness as the wines have matured. Flavoury wines intended for food, they began as idiosyncratic collectors' items in the mid-1980s but, as the winemaking style has matured, they have become superb alternatives to the fierce fruit and acid of classic New Zealand Sauvignon Blanc.

1986
FUMÉ

12.6% alc/vol; 100% Sauvignon Blanc; Kumeu district,
Auckland region; partial barrel fermentation and oak aged.
Winemaker: Michael Brajkovich

A toasty bottle age nose with distant hints of asparagus introduces this light gold wine. Mellow, and just at the edge of richness, it is clean and fresh, with some nice, subtle flavours, but it is drying out and losing any depth it once had. Faded, not jaded.

1987
NOBLE DRY

12.5% alc/vol; 100% Sauvignon Blanc; Kumeu district,
Auckland region; partial barrel fermentation and oak aged.
Winemaker: Michael Brajkovich
Best drinking: 1995–97?

Pretty in light, bright gold, this wine has an amazing bouquet some would call 'over the top', more a display of aromatic virtuosity than anything as sweet-sounding as a bouquet. Knee-deep in a flood of aromatic orange peel and honey, with a foaming collar of dusty oak, it is a smell that is fascinating, inviting and disturbing all at once. This is followed by a taste as light as sunshine, clear, almost fresh in texture, but struck through with a shaft of pure, citrus-edged beeswax, a flavour that sticks and stays, lingering long in a dry, delicate finish that is Oriental in its dried citrus and spice nuances, and its exotic character. Quite bizarre, this is like a wine from some ancient civilisation, a different age, maybe even a different planet, with aromas and tastes that defy easy classification and so risk ridicule in the strictly ordered world of wine. It should not be dismissed by small-mindedness, however, for it would be superb with the right food, and at eight years old is still demanding attention. Who knows what it will do in the future?

1988

*12% alc/vol; 100% Sauvignon Blanc; Kumeu district,
Auckland region; partial barrel fermentation and oak aged.
Winemaker: Michael Brajkovich
Best drinking: 1995*

This light gold wine is similarly exotic, trumpeting aromas of orange peel and honey, but it has a calming influence of richness that moderates these scintillating notes, and invests the wine with a fine, softening texture that fills the mouth with more than just the jangle of unusual flavour. From the bouquet, where orange and honey set aside competition for co-ordination, to the rounded, spreading palate, this is a more harmonic performance, with clarity and softness working to mellow and enhance the effects of flavour. A dry finish that is shorter than expected does detract from what is another fascinating wine, one worthy of full attention.

1989

*12.5% alc/vol; 100% Sauvignon Blanc; Kumeu district,
Auckland region; partial barrel fermentation and oak aged.
Winemaker: Michael Brajkovich
Best drinking: 1995–99*

Beautifully fragrant, this bright, straw-coloured wine smells winey, with a froth of toasty bottle age and oak on the top, and a mouth-watering, clear-edged precision. Full, fresh and clear, its warm, straw and hay flavours are deep and lingering, dry, but with a ripe feeling among the mellowing touches of light richness that mingle with the oak. A clever juxtaposition of warmth and freshness is the key to this wine's easy feeling and inviting character, an appeal that is enhanced by subtlety and myriad nuances of flavour, citrus, straw, and mild nuts among them. Deep, long, gracefully fine wine.

1990

*12% alc/vol; 100% Sauvignon Blanc; Kumeu district,
Auckland region; partial barrel fermentation and oak aged.
Winemaker: Michael Brajkovich
Best drinking: 1995–96*

Light-coloured wine with a yellow-straw hue and a bouquet reminiscent of fresh hay, with autumn characters and a clarifying freshness. Clean, light wine, slightly citric, with excellent length of flavour and nice oak notes that contribute mild richness, depth and a

soft resonance. Warm, steady, pleasant wine in a lightweight frame.

1991

*12.5% alc/vol; 100% Sauvignon Blanc; Kumeu district,
Auckland region; partial barrel fermentation and oak aged.
Winemaker: Michael Brajkovich
Best drinking: 1995–97*

Perfect straw colour, and a fine, dusty, savoury nose faintly tinged with pleasantly savoury, straw-hay characters. Very quiet wine, not light, but reserved, with a gracefully warm, round texture that fills the mouth with delicacy. Soft, long-flavoured, pleasant wine.

1992

*12.5% alc/vol; 86% Sauvignon Blanc, 14% Semillon;
Kumeu district, Auckland region; partial barrel
fermentation and oak aged.
Winemaker: Michael Brajkovich
Best drinking: 1995–2003*

A wine of straw-cosseted fruit, with its deep, mellow tawny-yellow colour, aromas of savoury freshness in harmony with ripe, tropical fruit, and fine, similarly succulent and dry flavours. This is lovely wine, managing to blend the dry summer features of aromatic straw with the sweet, ripe succulence of delicately perfumed jungly fruits like babaco, and then hanging on to the harmony right at the end of the long, graceful finish. It is like a harvest festival of subtle flavour, enriched by concentration and sweetness at its heart, a mildly silky texture, and tense, fine structure that manages to be supple as well as firm. Simply superb wine, a flavour jewel with many facets, the finest of which is subtlety.

1993

*13% alc/vol; 70% Sauvignon Blanc, 30% Semillon; Kumeu
district, Auckland region; partial barrel fermentation and
oak aged.
Winemaker: Michael Brajkovich
Best drinking: 1996–2005*

Light and very clear, with a lovely, aroma-laden nose that sings of red capsicum and sun-ripened hay, with a supporting baritone of soft, savoury oak. Beautifully soft and fresh by turns, it strokes and tingles in your mouth, with a welling warmth and depth of concentrated flavour that is most impressive. Kept civilised by fine winemaking that elongates and tempers its size and fruit sweetness with oak, it has the poise of an aristocrat, but lacks no enthusiasm or energy. Still young enough to be quite closed and as yet not showing all its flavour nuances, it is full of promise for the future.

MATUA VALLEY RESERVE SAUVIGNON BLANC

This is the best of Matua Valley's Sauvignon Blancs, using the ripest available fruit and usually exhibiting tropical rather than herbaceous characters. Not made every year, it is a wine that can be particularly impressive, although it is only recently that a specific style seems to have evolved for this label.

1986

12% alc/vol; 100% Sauvignon Blanc.
Winemaker: John Belsham
Best drinking: 1995

Light yellow-straw colour, complemented by a very attractive, gentle bouquet with subtle asparagus, meal and shortbread notes. There is a refreshing lightness about this wine, which is delicate rather than watery, enhanced by a tang of fresh acidity that is slowly mellowing with age. There are distinct flavours of cape gooseberries among the mellow tones of other fruit and traces of nuts, completing an entirely charming wine, in need of the company of gentlefolk.

1989

11.5% alc/vol; 100% Sauvignon Blanc.
Winemaker: Mark Robertson
Best drinking: 1995

Light gold, clear and bright, with a strident, sour-edged, bramble leaf and tomcat bouquet, vaguely touched with toast. Fresh, light and pleasant wine, a bit simple, with some faint passionfruit flavour and a light finish.

1990

11.5% alc/vol; 100% Sauvignon Blanc; Waimauku district,
Auckland region.
Winemaker: Mark Robertson
Best drinking: 1995

Yellow-straw-coloured wine, its bouquet is aromatic with orange peel and a tinge of oak. Soft in the mouth, with a hint of sour milk, it is light but with enough flavour bits and pieces to be interesting if not memorable. It fades away rather quickly.

1991

12% alc/vol; 100% Sauvignon Blanc; Waimauku district,
Auckland region.
Winemaker: Mark Robertson
Best drinking: 1995–98

Beautiful to look at, and to smell, its colour the ripe sandy yellow of straw, its bouquet fresh with succulent, subtle fruit aromas that hint at papaya and guavas, with a sweet, slightly creamy oak character in support. Beautifully balanced, long, very even wine, it is supple and graceful, filled with tropical and savoury flavour nuances, but with a background of intensity that makes it seem as though it has the benefit of essence of ripe Sauvignon. Flavours and silky softness hang on to the end, leaving a delicate but very satisfying finish, enlivened as the whole wine is by a tang of freshness.

1992

12.5% alc/vol; 100% Sauvignon Blanc;
Hawke's Bay region.
Winemaker: Mark Robertson
Best drinking: 1995–2000

Light, bright straw, with asparagus and rich hay-like aromas, mixed with spiced oak and a hint of mealiness. Lovely, ripe, viscous flavours, suggesting passionfruit, guava and other tropical delights, with a slightly abrasive, Sauvignon Blanc character chiming in at the same time as the lively freshness of clean acidity. Fine stuff, deep, angular and concentrated at times, yet with inviting softness at others, it appears very young, almost stroppy, with lovely fruit flavours and subtlety from beginning to end that suggest it has an excellent future.

1993

12.5% alc/vol; 100% Sauvignon Blanc; Waimauku district,
Auckland region.
Winemaker: Mark Robertson
Best drinking: 1995–2001

Fresh, new apple-scented wine, its bouquet trimmed with lime and a subtle nuance of five spice powder among the oak. Limy, leafy suggestions on the palate too, which is supple enough, with softly spiced oak, elements of melon and peach, and some slightly creamy, nut kernel and fresh milk characters peeping out from the fresh, lively facade. Fine wine, with depth and concentration, energy, length, all the bits to promise a long and interesting life, but succulent enough to enjoy a fresh glass or two already.

MONTANA MARLBOROUGH SAUVIGNON BLANC

This is the wine that led the way for Sauvignon Blanc in New Zealand, and made Marlborough's international reputation as a fine wine-growing region. Its vibrant clarity and fresh, energetic flavour have become the Sauvignon Blanc standard for the region, and to many wine drinkers this is the epitome of the style. Machine harvested and processed in stainless steel, it is also an excellent example of the wine quality that can be achieved with ideal vineyard conditions and modern winemaking technology. Also, it is quality that is available at a reasonable price; one of Montana's achievements has been its ability to make fine wines that meet international standards, at a price well below the norm.

1980

10.5% alc/vol; 100% Sauvignon Blanc;
Marlborough region.
Best drinking: 1995–96

Light gold-green colour, with a green capsicum nose that is fresh, clean and still powerful, and just a tinge of bottle age character that comes on the freshly baked shortbread and warm toast. A clear, clean mouthful with gooseberry and lychee flavours, that ends with a disappointing, fading softness. A wonderful drink in spite of this, fresh as spring, aromatically inviting, its flavours delightful almost to the very end.

1981

10.5% alc/vol; 100% Sauvignon Blanc;
Marlborough region.
Best drinking: 1995–96

This light, golden wine has a dusty, toasty nose with a light bouquet that hints at lychees and mild toast. Clear and fresh, with very interesting aged fruit flavours at its heart, it is lively and lingering, building up an excellent momentum of delicacy that delivers a most satisfying, bright finish. Light but still sprightly.

1984

11.5% alc/vol; 100% Sauvignon Blanc;
Marlborough region.
Best drinking: 1995–96

Fresh, green-gold wine, with a strong aroma of ripe hay and canned peas. The flavours, too, are rich with asparagus and canned peas, with a full, almost unctuous, mealy-edged finish. Still in good shape, if rather obvious.

1985

12% alc/vol; 100% Sauvignon Blanc; Marlborough region.
Best drinking: 1995–97

A fresh, bright wine, even at 10 years old. Its golden colour retains a green edge, and the light bouquet is notably clear, with freshness enlivening the mellow hints of bottle age. The palate is still alive with fresh, sweet-seeming fruit, now embellished with lovely warm toast characters, but still holding its ripeness on into a lingering finish. Very good wine, its fruit flavours fine enough to allow the toasty nuances of age to

emerge as delicate touches, its tastes excellent right now.

1986

12% alc/vol; 100% Sauvignon Blanc; Marlborough region.
Best drinking: 1995

Light golden colour, with a fresh, slightly mellow, canned peas aroma. Very fresh in the mouth, it fades somewhat, but manages to leave some of the taste of ripe lychees lingering at the end. Clean, with moderately interesting complexities of age, this bottle seems to be nearing the end of its useful life.

1987

12% alc/vol; 100% Sauvignon Blanc; Marlborough region.
Best drinking: 1995–97

The honeyed, perfumed bouquet is unusual, but rather interesting, filled out with nuances of dried apricots and peaches. The light palate also has flickers of intense flavour, but is generally light, clean and very dry. Idiosyncratic wine, it is rather attractive if you can overcome your Sauvignon Blanc expectations.

1988

12% alc/vol; 100% Sauvignon Blanc; Marlborough region.
Best drinking: 1995–99

Yellow, bright, light in hue, with a fragrant bouquet that is a creamy blend of toast and ripe gooseberry fruit. Fresh, clean and fat with fruit from beginning to end, it smells and tastes ripe, with all the supple textures and juicy flavours that implies. Lychees and gooseberries are everywhere in the palate, which maintains its fresh clarity but manages to fuse this with an intriguing softness. A real charmer, with the first notes of toast just beginning to show, but none of the anticipated canned peas character.

1989

12.5% alc/vol; 100% Sauvignon Blanc;
Marlborough region.
Best drinking: 1995–2000

Very good wine from beginning to end, it has balance, fruit and the liveliness of Sauvignon Blanc without its aggression. On the nose there is no dominant character, other than freshness, which pervades the balancing notes of mellow, ripe fruit and the shortbread aspects of bottle age. It offers an initially fresh mouthful, too, that at first appears simple, but gradually the fruit and bottle age flavours emerge in a lovely network of subtle nuances. Although becoming leaner with age, it is still a neat blend of tense, vibrant clarity and richer fruit, lychees and toast.

1990

11.5% alc/vol; 100% Sauvignon Blanc;
Marlborough region.

Light, lemon-yellow colour, faded aromas and a fresh, simple, very light palate that is just a shadow of Sauvignon Blanc. Fresh enough, but lacking flavour.

1991

12% alc/vol; 100% Sauvignon Blanc; Marlborough region.
Best drinking: 1995–2003

Pale lemon-coloured wine, its bouquet is a forceful amalgam of grassy, herbaceous, red capsicum aromas that are almost explosive. The palate is less obstreperous, with signs of some tropical characters such as passionfruit, and a more fulsome richness of flavour that is very attractive. At its brilliant best, this is Sauvignon Blanc at the stage when the razor has gone and all the charm of ripe fruit is out on display. The finish, neat, clean and touched by fruit succulence, completes a fine performance.

1992

11.5% alc/vol; 100% Sauvignon Blanc;
Marlborough region.
Best drinking: 1995–96

Pale, tinged with lemon-yellow, its fragrance is alive with mouth-wateringly fresh gooseberry and capsicum aromas. The light palate has suggestions of citrus and flowers among the capsicum, and finishes fresh, light, clean. Pleasant wine, lively and pretty enough.

1993

12.5% alc/vol; 100% Sauvignon Blanc;
Marlborough region.
Best drinking: 1995–98

Pale lemon in colour, with a light, fresh, lifted fragrance that has bits of capsicum and gooseberry fruit among the crisp acidity. The palate is less fresh than the bouquet, tender rather than soft, with a suggestion of passionfruit and a long, slightly austere finish. Smart wine, quite delicate in flavour and not overtly zingy.

1994

12% alc/vol; 100% Sauvignon Blanc; Marlborough region.
Best drinking: 1996–2005

The ripe, full bouquet of this pale-looking wine shows it to be full of youthful exuberance and still clinging to the banana aromas of fermentation it will shake off as it ages. An abundance of sweet, jolly fruit in the mouth, vigorous and mouth-filling enough to counter an edge of fresh acidity, it lingers long with traces of gooseberry and some tropical suggestions.

MORTON ESTATE BLACK LABEL FUMÉ BLANC

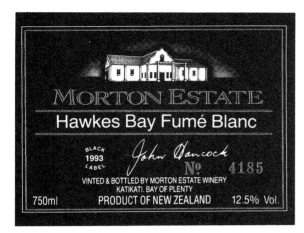

This is a rich flamboyant Sauvignon style. With fruit and oak in abundance, it has always been an alternative style for New Zealand, but has secured a loyal following among wine drinkers who prefer their Sauvignon Blanc to be less acidic and lively.

1984

11.6% alc/vol; 100% Sauvignon Blanc; 100% Hawke's Bay region; 100% barrel fermented; aged 9 months on lees in new French 225-litre barriques.
Winemaker: John Hancock
Best drinking: 1995

Pretty, light, bright and very yellow. Fine and toasty on the nose, just a tad composty, with mellow, hay-like characters. A fresh, clear, light wine, pleasant and interesting, with a just a twist of Sauvignon enthusiasm at the finish, but it is clearly drying out with age.

1985

12.9% alc/vol; 100% Sauvignon Blanc; 100% Hawke's Bay region; 100% barrel fermented; aged 9 months on lees in new French 225-litre barriques.
Winemaker: John Hancock
Best drinking: 1995

Plump, bright yellow wine, lightish. The nose is very toasty but still fresh, with a lifted fragrance that is vaguely herbaceous. Sweet fruit on the palate, with grassy tones, it is quite delicately flavoured but the wine itself is big and warm. Luckily, the delicate flavour does linger on at the finish, keeping the warm alcohol from becoming aggressive, but the wine lacks a sense of harmony.

1986

13% alc/vol; 100% Sauvignon Blanc; 100% Hawke's Bay region; 100% barrel fermented; aged 9 months on lees in new French 225-litre barriques.
Winemakers: John Hancock and Steve Bird
Best drinking: 1995–96

The colour of polished brass, this wine surprises with a hearty bouquet that manages to be both rich and fresh, with characters of toast and ripe, lush fruit balanced by a lively lightness. Clean and pleasant on the palate, the freshness is again apparent, as is toasty bottle age and remnants of ripe fruit flavours that loiter at the finish. The toast does dominate the palate, but the shadow of succulence provided by the fruit makes this a rather intriguing wine, one that keeps reviving itself with freshness.

1988

11.9% alc/vol; 100% Sauvignon Blanc; 100% Hawke's Bay region; 100% barrel fermented; aged 4 months off lees in new French 225-litre barriques.
Winemakers: John Hancock and Steve Bird
Best drinking: 1995

This shiny wine is laden with aromas of toast and quince-like fruit, with lashings of similar fruit on the palate along with a hearty portion of orange peel. They are not succulent flavours, however, and there is a leanness about the wine that ends in a dry, crisp finish. Light, pleasing and fresh, with lingering citrus peel.

1989

13.5% alc/vol; 100% Sauvignon Blanc; 100% Hawke's Bay region; 100% barrel fermented; aged 4 months off lees in new French 225-litre barriques.
Winemakers: John Hancock and Steve Bird
Best drinking: 1995–97

Its soft, yellow colour looks most attractive, a quality

endorsed by the bouquet, which is fragrantly perfumed with hints of tropical fruit and toasty aromas. Succulent in the mouth, clean and fine, the fruit is juicy sweet, pleasantly touched with oak to give a mellow dimension to the soft ripeness and the fizzy enthusiasm of Sauvignon Blanc. Very neatly made wine, balanced, inviting, it charms with its sophistication as much as it does with its lovely fruit.

1991

12.5% alc/vol; 100% Sauvignon Blanc; 100% Hawke's Bay region; 100% barrel fermented; aged 4 months off lees in new French 225-litre barriques.
Winemakers: John Hancock and Steve Bird
Best drinking: 1995–2000

Light, lemony straw in colour, with a hint of green and a clear, citric-tropical bouquet, this is lovely wine, with neatly placed oak to complement its distinctly tropical nature. Almost overflowing with fruit, it has hints of limes, passionfruit, papaya, even pineapple in its fruit salad palate, all dusted with vanilla and oak and a brisk rush of Sauvignon Blanc energy. Long, dry, with the flavour pushed right to the very edges of every part, this wine is quite complete, just hearty enough to hold the abundant fruit, and fresh enough to maintain a healthy liveliness throughout.

1993

12.5% alc/vol; 100% Sauvignon Blanc; 100% Hawke's Bay region; 100% barrel fermented; 100% malolactic fermentation; aged 4 months off lees in new and used French 225-litre barriques.
Winemakers: John Hancock and Steve Bird
Best drinking: 1995–2005

Clear, fresh, sandy, straw-coloured wine, with a very fruity, herby, aggressive bouquet that has nuances of vanilla-scented oak and brisk nettles, even peaches in places. A delicious sweet fruit palate counters the brisk character of the variety, which is quite aggressive and very fresh-edged, but never overcomes the savoury roundness of oak and the succulence of fruit. Very balanced, charming, warm-hearted wine with a tidy finish and an abundance of soft fruit.

NEUDORF FUMÉ BLANC

In recent years this label has emerged as one of the élite in a category which, given the reputation of the nation's Sauvignon Blancs, is arguably the most demanding in New Zealand. Like other Neudorf wines, it is invariably a picture of lively fruit flavour and poised winemaking.

1988
SAUVIGNON BLANC

12.5% alc/vol; 100% Sauvignon Blanc; 100% Moutere district, Nelson region; harvested 2 May 1988.
Winemaker: Tim Finn
Best drinking: 1995–96

Light, sandy, straw-coloured wine that looks very young. The bouquet is a subtle blend of canned peas and nettles, with a touch of spice. A very quietly spoken wine, with nice texture, grumpy flavours, a noticeable alcoholic warmth and a buzz of enthusiasm at the very end. Slightly opaque, reflective, clean, vaguely fresh.

1989
FUMÉ BLANC

*11.8% alc/vol; 85% Sauvignon Blanc, 15% Semillon;
100% Moutere district, Nelson region; harvested
20 April 1989.
Winemaker: Tim Finn
Best drinking: 1995*

Pale, sandy-straw colour, and a brisk, hay-like aroma
that is chip dry and vaguely mellow like midsummer.
A rather lovely wine, delicately flavoured with a fresh
feeling that ends with a buzz, and a surprising
incursion of kerosine characters. Clear and appealing,
it fades gently.

1990
MOUTERE SAUVIGNON BLANC

*13% alc/vol; 92% Sauvignon Blanc, 8% Semillon; 100%
Moutere district, Nelson region; harvested 17 and 30 April
1990; 50% aged in oak for one month.
Winemaker: Tim Finn
Best drinking: 1995–97*

Perfumed, aromatic wine that evokes macrocarpa
hedges and toast, with a savoury trim, but is never
strident. Precisely made, with shafts of hay through the
palate, neat weight and an elongated, crisp, lively feel
that leaves behind a fresh tingle of enthusiasm and a
tidy astringency. Again delicately flavoured, fine, with
firm textures and a hearty backbone of warmth, it is
beautifully poised, its depth and presence completing
a very well-composed wine.

1991
NELSON-MARLBOROUGH
SAUVIGNON BLANC

*12% alc/vol; 88% Sauvignon Blanc, 12% Semillon; 50% of
Sauvignon Blanc and 100% of Semillon from Moutere
district, Nelson region, 50% of Sauvignon Blanc from
Marlborough region; harvested 27 April 1991 in Moutere,
2 May in Marlborough.
Winemaker: Tim Finn
Best drinking: 1995–97*

Light in colour, a pale, sandy hue that is clear and
bright. The bouquet is mellow, mealy and fresh with
cooked asparagus aromas and a clean tang of minerals,
it wells up from the glass, predicting the momentum
of flavour that the palate delivers. Very good wine, with
excellent fruit weight and a suave texture to

complement the brisk, clean, lively nature of
Sauvignon Blanc. Still with a youthful vigour, it also
has the level of integration and mellow flavour of early
bottle age, aspects that complement the sweet heart
of fruit and deliver greater complexity. Well balanced,
light, but never thin, it has an easy elegance and
charm.

1992
NELSON SAUVIGNON BLANC

*13% alc/vol; Sauvignon Blanc and small amount of
Semillon; 100% Nelson region, 50% of Sauvignon from
Moutere, 50% from Richmond, 100% Semillon from
Moutere; harvested 5 May 1992 at Moutere, 24 April
at Richmond.
Winemaker: Tim Finn
Best drinking: 1995–2000*

Light, vaguely green wine with peas and hay aromas
in a bouquet that is a contradiction of freshness and
mellow ripeness, spiced with a pinch of nutmeg.
Pleasing fruit concentration helps the macrocarpa
hedge character of the palate, accommodating its
briskness and natural freshness, facilitating length and
presence. Super wine for food, it has weight and
flavour in abundance, depth, length — in fact enough
structural momentum to keep pace with the stroppy
adolescent flavours and aromas.

1993
NELSON SAUVIGNON BLANC

*12% alc/vol; Sauvignon Blanc and small amount of
Semillon; 100% Nelson region, 50% of Sauvignon Blanc
from Moutere, 50% from Richmond, 100% Semillon from
Moutere; harvested 14 May at Moutere, 8 and 24 April at
Richmond.
Winemaker: Tim Finn
Best drinking: 1995–97*

Pale, greenish gold, light and bright, with a fragrant,
floral bouquet showing hints of pine, aromatic hay,
limes and the vague plumpness of melon. Packed with
lovely fruit, the flavour of passionfruit and papaya,
enlivened here and there with a pine character and a
bright, lingering energy that is juicy fresh and full of
promise. Very precise wine, it is neither big nor thin
and, while its flavour is always present, it is never
overwhelming, or even assertive, just lively.

1994

13% alc/vol; 100% Sauvignon Blanc; 100% Nelson region,
50% from Moutere, 50% from Richmond; harvested
15 April and 10 May at Moutere, 25 April at Richmond.
Winemaker: Tim Finn
Best drinking: 1996–2003

Very pale, just touched with a hint of green. An excellent, ripe wine full of life and the pleasure of bright, energetic fruit. There is lime, nettles and fruit salad on the nose, which is not yet fragrant but has a hard core of concentration that suggests it soon will be. Very sweet-seeming limes and passionfruit appear instantly in the mouth, and the mid-palate is an abundance of tropical fruit salad, juiciness and brisk clamour, which tails off to a superb finish layered with fruit, gentle astringency and brisk freshness. Very good wine indeed, weighty, deep, full of exuberance and ripe fruit and tailored with class that never permits the undoubted energy to dominate.

OYSTER BAY SAUVIGNON BLANC

Delegat's Marlborough label gained quick recognition with these vibrant, energetic wines, which just as rapidly became one of the most difficult wines to buy, either in New Zealand or on export markets. The small vintages of the early 1990s have compounded the problem, but its reputation as a class wine seems secure.

1990
MARLBOROUGH SAUVIGNON BLANC

12.5% alc/vol; 100% Sauvignon Blanc;
Marlborough region; harvested 8 April 1990.
Winemaker: Brent Marris
Best drinking: 1995–97

Light, golden straw colour. Very toasty, fresh bouquet of aged, ripe Sauvignon Blanc introduces a smart wine with nicely supple, deep flavours, brambly characters that come from the heart, and last to the very end. Slightly dry, astringent finish, but fresh and clean all the way. A classy wine aged to delicate beauty with freshness and momentum, it has neat fruit and friskiness in excellent balance, and a lingering charm at the end.

1991

11.3% alc/vol; 100% Sauvignon Blanc;
Marlborough region; harvested 10 April 1991.

Winemaker: Brent Marris
Best drinking: 1995–96

Rich, straw-coloured, clear, bright wine with a slightly toasty, limy bouquet that has a mineral note to it, as well as some subtle spice. Fresh and clean on the palate, with fading flavours that repeat the minerals and lime characters, finishing crisp, with a faint echo of flavour.

1992

11% alc/vol; 100% Sauvignon Blanc; Marlborough region; harvested 5 May 1992.
Winemaker: Brent Marris
Best drinking: 1995–96

Clear, bright-looking wine, the colour of straw, it has a fattish bouquet, suggestive of lanolin, with a faint whiff of green peas. Fresh, clean and very light, it is nicely balanced with a tracery of subtle flavours, and a keen balance that never quite succumbs to the fresh acidity. Long, delicate, light finish.

1993

12% alc/vol; 100% Sauvignon Blanc; Marlborough region; harvested 6 May 1993.
Winemaker: Brent Marris
Best drinking: 1995–2000

A bright, light straw colour that suits the hay-like bouquet. This wine is clarion clear, with a heart of intense fruit character that is mildly limy, with mineral overtones, and savoury hay-straw flavours. Very lively, fresh-feeling and zippy, but never aggressive, it has a long, lingering finish that maintains the intensity all the way, and repeats the intriguing, dry, savoury and hay flavours. Very appealing, and just sturdy enough to impress.

1994

13% alc/vol; 100% Sauvignon Blanc; Marlborough region; harvested 13 April 1994.
Winemaker: Brent Marris
Best drinking: 1995–2002

Water clear wine, with a very faint touch of mint on the nose among the fresh, nettly aromas and some richer tones of red capsicum. Supple and fresh, with plenty of guts and flavour for a young wine, it is very frisky, with a clear, crisp finish, moderate length and a trailing freshness of flavour and acidity.

STONELEIGH VINEYARD MARLBOROUGH SAUVIGNON BLANC

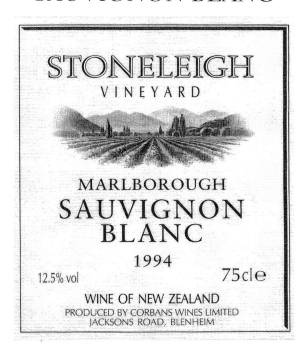

Since its release in the mid-1980s, this has become one of New Zealand's most widely recognised wine labels. Its consistent quality and light, mellow herbaceousness have established it as a most respectable wine, one that is less assertive than most Marlborough Sauvignon Blancs, but still retains the region's characteristic vigour and freshness. It does seem to be at its best when young and fresh, for it ages with less grace than most.

1987

12% alc/vol; 100% Sauvignon Blanc; Marlborough region; harvested 25 April 1987.
Winemaker: Glenn Thomas

Light-coloured, brassy, green-tinged wine with a light nose that hints at canned peas and other fading, mature, herbaceous characters. Tender on the palate, mellow, with a vague touch of toast and a fresh, watery finish. Interesting, but well past its best.

1988

12% alc/vol; 100% Sauvignon Blanc; Marlborough region; harvested 4 May 1988.
Winemaker: Glenn Thomas
Best drinking: 1995

Yellow-golden wine, that has a mellow, toasty bouquet laced with canned peas aroma and a charming touch of freshness. Still pleasant and alive, softer than it seems, with a mild, vaguely spicy character, and an easy, clean finish.

1989

12% alc/vol; 100% Sauvignon Blanc; Marlborough region; harvested 31 March 1989.
Winemaker: Alan McCorkindale
Best drinking: 1995

Hay-coloured with a lively green light in it. On the nose its mellow, lightly spicy character adds interest to the ripe red capsicum aroma. Very soft and pretty palate, and it retains an air of freshness although it is fading away at the edges, and is less than fresh at the finish.

1991

12.5% alc/vol; 100% Sauvignon Blanc; Marlborough region; harvested 16 April 1991.
Winemaker: Alan McCorkindale
Best drinking: 1995–97

Lovely wine, with a pretty colour like that of ripe hay, and a bouquet rich in the aromas of red capsicum, hay and other mellow, herbaceous characters, given a lift by an attractive waft of strange, perfumed, quite exotic fragrance. Very clean and bright, but delivering a mouthful of flavour that is round, ripe and mellow, with enough momentum to carry it on into the finish. Very moreish wine, mouth-watering fresh, tasty, leaving behind a mildly resonant finish.

1992

12.5% alc/vol; 100% Sauvignon Blanc;
Marlborough region; harvested 2–26 April 1992.
Winemaker: Alan McCorkindale
Best drinking: 1995–96

Pale, lemony, straw-coloured wine, with a mellow, grassy character on the nose and in the mouth, but restrained by an unusual, soft, buttery quality. Tastes older than its vintage suggests, but a pleasant wine for all that, mild and slightly quirky.

1993

11.5% alc/vol; 100% Sauvignon Blanc;
Marlborough region.
Winemaker: Alan McCorkindale
Best drinking: 1995–97

Very pale to look at, this wine has a lively, frisky, gooseberry bouquet that is mellowed slightly by a faint hint of ripe red capsicum. Very supple for such an enthusiastic wine, but never far from the exuberant freshness of its acid edge and touch of intensity, it has plenty of flavour in the gooseberry, capsicum, cut grass area, and it leaves behind a tingle that almost suggests too much acidity. Exciting wine for its texture and liveliness, it makes demanding company.

TE MATA ESTATE CAPE CREST SAUVIGNON BLANC

Te Mata is best known for its stunning red wines, but none of its small range is less than impressive, and all reflect the estate's individual approach to excellence. Unlike most other New Zealand Sauvignon Blancs, this wine is made for depth and length, rather than enthusiasm, with the accent on structure as much as mature Sauvignon flavours.

1987

12% alc/vol; 100% Sauvignon Blanc; Hawke's Bay region, Cape Crest Vineyard; hand harvested 10 April 1987.
Winemaker: Peter Cowley
Best drinking: 1995–97

Light-coloured wine, with an attractive, delicate aroma that is fringed with citrus peel, mild toastiness and a touch of mineral tang. Toasty on the palate as well, with hints of citrus and minerals, even a suggestion of smoke among the waves of flavour nuance that are steadily delivered, as if from a deep well. Not big wine, but strong and clear, its cleverly crafted, subtle flavours gently welling up from a pool of clarity and easy, fine-grained freshness.

1989

13% alc/vol; 100% Sauvignon Blanc; Hawke's Bay region, Cape Crest Vineyard; hand harvested 20 March 1989.
Winemaker: Peter Cowley
Best drinking: 1995–97

Light straw colour, touched with gold, and showing a slight tinge of canned peas in its firm bouquet. With nice, plump fruit flavour at the heart of the palate, edged with peas, and showing a crisp mineral quality, it is serious, restrained wine, with touches of toasty bottle age showing through. Good depth and length give it a sense of quality, but it is as dry in character as it is in texture.

1990

12.5% alc/vol; 100% Sauvignon Blanc; Hawke's Bay region, Cape Crest Vineyard; hand harvested 17–18 April 1990.
Winemaker: Peter Cowley
Best drinking: 1995–98

Light, straw-coloured wine with an almost pungent aroma of smoky, mineral flintiness, shafts of toast and a background of mature fruit richness. Orderly, never flamboyant wine, but deeply satisfying with its traces of sawdust, marmalade and fruit sweetness on the palate and a growing crowd of flavour nuances that cluster around the finish. A long, clear, sometimes subtle wine with strength of character and a sustained finish that toys with ideas of richness.

1991

13% alc/vol; 100% Sauvignon Blanc; Hawke's Bay region, Cape Crest Vineyard; hand harvested 3–4 April 1991.
Winemaker: Peter Cowley
Best drinking: 1995–99

Pale to light straw, with a faint glitter of gold in it, this is pretty wine with an enigmatic streak. Complex aromatic, minerally, toasty characters occupy the nose, and the taut, edgy palate, all kept under control by a feeling of austerity in the long, cool structure and quiet strength. Again a very orderly wine, but with enough mystery and subtlety to be intriguing, and the length to impress as well as to satisfy.

1992

13% alc/vol; 100% Sauvignon Blanc; Hawke's Bay region,
Cape Crest Vineyard; hand harvested 27 April 1992.
Winemaker: Peter Cowley
Best drinking: 1995–2000

Very glamorous wine indeed, although its light straw colour does not arouse such expectations, but the mature tropical aromas of passionfruit and very ripe papaya do. There are subtleties of vanilla spice and savouriness embedded in the supple, luscious texture of the bouquet and the palate, but they are kept on a tight rein, all the time straining to be let loose. Dry and long, it is structurally perfect, with alcohol, acid and an elegant balance between these and the fine-grained fruit that runs so deep. It feels almost as aristocratic as Chardonnay, just missing a quantum of richness. Terrific wine.

1993

12% alc/vol; 100% Sauvignon Blanc; Hawke's Bay region,
Cape Crest Vineyard; hand harvested 14 May 1993.
Winemaker: Peter Cowley
Best drinking: 1995–99

Straw-coloured, fresh, bright-looking wine with a deeply delicious character on the nose and in the mouth. The aromas are not specific, but they are succulent, sweet, mellow, ripe in all the notes of fruitful autumn, complemented by creamy, light richness. The palate, too, is ripe, with a touch of charming lightness that becomes serious at the end, with a long, dry, firm finish which has a smoky, mineral character about it. Wine that begs to be drunk with food.

TE MATA ESTATE CASTLE HILL SAUVIGNON BLANC

The fruitier of the two Te Mata wines, but not necessarily a lesser wine for that, Castle Hill is more approachable when young, but gives nothing away in structure or in aging potential to its less enthusiastic partner.

1987

13% alc/vol; 100% Sauvignon Blanc; Hawke's Bay region,
Castle Hill Vineyard; hand harvested 21–23 April 1987.
Winemaker: Peter Cowley
Best drinking: 1995–97

Polished straw-coloured wine, its clarity matched by a bright bouquet that is full of the aroma of lime marmalade, lined with a dusty layer of toast. Suave stuff, matched by a rich, long, supple palate with a bag of flavour nuances that run very deep: limes and marmalade and minerals, washed with mellow tones of bottle age and the softening succulence of ripe fruit. Warm wine, with a cooling freshness, and a steady, quiet, almost introspective nature that is at odds with Sauvignon Blanc's reputation, but manages to leave a strong impression of depth and substance.

1989

13% alc/vol; 100% Sauvignon Blanc; Hawke's Bay region, Castle Hill Vineyard; hand harvested 29–31 March 1989.
Winemaker: Peter Cowley
Best drinking: 1995–99

Its mellow aroma spiced with savoury, toasty characters and rich, mature fruit is matched by equally softened, poised fruit flavours to make this a particularly toothsome wine. It genial spread is enlivened by a frisky edge of Sauvignon Blanc briskness and a tingle of acidity, all swirling in and out of a tide of complexities. Lovely stuff, with more substance than its surface charms first imply.

1990

12% alc/vol; 100% Sauvignon Blanc; Hawke's Bay region, Castle Hill Vineyard; hand harvested 28 April and 1 May 1990.
Winemaker: Peter Cowley
Best drinking: 1995–98

An even, steady bouquet with a slight hint of orange peel and dusty spice. Soft, slightly creamy palate with quite chunky fruit and a mineral austerity that comes on like distant smoke in the finish. Very evenly paced throughout, its various characters coming and going, this is attractive wine, with background style and moderate momentum.

1991

12.5% alc/vol; 100% Sauvignon Blanc; Hawke's Bay region, Castle Hill Vineyard; hand harvested 22–24 April 1991.
Winemaker: Peter Cowley
Best drinking: 1995–2001

Light, fresh-looking wine with a pale straw hue, its aroma mellow and mineral-like. There is a mineral quality about the flavour, too, which is fresh, lively, with an excellent feeling of elongated, sinuous texture spread with ripe, succulent fruit nuances. Has a very real presence that verges on strength, and subtlety that extends through and fades slowly. Neat wine, beautiful to drink, cleverly balanced, aristocratic in form, but with a friendly nature.

1992

12% alc/vol; 100% Sauvignon Blanc; Hawke's Bay region, Castle Hill Vineyard; hand harvested 1–4 May 1992.
Winemaker: Peter Cowley
Best drinking: 1995–2003

Full, very ripe, aromatic bouquet that is just gaining a frill of complexity around notes of lychee, cape gooseberry and red capsicum. Wonderful, similar flavours follow, enhanced by intensity, fine grain and fresh, lively tension to the point of exuberance. The fruit flavours are a real presence in this wine, right to the last trail of finish that leaves a subtlety of ripe quince. Very svelte wine, brightened up by fresh clarity, refined by subtle winecraft, it is quite delicious.

1993

11.5% alc/vol; 100% Sauvignon Blanc; Hawke's Bay region, Castle Hill Vineyard; hand harvested 14–17 May 1993.
Winemaker: Peter Cowley
Best drinking: 1995–97

Pale, green-tinged straw colour, with a ripe gooseberry nose that is even, moderately deep and ripe. The palate, too, is ripe, deeper and fuller than the bouquet, with a trailing clarity that washes the wine with freshness and leaves a firm tingle at the end. This character is not quite crisp, not assertive, and always in harmony with its lively, ripe fruit partners and their soft heart. Tender and lively at once, it offers a very pretty glassful.

VAVASOUR RESERVE MARLBOROUGH SAUVIGNON BLANC

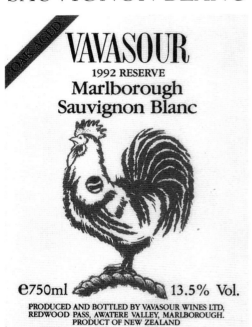

Glenn Thomas is responsible for establishing more élite Sauvignon Blanc labels than any other winemaker in New Zealand, and here at Vavasour he has created what many see as his finest wine from this variety. Certainly it is an impressive example of consistency and complexity that underscores Thomas' fine touch with the volatile personality of this grape when it is grown in Marlborough conditions.

1989
FUMÉ BLANC

13.5% alc/vol; 100% Sauvignon Blanc; Marlborough region; harvested 16 March 1989; 100% barrel fermented in all new French oak 225-litre barriques; aged 3 months in new French barriques.
Winemaker: Glenn Thomas
Best drinking: 1995–99

With its ripe, even-textured, moderately rich bouquet and fig-like aromas, this wine first appears big, and the initial taste confirms this, with a wad of sweet fruit and washes of ripe, almost tropical fruit flavours. The finesse of the wine takes over from here, as the freshness and clarity subdue the fruit and allow more of the easy, satin textures to assert themselves, and the oak to make its presence felt. Very warm, viscous wine, it would be solid if it were not for its fresh components and very long, clean finish. A classy performance that is also a delicious drink.

1990

12.8% alc/vol; 100% Sauvignon Blanc; Marlborough region; harvested 3 April 1990; whole bunch pressed; barrel fermented in used 500-litre puncheons and new 225-litre barriques, all French; aged 3 months in new and used oak barrels.
Winemaker: Glenn Thomas
Best drinking: 1995–96

Pale, sandy straw colour, fresh and bright, with an aromatic, horse manure character on the nose that is distinctive and not as bad as it sounds, but warm and mellow in a definite, vegetative way. Big wine, with fine-grained oak and a lightness of touch that is appealing, and nice moments of citrus and fresh acidity throughout, features that brighten its nettly flavours and slightly soft texture. Clean, brave wine.

1991
RESERVE SAUVIGNON BLANC

13.5% alc/vol; 100% Sauvignon Blanc; Marlborough region; harvested 26 April 1991; whole bunch pressed; 60% barrel fermented in new and used oak; 20% malolactic fermentation; aged in oak 8 months.
Winemaker: Glenn Thomas
Best drinking: 1995–2001

Fresh, fragrant wine shot with lime blossom aromas and shafts of sweet oak, harmonised by aromatic fruit complexities. Pleasant fruit on the palate, lightly sweet, ripe-flavoured touches that embellish its big body in partnership with limy citrus characters and a quiet undercurrent of richness. A very classy wine, this one, its slightly abrasive Sauvignon Blanc nature restrained by elegant, lingering oak, and lovely textures that turn freshness and power into grace. Not many Sauvignon Blancs make it to elegance, but this one does.

1992

*13.5% alc/vol; 100% Sauvignon Blanc; Marlborough
region; harvested 25 April 1992; whole bunch pressed; 30%
malolactic fermentation; aged in oak 8 months.*
Winemaker: Glenn Thomas
Best drinking: 1995–96

Herbs and aromatic oak nose, lively and mellow by
turn. Lovely, supple-textured, almost creamy palate,
its svelte quality lasting right to the end, holding
together a wine that has quite simple fruit flavour, limy
in character, with rather stern acidity and a tough
nature. Subtle, rather charming oak nuances make
regular incursions, keeping up the appearance of
quality, but are never fully convincing. Deft winemaking here.

1993

*12.5% alc/vol; 90% Sauvignon Blanc, 10% Semillon;
Marlborough region; harvested Sauvignon Blanc
11 May 1993, Semillon 24 May; whole bunch pressed;
40% malolactic fermentation; aged in oak 7 months.*
Winemaker: Glenn Thomas
Best drinking: 1995–99

Another gracious wine from this collection. Ripe and
mealy on the nose, with the lift of nettly aroma, citrus-
tinged acidity, and a creamy camembert cheese
dimension, it is finely balanced between fragrance and
aroma. Full of creamy flavours, spiced with fresh limes
and a trace of oak, it finishes well, holding its heart of
concentrated fruit, with fragrance a lingering feature.
Good wine.

SPARKLING WINES

SPARKLING WINES HAVE BEEN A PRESENCE IN NEW ZEALAND FOR A long time, certainly in the form of Mission's Fontanella, which had the field to itself until production ceased early in the 1970s. Later, Mate Selak took up the challenge at Selaks in West Auckland, before Montana made a significant investment in bottle fermentation technology for their Lindauer wine, a development that was seminal in creating a market for high-quality sparkling in New Zealand, and establishing a wine of international standard.

Daniel le Brun also made a substantial contribution when he became the first to establish a winery dedicated to méthode champenoise production, his success forcing the industry to see this as a serious wine. Le Brun, originally from Champagne in France, was also adamant that his choice of Marlborough as the source for his wine was based purely on the area's potential for growing wines of the highest quality.

This has been borne out by the subsequent emergence of Marlborough as the pre-eminent méthode champenoise region in the country; it is home to Montana-Deutz Marlborough Cuvée, Pelorus, Domaine Chandon's Marlborough Brut and Nautilus, as well as le Brun.

Because of the tradition for making this style as a non-vintage wine, a number of the best wines made in New Zealand, such as le Brun non-vintage, and Montana-Deutz Marlborough Cuvée and Blanc de Blancs, cannot be represented in a vertical-tasting format. This does not prevent their being classified as fine wines, but does make it difficult to describe their progress as wines.

All fine sparkling wines made in New Zealand are bottle-fermented, using méthode champenoise techniques, and all are a blend of Pinot Noir and Chardonnay wines, although these are rarely made with fruit from the intensely flavoured clones that are the principal source of fine Chardonnay and Pinot Noir.

CLOUDY BAY PELORUS

From the first release, this has been a perfect example of top-class sparkling wine — complex, elegant and deeply flavoured. Carefully made to show off the deep, clear flavour characteristics of Marlborough-grown fruit against a background of beautifully proportioned yeast and other winemaking interventions, it has been universally acclaimed as one of New Zealand's finest. This image has been further enhanced by superb packaging, probably the finest on any wine made in New Zealand, and certainly a match for the best the French can offer in the exclusive territory of prestige sparkling wines.

1987

13% alc/vol; 50% Pinot Noir, 50% Chardonnay.
Winemaker: Harold Osborne
Best drinking: 1995–96

A steady bead of even, smallish bubbles climbing steadily through a moderately ripe straw-coloured wine makes for a very attractive appearance, almost as if polished for a presentation. The bouquet, too, is in fine condition, toasty, yeasty and aromatic, ripely mellow but tinged with the freshness of an orangy, citric tone that is a bright flicker of life among the faint crackle of bubbles. The bubbles and citric flavour fill the mouth with a lively effervescent foam balanced by a richness of flavours that suggest mushrooms and an earthy hint of leaf litter, flavours which linger on to a soft, lasting finish. Neatly balanced with fresh and mellow textures as well as sparkle, and lovely tones of mature citrus mingled

with the mushrooms and mealy yeast, this is a subtle, well-crafted, most satisfying wine.

1988

13% alc/vol; 50% Pinot Noir, 50% Chardonnay;
Marlborough region.
Winemaker: Harold Osborne
Best drinking: 1995

Sandy, plump, straw-coloured wine with a steady, even bead of regulation bubbles, its bouquet is enchantingly aromatic, with smoky, citrus overtones and a more subtle, mellow heart of creamy, salt-tanged yeast. A very relaxed, frothy palate with a stream of fizz coming from deep within it, and lovely passing flavours including ripe oranges, toast and vaguely salty oatmeal. Very soft, with shadows of ripeness and a passing hint of mushrooms, it makes for an easy, dusky drink.

1989

13% alc/vol; 50% Pinot Noir, 50% Chardonnay;
Marlborough region.
Winemaker: Harold Osborne
Best drinking: 1995–98

A steady, measured stream of bubbles through a ripe straw colour introduces a wine that is mouth-wateringly delicious from first sniff to the last echo of flavour. The bouquet is lively and mealy at once. The fragrance has so much mealy aroma and highlights of smoke and creamy, slightly sour camembert that it verges on the pungent, but is kept in check by a piquant freshness enhanced by the aroma of ripe oranges. Finely flavoured and equally fine in texture, with depth, and a fascinating hint of austerity that completes a four-way balance with frisky bubbles, freshness and the mellowness of yeast and cream. The pleasant harmonies of flavour are sustained right through, leaving a final impression of a superbly complex, layered, resonant wine that is gracefully balanced yet full of life and promise for the future.

1990

13% alc/vol; 50% Pinot Noir, 50% Chardonnay;
Marlborough region.
Winemaker: Harold Osborne
Best drinking: 1995–98

The steady, small bubbles and plump straw colour are not too different from earlier vintages, but the bouquet is more immediately friendly, with an aromatic, orangey nose complete with subtle, suggestive extensions of toffee, cream cheese, oatmeal and smoke. The palate is tense yet quite deliciously juicy with orange details, real warmth and gently balancing astringency, leaving a tingling sensation of vigour and easy texture, but without the fine balance of the 1989. Delicious wine, however, with an air of class and charming, ripe texture that strokes while the bubbles fizz.

1991

13% alc/vol; 50% Pinot Noir, 50% Chardonnay;
Marlborough region.
Winemaker: Harold Osborne
Best drinking: 1996–2001

Green-tinged straw-coloured wine, with bubbles marching at regulation pace and spacing in long, relentless lines. An effervescent, limy, youthful nose that is already glittering with a lively array of flavours recalling citrus, yeast and savoury smokey emerging from a bouquet of substance and still quiet depths. Sweetish, broad, finely textured palate has deep but still undefined characters in a mélange of flavour and texture that is dense yet easy all the way to the finish. Freshness and long, long flavour hang around after each sip, implying a promising future for this already impressive wine, one with graceful balance, effortless complexity and warmth to match its crisp tenor.

DANIEL LE BRUN BLANC DE BLANCS

The fruit in le Brun wines is the base on which the extravagances of bottle-fermented sparklings are built, and with this Chardonnay Daniel le Brun has used the creamy sweetness of the grapes to the full, enhancing them with yeast and other embellishments, but always letting the fruit lead. In spite of this, yeast is still a major feature of the style, and the wines are at their best when the two components find equilibrium.

1985

12.6% alc/vol; 100% Chardonnay; Marlborough region;
on lees in bottle 3 years.
Winemaker: Daniel le Brun

Light, golden colour, with a steady stream of even, tiny bubbles, this wine has a slightly oxidised character and an acetic tinge. Short, dry and austere, it is well past its best.

1986

12.6% alc/vol; 100% Chardonnay; Marlborough region;
on lees in bottle 3 years.
Winemaker: Daniel le Brun
Best drinking: 1995

Pale gold, with steady bubbles of various sizes, from tiny to moderate, and a yeasty, nutty bouquet that has a cleverly refreshing, light touch. Good, even flavours that are yeasty and camembert creamy with a pleasing nuttiness, even earthy in places, and an unusual sharpness that is not citric. Round and pleasant wine, still effervescent, but the flavours are fading somewhat.

1987

12.6% alc/vol; 100% Chardonnay; Marlborough region;
on lees in bottle 3 years.
Winemaker: Daniel le Brun
Best drinking: 1995–96

Frothy, ripe straw wine with steady, tiny bubbles that rush up in regular rivers of gas. Fresh, shortbread bottle age with hints of toast, an edge of freshness and temptations of yeast fragrance that are plump and juicy almost to the point of fatness. This wine is very much alive, clean yet mellow, with a creamy ripeness in the mouth that gives way gradually to an austere, dry finish engraved with shadows of yeast and sweetness. Completely integrated, it has a pervasive fineness that at all stages appears perfectly turned, crafted for grace, with its full measure of flavour subtleties that slide into each other just before they are positively identified.

1988

12.6% alc/vol; 100% Chardonnay; Marlborough region;
on lees in bottle 3 years.
Winemaker: Daniel le Brun
Best drinking: 1995–96

Bright straw with a very fine bead that is a neatly regulated procession of steady, small bubbles. Beautifully aromatic, the bouquet is nutty and creamy at once, light, sweetly poised, with suave subtleties and a distant echo of summer oranges. In the mouth the fizz is honest, the flavours sweet and tender, with a lovely, smooth texture and a long, graceful finish that tapers away without rush, leaving an impression of soft charm. Quite delicious, lingering wine to savour, at every turn it seems to be in proportion, no flavour or texture pulling too much in any direction, and delivers its abundance of flavour subtleties with ease.

1989

12.6% alc/vol; 100% Chardonnay; Marlborough region;
on lees in bottle 3 years.
Winemaker: Daniel le Brun
Best drinking: 1995–99

Glittering, straw-coloured wine, with light, even, tiny bubbles in suitable streams. A very yeasty nose, complemented by fresh, creamy nuts and buttermilk characters and a crisp fragrance that is almost apart from the body of the bouquet. The bubbles are persistent in the mouth, without being frothy, and

there is excellent fruit weight that is sweet but never fruity, offset by delicious mealy, nut kernel yeast characters, fresh peeled orange and a vague concentration that hints at Marmite. Texture and flavour nuance are svelte and very impressive, layered in depth through the palate, and keeping up momentum right to the finish and beyond, all the time tickled by bubbles. Fine, lovely stuff.

1990

12.6% alc/vol; 100% Chardonnay; Marlborough region;
on lees in bottle 3 years.
Winemaker: Daniel le Brun
Best drinking: 1996–99

Bright, light, yellowish straw wine, with busy, tiny bubbles in steady streams and quite momentous fruit on the nose, sweet, creamy and ripe, almost glossy. There is a balancing finesse of yeast, traces of nuts, even a hint or two of unripe camembert and a sprinkling of salt intensity, all stepping across from bouquet to palate with ease, but the pervasive character is ripe fruit of the creaming soda sort. Still very close-grained, deep and lively, it seems too young to drink yet, but is very pleasurable in spite of that, succulent, plump, teasing with its bubbles and promising to unravel strands of subtleties with time.

DANIEL LE BRUN VINTAGE

French Champagne fans would claim that this is the best of the le Brun range, with its typical barrage of deep-seated fruit flavours juxtaposed against the full range of yeasty characters it is possible to extract. Big but never overpowering wine, it has become a standard against which other New Zealand sparklings are judged for strength and balance of yeast and fruit character.

1986

*12.6% alc/vol; 40% Chardonnay, 60% Pinot Noir;
Marlborough region; on lees in bottle 3 years.
Winemaker: Daniel le Brun.*

Mild gold, with a steady stream of bubbles. Oxidised, light, slightly acetic, flat in flavour if still fizzy.

1989

*12.6% alc/vol; 40% Chardonnay, 60% Pinot Noir;
Marlborough region; on lees in bottle 3 years.
Winemaker: Daniel le Brun
Best drinking: 1995–97*

Mellow gold, with tiny, orderly bubbles doing what they must, in line and evenly spaced. A fine, wonderfully aromatic bouquet that is earthy, smoky, mushroom-laden with forest floor nuances and inlaid with Marmite yeastiness sets up this yummy wine. Its hearty mouthful is rippling with flavours and fizz: creamy nut kernels, mealiness, mushrooms, with tinges of orange and soy sauce. A very savoury, lively, positive wine with its notable enthusiasm in step with the aromas and flavours that fill it to the very edges. Bold, lively, lingering, even inspiring, like Satchmo giving life to a trumpet.

1990

*12.6% alc/vol; 40% Chardonnay, 60% Pinot Noir;
Marlborough region; on lees in bottle 3 years.
Winemaker: Daniel le Brun
Best drinking: 1996–2000*

Fresh straw colour with an even, lively bubble that maintains its steady precision in spite of its obvious enthusiasms. The bouquet is youthful, just beyond the green and gangly stage, with big, sweet, smoky fruit that has hints of Marmite, yeast, cream and nuts, with dusty mushroom nuances. The palate, too, is sweet with ripe fruit, alive with almost fiercely buzzing bubbles, deep and dense, but very delicately balanced and showing neat finesse that holds through the palate and on into a lingering, smoky, yeasty finish. Very dense, elongated, fine wine that needs a bit more time to unravel itself so that it can show off.

MORTON ESTATE VINTAGE

Morton Estate were the first North Island winery to produce regularly a high-quality sparkling wine of consistent quality, and remain the most highly regarded sparkling wine makers north of Cook Strait. The style has always been more closely associated with fruit than with yeast, based as it is on Gisborne Chardonnay, on ebullient, ripe flavours that are typically the opposite of what méthode champenoise drinkers would call classic. By paying attention to balance and finesse, however, the Morton style has created another option for fizzy drinkers who want the best, but enjoy lush fruit as much as some treasure the taste of busy yeast.

1983
CHAMPAGNE

12.5% alc/vol; 70% Chenin Blanc, 30% Chardonnay; Gisborne region; on lees in bottle 6 years. Winemaker: John Hancock.

Yellow, with a pop and a light fizz on opening, but with very lazy bubbles in the glass. It has a fresh-edged bouquet, with biscuit aromas and the fading flatness of oxidisation, offset by a modicum of creaminess and lots of toast that makes it pleasant if not exciting. Very gentle fizz in the mouth but a quite brisk, almost aggressive, herbal flavour among the toast and softness.

Traces of acidity show there is life in the old thing yet, but it no longer has much stamina to keep in at the finish. Very interesting.

1985

12.5% alc/vol; 60% Chardonnay, 40% Pinot; Gisborne region; on lees in bottle 3 years. Winemaker: John Hancock Best drinking: 1995

Yellow-gold in colour, this wine has gentle, tiny bubbles that fizz quietly to their own waltz music, and a fragrant-edged, toasty, earthy, mellow bouquet that is in places reminiscent of wine biscuits. This wafty introduction in no way prepares you for the subsequent big mouthful of flavour and bubbles, rich with yeast, oodles of toast, slices and crumbs, and a lingering finish that holds sack and mild yeastiness in equal parts among the toast. Austere in places, it has a certain fading style, gracious if not graceful, with a vague memory of grapefruit flavour adding marmalade to the toast, and leaving an impression that, in its youth, it was probably a wild, rumbustious thing considered over the top by effete judges.

1986

12.5% alc/vol; 100% Chardonnay; Gisborne region; undisgorged. Winemakers: John Hancock and Steve Bird Best drinking: 1995

Foaming big bubbles clutter the fresh yellow wine with holes, giving foam to the clean, clear, yeasty-mealy nose with its shots of peachy fruit against the sweet and savoury background aromas. An abundant, creamy mouthful of flavour running rampant through the equally exuberant fizz, a party of toast, cream, nuts, yeast, grapefruit and peaches mixed to super-duper proportions, it spreads to every corner of your mouth, and although it does not linger long at the finish it certainly leaves an impression. Has swagger rather than finesse, but it is never clumsy or rough, always delivering what it promises. A lot of fun from beginning to end.

1987

12.5% alc/vol; 85% Pinot, 15% Chardonnay; Pinot from Hawke's Bay region, Chardonnay from Gisborne; on lees in bottle 3 years.

Winemakers: John Hancock and Steve Bird
Best drinking: 1995–97

Polished-looking wine, copper-gold with orderly bubbles marching steadily up through the glowing beverage where they mingle at last with a bright, delicate bouquet that is fine and minerally with some pretty, floral fragrances and crisp toastiness. Good, honest bubbles in the mouth too, and a fine, restrained palate with depth of flavour and a lovely texture that is not quite rich, but rather effortlessly smooth, punctuated by precise bubbles. The finish is very, very long, fine again, slightly austere, but delicately laced with flavour that hangs on tenaciously—nuances of ripe grapefruit, smokiness and vague strawberry subtleties which have emerged from the palate's depths. Superb wine, flavourful, but never short on finesse, it lacks only the sort of yeast flavours a purist would demand.

1988

12.5% alc/vol; 50% Pinot, 50% Chardonnay; Pinot from Hawke's Bay region, Chardonnay from Gisborne; on lees in bottle 2–3 years.
Winemakers: John Hancock and Steve Bird
Best drinking: 1995

Light, yellow-gold wine with steady, tiny bubbles and a fresh yet soft bouquet larded with mature yeast aromas and a fresh fruit background that includes a healthy measure of orange peel. The palate is also soft, light and a little one-dimensional, but with good bubbles and a pleasant citric character that maintains its appeal. Nicely astringent at the end, it is good, well-behaved wine, but you would not take it to a party.

1989

12.5% alc/vol; 40% Pinot, 60% Chardonnay; Pinot from Hawke's Bay region, Chardonnay from Gisborne; some malolactic fermentation; on lees in bottle 2–3 years.
Winemakers: John Hancock and Steve Bird
Best drinking: 1995–99

A pale, lemon-yellow wine with a hard-working set of regularly performing, tiny bubbles that proceed with precision to the surface of each glassful. This formality is followed by a quite beautiful bouquet that is complex and mellow, but suitably fresh, fragrant with toast and some creamy, nut kernel aromas, a measure of smoke and vaguely peach-like fruit. The full palate is lovely and creamy, citric, and backed by a curtain of sweetness from ripe fruit, a pleasant balancing astringency and some subtle nuttiness. Big in flavour, it lingers long and shows restraint towards the end, promoting an overall sense of elegance that overcomes its fullness. An easy, delicious, fine-textured wine that is very satisfying.

1990

12.5% alc/vol; 20% Pinot, 80% Chardonnay; Pinot from Hawke's Bay region, Chardonnay from Gisborne; serious malolactic fermentation; on lees in bottle 2–3 years.
Winemakers: John Hancock and Steve Bird
Best drinking: 1995–98

Copper-tinged yellow-gold wine that is bright enough for the steady little bubbles positively to glitter through it. Sweet, aromatic, fruity, camembert cheese bouquet that is kindly and warm, with a certain mildness that appears almost lazy. Round and juicy in the mouth, there is plenty of creaming soda character fruit to give a mouth-filling, juicy buoyancy to the cream cheese texture and mellowness of yeast, completing a wine that is almost too succulent to be sparkling wine, if it were not for a saving measure of fresh acidity and some mildly nutty-furry nuances kicking in at the finish. A plump, pretty thing, ripe for drinking now, but possibly growing into a more refined bottle with some time.

1990
BLACK LABEL

12.5% alc/vol; 100% Pinot; Bay of Plenty region; 100% barrel fermentation; malolactic fermentation; on lees in bottle 4 years.
Winemakers: John Hancock and Steve Bird
Best drinking: 1996–2000

Fresh, light lemon-yellow, with a steady stream of attractive little regular bubbles and a very fragrant, toasty, oaky, smoky bouquet that is rich with tones of ripeness. The palate is fine and ripely fragrant, with creamy nut kernel and camembert characters adding round texture as well as depth to a beautifully proportioned mid-palate. The tidy balance of flavours and texture is maintained right through to a long, savoury, fine finish that has just a touch of sweet fruit to its dryness, alongside a faintly astringent twist. Superb wine, neatly crafted, its barrage of lightly defined, deeply ingrained flavours moving in and out among the persistent bubbles, matching with yeast and buttery textures the freshness and slight citric character that give it lift.

BOTRYTISED
SWEET WINES

THE WINES IN THIS SECTION ARE ALL MADE FROM GRAPES THAT HAVE BEEN affected by the mould *Botrytis cinerea*. Where applicable, other sweet wines are included under specific varietal listings but, because botrytis considerably reduces the identifiable, varietal character of wine, replacing this with its own characteristics, botrytised sweet wines become a category apart.

Because of the unpredictability of conditions suitable for the growth of *Botrytis cinerea*, and consequently the production of high-quality sweet wine, this is a relatively small category. Although a number of single wines have been made in occasional vintages by various winemakers, only the four listed here can be said to have made a concerted effort to produce such wines on a regular basis, and with any degree of consistent success. In spite of these limitations, there is enough evidence to indicate that New Zealand has the potential to produce botrytised sweet wines of a very high standard.

The styles made have been predominantly Germanic in character, using the delicate floral notes of Riesling as a basis for sweet, fresh, low-alcohol, unwooded wines. Some development has been initiated with barrel fermentation and higher alcohol styles, and some very interesting wines made from Chardonnay, as well as Semillon and Sauvignon Blanc. These remain in the minority, however, and exist mostly as an indication for the future direction of sweet winemaking in New Zealand, rather than as a significant part of the current, fine sweet wine repertoire.

Compounding the problem is the quantities made, which are inevitably small because few winemakers have been prepared to commit themselves to substantial crops of botrytised fruit, or to the meticulous detail demanded in the winery.

Given these conditions, the following selection has been made giving full consideration, not only to the wines themselves and their consistency over a number of vintages, but also to the overall performance and size of the wineries producing them. Some very good wines have been left out, even some with a relatively long history, because tiny quantities alone are not enough to establish a credible, sustainable fine wine reputation. Unless a winery shows the potential to expand to a reasonable production size, or has a fine wine reputation broad enough to include tiny quantities of something special, it would be misleading to include it under the fine wine title. It should be noted that the smallest of the famous Sauternes properties produces at least 1000 cases each vintage, and even among Germany's tiny properties, such as the famous Weingut Egon Müller-Scharzhof estate, at least 600 cases are produced under the most difficult circumstances.

The following wines are all made by producers whose wines are included in other sections of this book and, with the possible exception of Dry River, are likely to continue making fine botrytised sweet wines in reasonable quantities.

CORBANS PRIVATE BIN NOBLE RHINE RIESLING

Corbans have played an important part in the development of botrytised sweet wines, a programme that culminated in the 1986 Noble Riesling which, through its regular competition success, has been one of the most widely publicised of all New Zealand sweet wines. Its quality has also served as a standard for many other producers embarking on sweet wine-making, and it must be seen as a seminal wine in the evolution of this style in New Zealand.

1986

12.3% alc/vol; 100% Riesling; Marlborough region;
harvested 14 June 1986.
Winemaker: Glenn Thomas
Best drinking: 1995–2000

Creamy, delicate, lifted fragrance comes from this golden-coloured wine and the bouquet has tones of the Blues, with its smoky character and mellow harmonies, complete with whiffs of pine and caramelised honey. The palate is alive with sweetness

and intense flavours, trimmed with a concentrated moment of orange peel, racy honeywax, cream and sweet, ripe apricots. Concentrated, rich, long and suavely supple, for all its intense sweetness and pastry-like layers of flavour it has remarkable freshness, and a fine, always slightly aromatic elegance that gives it a real feeling of style. Superb wine, tasting as if its flavour depths are bottomless, feeding an endless stream of nuances to the surface, where they continue to echo.

1988

11.9 % alc/vol; 100% Riesling; Marlborough region;
harvested 2 June 1988.
Winemaker: Glenn Thomas
Best drinking: 1996–98

Light, golden-coloured wine, lush with ripe aromas on the bouquet, which are complemented by just a hint of lime, honey, cream and some dried fruit. Very fresh in character, this is a lively, light sweetie, with a heart of dried apricots but a little short of concentration and silky texture. Extremely sweet, with a pinch of astringency balancing off the finish, and mouth-watering, limy clarity.

1989

12% alc/vol; 100% Riesling; Marlborough region;
harvested 18 May 1989.
Winemaker: Alan McCorkindale
Best drinking: 1997–2001

Light gold and lightly aromatic, with fragrances of dried flowers and honey, and a tasty hint of *crème brulée* for extra interest. Fresh to the point of being lively, restrained by a steady stream of fruit flavours, moderate intensity and an even balance of components. Its flavours are very ripe, with persistent suggestions of peaches throughout, and a lightly flippant texture. The neat border of intensity is a real pleasure, and the finish is moderately long, with more peaches and a final touch of *crème brulée*. Well constructed, delectably flavoured, fresh-feeling wine.

1990

10% alc/vol; 100% Riesling; Marlborough region;
harvested 22 May 1990.
Winemaker: Alan McCorkindale
Best drinking: 1995–96

Ripe straw-coloured wine, bright and clear, with soft

honey aromas, heavy with floral characters and a sense of viscosity. Sweet on the palate, very fresh, with beeswax flavours and clean, honest appeal. Lime and honey are its dominant features, and it finishes with a brisk astringency that fades quickly with the light flavours. A pleasant, light, pretty little sweetie with a modicum of attractive complexity.

DRY RIVER
SELECTION SERIES

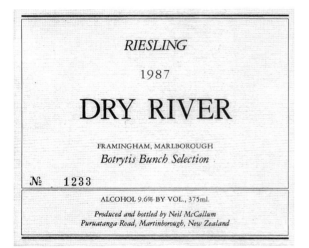

RIESLING

1987

DRY RIVER

FRAMINGHAM, MARLBOROUGH

Botrytis Bunch Selection

№ 1233

ALCOHOL 9.6% BY VOL., 375ml.

Produced and bottled by Neil McCallum
Puruatanga Road, Martinborough, New Zealand

Meticulously crafted, the Dry River range is typically Germanic in its winegrowing philosophy. This is closely related to fruit ripeness and individual selection of grape varieties, bunches and berries, which are subsequently vinified and marketed separately. They comprise the largest range of wines in this category, although most are made only in tiny quantities. They nevertheless maintain a very high standard across the range, and have an influence on the wider wine community that is far greater than the size of production would normally suggest.

1987
BOTRYTIS BUNCH SELECTION RIESLING
9.6% alc/vol; 100% Riesling; Framingham Vineyard; Marlborough region.
Winemaker: Neil McCallum
Best drinking: 1996–98

Light, bright, glossy gold in colour, this wine has a waxy, deliciously perfumed nose that is alive with floral fragrances, touches of orange peel and mushroom hints among the lively fruit. Intense, fresh limes and cream palate with an even, slightly silky viscosity and a heart of apricots and candied orange peel. Creamy, almost frothy with fruit, it has bright intensity and lingering freshness, but the flavours stop a little short, and the intensity is impressive to start with, but fades off quickly partway through. A lovely drink, full of life and delicious flavour, with more finish and structure it would be superb.

1989
BOTRYTIS BUNCH SELECTION RIESLING
9% alc/vol; 100% Riesling; Framingham Vineyard; Marlborough region.
Winemaker: Neil McCallum
Best drinking: 1998–2014

Bright, yellow-straw wine, with a waxy, fragrant, floral bouquet that is unlined by a note of concentrated fruit. Immediately very intense, its concentrated flavours threaten to take over the finer, fragrant characteristics, but gradually the silky, suave texture asserts itself, and with it come touches of lime and a nicely dry complexity of subtle flavours that hint at straw, ripe apricots and peaches. In spite of its rich sweetness, there is a pervasive sense of lightness spun about a core of flavour intensity that lingers on at the very end like an echo of its fierce beginning. Fresh as a baby, full of life and gushing sweetness, the wine is ideally balanced, with abundant sugar never being allowed to dominate, while complex flavours form an intricate pattern against its effortlessly smooth texture. Very fine, deep, high-toned and still remarkably youthful, it hold tremendous promise for future bottle age, when its sweetness and balance should support a glorious array of flavour nuances arising from such fierce concentration.

1990

BOTRYTIS SELECTION RIESLING

9% alc/vol; Boldervine Vineyard; Marlborough region.
Winemaker: Neil McCallum
Best drinking: 1996–2003

Pale, yellow gold, with an intense, fragrant bouquet that is a richly embellished with aromas suggestive of caramel, clotted cream and flowers. It is intense on the palate as well, with a deeply embedded, concentrated core of fruit flavour that gives off nuances of beeswax, juicy freshness and subtle cream. A silky texture enhances the juicy fruit qualities, contributing a feeling of light richness and a sense of fruit rolling across the mouth in soft waves of succulence. The brightness of intense concentration is not suppressed by this effect, and serves to moderate the wine's tendency to easy succulence with clarity and energy, factors that linger on in a very long, graceful finish. This wine is all elegance and finesse.

1990

BOTRYTIS BERRY SELECTION CHARDONNAY

9.5% alc/vol; 100% Chardonnay; Seton Vineyard,
Martinborough district, Wairarapa region.
Winemaker: Neil McCallum
Best drinking: 2000–2020

Bright, polished wine the colour of new brass, it seems from the beginning to be enormous, in spite of its light alcohol, so powerful is the presence of intense flavour and overflowing sweetness. The bouquet is all intensity and sweetness, with lashings of honey and a creamy richness with bite that implies *crème brulée*. The palate, too, has such intensity as to be an immediately fierce presence in your mouth, only to be eased by a voluptuous, satin-like texture and mouth-watering freshness. Again this is a superb piece of elegant winemaking, with all its abundance complemented by equally assertive, balancing components. The almost outrageous sweetness is juxtaposed against such intensity of aroma and flavour, such exhilarating acid, and a most sensuous, richly glossy texture, that at the end of its long, long finish it seems to have been an experience in lightness rather than a collection of superlatives. Within all this extravagance, subtleties of fresh limes, beeswax, cream, orange peel are beginning to fill in some delicious detail against that magnificent background, and there should be some wonderful future drinking in store for those lucky enough to have this wine in their cellar. A simply sensational wine.

1990

GEWÜRZTRAMINER SELECTION

13.2% alc/vol; 100% Gewürztraminer; Dry River Estate,
Martinborough district, Wairarapa region.
Winemaker: Neil McCallum
Best drinking: 1997–2005

Light, yellow-straw wine, intensely aromatic, with a seasoning of light cinnamon and clove spices, and a tang of ginger. A neat sweetness pervades the palate, not overt, but supporting the ripe lychee flavours and soft, almost oily texture, which are in turn balanced by a big, warm, brisk finish when the alcohol kicks in. Powerful, attention-grabbing wine, with a considerable future, it is already beginning to show flavour complexities such as orange peel and hints of cream among the fruit and spice. There is real depth and generosity here.

1991

BOTRYTIS BERRY SELECTION MÜLLER THURGAU

10.5% alc/vol; 100% Müller Thurgau; Marlborough region.
Winemaker: Neil McCallum
Best drinking: 1995–2000

Glossy, green-gold, polished wine, with a fruit, muscat raisin bouquet, complete with beeswax complexities and sweet lashings of floral fruit. The concentrated, very sweet, almost overwhelming forepalate has oodles of concentrated flavour that is lavish with raisin-like characters. Light but extremely sweet and concentrated, this is an intriguing, rather than an impressive wine, a very tasty experience that leaves a clinging residue of flavour, rather than a lingering finish, always dominated by sugar. Very toothsome wine candy.

1991

BOTRYTIS BUNCH SELECTION GEWÜRZTRAMINER

13.9% alc/vol; 100% Gewürztraminer; Dry River Estate,
Martinborough district, Wairarapa region.
Winemaker: Neil McCallum
Best drinking: 2001–2016

Light-looking wine, the colour of green-tinged, fresh straw, it has a bouquet that is fragrantly deep, growing in dimension even as you take it in, with waves of aroma and intensity welling up. These come complete with wax and orange peel subtleties, and an unequivocally beautiful floral note that is softness and spice at once. Sweetly concentrated on the palate, the wine's abundance is maintained through deep, concentrated fruit, rich texture, easy sweetness and an immensely powerful finish that is warm with alcohol and lively, seemingly immortal flavours issuing from deep within. Alive with flavours of apricots, mellow spices, roses and even some *crème caramel*, its melodramatic form moderated by the sheer beauty of its aromas and flavours, it is big and tender at once. A hearty wine that is enormously subtle, it is quite simply superb, from its grand opening to the last, lingering flashes of flavour.

GLAZEBROOK PENNY NOBLE HARVEST

Ngatarawa have specialised in making fine sweet wines that have more weight and power than others in this style, although these wines are based on Riesling grapes, which are normally more delicately flavoured. Ngatarawa's success suggests that variety alone is not enough; ripeness, concentration, weight of flavour, sweetness and the degree of botrytis infection are more important considerations in the evolution of a wine style in this category.

1987

12.5% alc/vol; 100% Riesling; Ngatarawa district,
Hawke's Bay region.
Winemaker: Alwyn Corban
Best drinking: 1995–2002

Bright, copper-orange wine, fragrantly scented with the perfume of apricot compote and honeywax, with slivers of orange peel and a touch of brisk energy that eludes accurate description. The whole bouquet is a wonderful balance of lavish, succulent fruit and perfume with an intense edge of botrytis fur, ripeness and clarifying acidity. The wine is very sweet and fiercely intense with flavours that repeat the apricots and beeswax of the bouquet, but are here complemented by a smooth, suave texture and light richness of touch which impart a degree of elegance. Among all this confusion of flavour and texture there is a co-ordinating clarity, a freshness that keeps a sense of order and style, without reducing any of the concentration of power of flavour or the caramel-flavoured finish. Wonderful sweet wine, with energy as well as sweetness and fresh balance.

1988

11.5% alc/vol; 100% Riesling; Ngatarawa district,
Hawke's Bay region.
Winemaker: Alwyn Corban
Best drinking: 1995–2000

Tawny, orange-copper-coloured wine, with a huge, fragrant, powdery orange peel bouquet, decorated with nuances of apricots and muscadelle raisins. Very fresh and intensely beautiful, its deep, concentrated flavours are decorated with a refreshing lilt of crispness that lingers on at the finish in a glittering trail of flavour nuances. Quite wild, almost unco-ordinated wine, it seems to be free of any controlling structure to the point of exhilaration, but never chaos, for while its caramel, orange and beeswax flavours all clamour for attention, the balance of parts always avoids awkwardness or clumsiness. Unusual, very attractive wine, sweet and clear, an amalgam of pleasures.

1991

12% alc/vol; 100% Riesling; Ngatarawa district,
Hawke's Bay region.
Winemaker: Alwyn Corban
Best drinking: 1996–2006

Glistening, golden wine, its beautifully fragrant bouquet sweetly tinged with honey aromas and a heady intensity that is paradoxically furry and very sweet, yet fresh and dry. The palate is sweetly supple, all silky texture and creamy flavour impregnated with moments of intensity and a pervasive, elegant freshness. Honeywax, bittersweet orange and faint spice can be found in there, as well as *crème caramel*, fruit succulence and even touches of apple and lime, making a poetry of flavours that lilts along to the wine's own pretty rhythms. Again it has an edge of wildness, an ebullient energy and clarity that produce a bright, flavour-filled finish that lingers for an inordinately long time. Very fine, extremely attractive wine with glamour as well as finesse, and an abundance of flavour, it should gain even more character with age.

1992

13% alc/vol; 100% Riesling; Ngatarawa district,
Hawke's Bay region.
Winemaker: Alwyn Corban
Best drinking: 2000–2017

A very strongly coloured wine, its straw hue embellished with lemon-lime hints, it has a bouquet that, for all its concentration and complexity, is a picture of grace, all the components sweetly meshed together: honey, lychees and orange peel, with vanilla as a robe of creamy, easy richness. The palate is already quite intricate, yet forceful, concentrated at the heart with very intense fruit complete with wax and honey overtones, succulence and soft, satin-like texture, all shot with a *crème brulée* note of crisp, fruit-embellished caramel. As well as the sugar balancing its freshness, this wine also has warm alcohol and slightly abrasive textural qualities that provide a more complex and complete structure than in earlier wines, introducing an air of virility as well of greater sophistication. Sweet, suave and full of life, its early grace becomes lithe elegance by the end, suggesting that this will mature into a quite spectacular wine.

MARTINBOROUGH VINEYARD LATE HARVEST

Martinborough Vineyard

CHARDONNAY

1993

LATE HARVEST

12% VOL 375ml

PRODUCED AND BOTTLED BY MARTINBOROUGH VINEYARD LTD,
PRINCESS STREET, MARTINBOROUGH, NEW ZEALAND.

PRODUCE OF NEW ZEALAND

Not normally seen as a particular feature of this winery, these sweet wines still represent a high standard of sweet winemaking, confirming both the reputation of the winery and the potential of this particular winegrowing district.

1987
SAUVIGNON BLANC POURRITURE NOBLE

12% alc/vol; 100% Sauvignon Blanc; Martinborough district, Wairarapa region.
Winemaker: Larry McKenna
Best drinking: 1995–97

Bright, shiny gold with moderate depth, this wine has a bouquet with a fresh edge and is filled with ripe, dusty botrytis aromas, apricots and orange peel and a distant intensity. Very sweet, honeyed wine, with suggestions of rosehip syrup on the palate, moderate intensity of flavour that is at times quite peachy and a lovely, frilly softness which rides right through to the very end. Sweetness tends to take over at the finish, but there

are a lot of lovely flavours in here, as well as some classic botrytis complexity, to make for a very pleasurable sipper.

1987
MÜLLER THURGAU LATE HARVEST

9% alc/vol; 100% Müller Thurgau; Martinborough district, Wairarapa region.
Winemaker: Larry McKenna
Best drinking: 1995–96

Polished golden in colour, this wine is fresh with quince aromas and has a softly floral intensity on the bouquet. The palate is slightly sour with lemon-like acidity, but this is balanced by a very sweet palate that gives a floral impression and has a frothy, not quite creamy texture. Light and easy sweetie, very forward, very sweet.

1991
RIESLING LATE HARVEST

10.5% alc/vol; 100% Riesling; Martinborough district, Wairarapa region.
Winemaker: Larry McKenna
Best drinking: 1996–2001

Light, yellowy golden wine, it has an intense apricot-dominated bouquet that is sweet and perfumed with hints of ripe fruit and orange peel, and an intriguing touch of nuttiness. The immediate extreme sweetness on the palate is gradually brought into check by fresh acidity and a barrage of little flavour complexities, so that the wine finishes long and complex, with a fluffy astringency which draws it out as it moderates the sweetness. Neat wine, full of interest and some delicious, delicate flavours.

1993
RIESLING LATE HARVEST

9.5% alc/vol; 100% Riesling; Martinborough district, Wairarapa region.
Winemaker: Larry McKenna
Best drinking: 1998–2007

Greeny gold and light in appearance, this wine also has lightness on the nose, in a freshly perfumed bouquet that is lined with intensity and shows faint hints of honeywax and orange peel. The palate is very sweet, fresh and fat with ripe succulence and fine, long, deeply sourced flavours, and a distant note of astringency that grows as the wine progresses, to finish as a drying influence on the pushy sweetness of the rest of the wine. Juicy, clean and quite lively in spite of its general lightness and fruity character, the wine's compact intensity suggests a full range of flavour subtleties in the future, and there is enough astringency and acid to keep the bouncy sweetness in check. Delicious even at this young age.

1993
CHARDONNAY LATE HARVEST

12% alc/vol; 100% Chardonnay; Martinborough district,
Wairarapa region.
Winemaker: Larry McKenna
Best drinking: 2003–2016

Fresh, light gold in colour and rich and ripe on the nose where the perfume of oak is mingled with the aroma of ripe fruit and the tang of botrytis. Mouth-wateringly fresh and creamy, with nutty overtones and gloriously sweet from the beginning, the palate is mostly potential because the wine is so young, but the vigour, freshness and succulent, satin-textured mouthful is so deep and concentrated, so well balanced, that there is no reason to imagine a future which is other than superb. This wine is very even, with excellent potential, and feels simply wonderful in the mouth. Already the long, fine finish is showing signs of developing complex flavours to mingle with the sweetness and mellow the fresh intensity that currently dominates this wine. Excellent stuff.

CABERNET
SAUVIGNON AND
PRINCIPAL BLENDS

BECAUSE OF THE STRONG BRITISH INFLUENCE ON NEW ZEALAND'S FINE WINE culture, Cabernet Sauvignon has been the principal red grape during the initial stage of the fine wine era in this country. The very close association between Britain and Bordeaux throughout history has led to an emphasis on Bordeaux varieties in general, and Cabernet Sauvignon in particular, as the most likely foundation for making fine red wine.

Since the 1960s, Cabernet Sauvignon has been planted and developed while other fine red varieties such as Pinot Noir, Syrah, and Nebbiolo have been almost totally excluded, and advances in quality red wine growing have been made predominantly through the refinement of Cabernet Sauvignon, rather than investigation of other varieties. In particular, Cabernet Sauvignon's winemaking potential has been improved by supplementing it with other traditional Bordeaux varieties used for the same purpose — Merlot and Cabernet Franc in particular, with some minority interest in Malbec and Petit Verdot.

Cabernet Sauvignon has also gained support in New Zealand's naive winegrowing environment by performing particularly well in the year of its first crop, and a number of red wine reputations were established, in the early quality wine years, by Cabernet Sauvignon wines made off four-year-old vines. Cooks, in particular, had a spectacular rise to fame with their 1973 Cabernet Sauvignon wine, which displayed many of the cassis-like fruit characteristics expected of good Bordeaux reds. Nobilos and McWilliams also had early success with Cabernet Sauvignon, enough to impress wine competition judges, and the gold medals they won encouraged other winemakers to plant the variety in every major winegrowing region in the country.

In spite of show successes, and early support from local wine enthusiasts, the Cabernet Sauvignon clones in use early on suffered from heavy virus infestations that limited the vines' ability to produce full-coloured, mature-flavoured fruit with appropriate sugar:acid balance for fine winemaking. This situation was compounded by naturally fertile soils and vigorous growing conditions, which encouraged the development of excessive herbaceous characteristics that the wines were subsequently unable to incorporate in a harmonious flavour balance; characteristics that became accentuated by bottle age. This last problem was a serious shortcoming when traditionally one of the prime reasons for Cabernet Sauvignon's claim to fine wine status is its ability to age with grace.

The result of these early complications was a succession of wines that were light in alcohol and colour and dominated by excessively herbaceous aromas and flavour. Given that winemaking was less than accomplished at the time, often relying on cheap American oak and showing little understanding of the particular structural requirements of red wine, it is not surprising that many were prepared to claim that New Zealand was not a suitable place for growing premium red wines.

It does appear that New Zealand's winegrowing climate is marginal for Cabernet Sauvignon, and that it will be fully ripened to mature flavour status in commercial quantities only in selected sites in warmer winegrowing regions, most notably those in Hawke's Bay. All but three of the leading Cabernet producers have their main vineyards in this region, the others being in Martinborough and Auckland. The variety is, however, also widely planted in Marlborough, and in Nelson and Canterbury, suggesting a tendency to plant irrespective of prevailing growing conditions, and giving more weight to the idea that New Zealand is not a natural source of premium red wine.

The quality of wines from the leading producers has already shown that red wine can not only be made competently from New Zealand-grown Cabernet Sauvignon, but can be made with the elegance, finesse, longevity and consistency expected of true fine wines. As a category, it may not have the depth or the range of wines made from such varieties as Chardonnay or Sauvignon Blanc, but the track record of a few properties shows that it may well match those in the future, as improvements in viticulture are consolidated and the sophistication of red winemaking improves.

The seminal development with Cabernet Sauvignon came in 1984, with the launch of the 1982 Te Mata Coleraine, a wine that showed none of the traditional problems of New Zealand Cabernet Sauvignon-based reds and revealed a level of winemaking skill previously unseen in this country. This was followed by a succession of fine Cabernet Sauvignon blends from Te Mata, taking it beyond the first-year vines syndrome, proving what was possible under New Zealand conditions, and inspiring a small but dedicated band of producers who were prepared to learn the lessons of making this demanding wine style.

First among the solutions was to get the grapes fully ripe, something Te Mata was able to do consistently in its ideally sited vineyards. Site selection has proved to be a factor in almost all of the leading producers, along with improved viticulture that has involved the elimination of virus infection, using good-quality French oak barrels to contribute to complexity and texture and adding Merlot and Cabernet Franc to the blends. Some straight Cabernet Sauvignon wines are still made, but the leading producers have almost universally resorted to at least a Merlot contribution in their best wines.

Of all the fine wine varieties in New Zealand, Cabernet Sauvignon has so far proved to be most sensitive to its growing conditions, with one region, Hawke's Bay, dominant in the leading wines made from this variety. Cabernet Sauvignon's longer history, however, makes it and its blends the leading fine red wine style in this country, a style that is typically fragrant, with a positive dimension of fruit flavour and depth, often tempered by a tinge of herbaceousness that is reminiscent of wine from the St Julien district of Bordeaux. These wines are typically New Zealand, however, in their fierce clarity, a feature that the best producers harmonise with warmth, ripe tannins and fine oak.

Cabernet Sauvignon has been present in New Zealand since the earliest days of winegrowing; records show that one clone was released from the experimental station at Momohaki in 1898. Most recently, however, Cabernet Sauvignon was brought in from the University of California at Davis in 1970, and from the same source in 1976, with others coming from Australia.

Merlot was also present by the end of the 19th century, and since the 1970s, with this variety, as with Malbec and Cabernet Franc, there has been more importation and evaluation of clones different from those already established in the country. As Cabernet Sauvignon's sensitivity to climate variation becomes apparent, Merlot and Cabernet Franc are becoming more important as a source of lesser wines, but Cabernet Sauvignon, with increasing support from these varieties, remains the dominant variety for the fine red wines of New Zealand.

ATA RANGI CÉLÈBRE

Paradoxically this was the first of the Martinborough reds to establish a reputation, and it remains the only fine red wine from the district not to be made from Pinot Noir. An unusual (for New Zealand) blend of Cabernet Sauvignon, Merlot and Syrah, it is typically high in alcohol and dark in colour, characteristics that have won it a strong following among red wine enthusiasts.

1986

13.7% alc/vol; 85% Cabernet Sauvignon, 15% Syrah;
Martinborough district, Wairarapa region;
aged for 16 months in 25% new and
75% used French oak 225-litre barriques.
Winemaker: Clive Paton
Best drinking: 1996

Very deep, dark mahogany in colour, this wine has an oldish, cold tea character, with toast and some lightly fragrant, still keen fruit. The palate is reasonably intense and deep, dry and complex, a little medicinal, with some fresh-tasting fruit still lingering about, making an altogether tasty wine that spreads its mellow texture to every corner of your mouth, with warmth and some gentle backwaters of flavour. It does have some discordant shafts of tea and compost herbaceousness, and a rather clunky finish with the tannins fairly simple, all brisk texture and no flavour, but its mellow conviviality more than compensates for these. A very nice drink.

1987

13.5% alc/vol; 85% Cabernet Sauvignon,
15% Syrah; Martinborough district, Wairarapa region;
aged for 16 months in 25% new and 75% used French oak
225-litre barriques.
Winemaker: Clive Paton
Best drinking: 1995–98

Deep, cherrywood-mahogany colour, with a vague dustiness on the bouquet, an unusual rancio character among aromas of leather, peas and coffee, and a distant fragrance. The palate is suddenly and forcefully sweet with ripe fruit, with flavours that are intense but cool, and very lively, and studded with pieces of leather and tobacco. This is a fruit presence rather than fruitiness, swirling like a vortex of flavour, against which the greenish, rather abrasive tannins struggle to make a successful balance, giving the wine a coarseness that seems out of keeping with the delicious, still fresh nature of the fruit, and the vague fragrance that lingers on at the finish. Almost delightful wine, marred by the tannins, but still a very rewarding bottle.

1988

13.5% alc/vol; 60% Cabernet Sauvignon, 20% Merlot,
20% Syrah; Martinborough district, Wairarapa region;
aged for 16 months in 25% new and 75% used French oak
225-litre barriques.
Winemaker: Clive Paton
Best drinking: 1995–2007

Deep, richly coloured wine with a mahogany tinge to it, and the first signs of polished tawny. Beautifully fine, richly textured bouquet, with leathery highlights, hints of tobacco, coffee and cassis as fragrant highlights. The palate is warm and very supple, a stroking singular body of svelte texture, moderate density and wonderfully long, fine, keen fruit flavours that have touches of cassis and leather. There is oak, too, something of a cheaper note in among the lavish fruit, and grainy, slightly green tannins that disturb the robe of fruit flavour, but the finish is soft, long, buoyant and juicy enough to keep these discomforts at bay, and leave the drinker revelling in sensual fruit and the charming nuances of bottle age. Delicious wine.

1989

13.5% alc/vol; 60% Cabernet Sauvignon, 25% Merlot, 15% Syrah; Martinborough district, Wairarapa region; aged for 16 months in 25% new and 75% used French oak 225-litre barriques.
Winemaker: Clive Paton
Best drinking: 1996–2005

Deep, rich red, glossy and bright with some tattered remnants of purple still hanging on. Quiet and chocolatey on the nose, with hints of coffee and oak and a unmistakeable freshness of fruit. Very suave and cool, with excellent, attention-grabbing fruit intensity and a graininess that imitates fine chocolate. Crisp, tight wine, its depth is most impressive, but it seems hardly to have aged at all, because the flavour subtleties are so deeply embedded in fruit. Tannins are fine textured, richer than earlier vintages, and the oak is nicely in harmony, but this is dense wine to the end, abundantly invested with fruit, suggesting a long future. Solid wine, but never clunky, it is impressive before it is personable.

1990

13.5 alc/vol; 55% Cabernet Sauvignon, 30% Merlot, 15% Syrah; Martinborough district, Wairarapa region; hand picked 31 March– 27 April 1989; aged for 16 months in 25% new and 75% used French oak 225-litre barriques.
Winemaker: Clive Paton
Best drinking: 1997–2009

Dark, deep, purply colour with some reddish tones creeping in, and a bouquet that is equally deep, dark and handsome, with brief flashes of coffee, rich fruit and pepper. Warm, almost Italian in its intense fruit character, but just a little too cool to be convincing, with patches of minerals and freshness among its supple, finely textured flavour and a grainy tannin texture that gains in momentum as the wine progresses

through to a flavoury, lingering, fresh-framed finish. Although it is never actually fruity, there is a pervasive presence that whispers fruit character in aroma, texture and sweet feel, a presence that has a lot of charm without being frilly, adding to the wine's depth and the impression that it will last long and gain from age.

1991

13.5% alc/vol; 50% Cabernet Sauvignon, 35% Merlot, 15% Syrah; Martinborough district, Wairarapa region; hand picked 6–18 April 1991; aged for 16 months in 25% new and 75% used French oak 225-litre barriques.
Winemaker: Clive Paton
Best drinking: 1999–2012

Deep and purple rich with cerise highlights, and a savoury-sweet fruit-laden bouquet with a solid slice of smoky, charry oak embedded in it. Very fruit-sweet, creamy textured, deep-flavoured wine, supple but tightly constructed, with a grip of good, ripe, cherry-flavoured tannins and a twist of still-green herbaceousness. The fruit has that fresh, keen edge to its intensity and, in spite of the cool appearance, there is some real warmth in this wine, warmth that carries through to the finish and beyond, supported by the gentle fur of tannin. Lovely and lively, it has a measure of sophistication that adds to its elegance and moderates the high-strung intensity of its fruit with a trim of complexity. Very smart wine indeed.

1992

13.5% alc/vol; 55% Cabernet Sauvignon, 25% Syrah, 15% Merlot, 5% Cabernet Franc; Martinborough district, Wairarapa region; hand picked 25 April–11 May 1992; aged for 16 months in 25% new and 75% used French oak 225-litre barriques.
Winemaker: Clive Paton
Best drinking: 2001–2008

Deep, bright, purplish red colour with a fragrant nose laced with blackcurrants and vanilla sweet oak, this wine is full of enthusiastic youth, warmth and a measure of peppery herbaceousness. There is heaps of sweet, currany fruit on the palate, warm alcohol and a collar of fruit intensity, balanced by grainy tannins and oak, altogether making a fresh, even-textured, comfortable wine that is very cleverly made. For all its youth, it finishes easy and well, its fruit and texture lingering on at the finish.

1993

*13% alc/vol; 50% Cabernet Sauvignon, 25% Merlot,
20% Syrah, 5% Cabernet Franc; Martinborough district,
Wairarapa region; hand picked 11–17 May 1993;
aged for 16 months in 25% new and 75% used French
oak 225-litre barriques.
Winemaker: Clive Paton
Best drinking: 1998–2005*

Deep, purple, ripe, glossy red with a peppery, oak-impregnated aromatic-fragrant bouquet bright with fresh, intense fruit and a suggestion of green leaves. Taut and very lively on the palate, with nice, sweet oak and a fresh, curranty fruit, it has a fierce brightness of flavour that verges on being intimidating, but is saved by some gruffly convivial tannins towards the end, giving length as well as a modicum of warmth to its overall character. This deft use of tannin is a sign of the winemaking skill that saves this wine from being two-dimensional, suggesting that once it overcomes its angular youthfulness it will become a much more charming, sedate, even elegant wine, perhaps lacking only in richness.

BABICH IRONGATE CABERNET SAUVIGNON/MERLOT

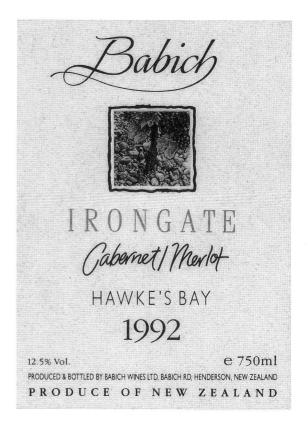

The Irongate label denotes Babich's prestige wines, grown in the Gimblett Road district of Hawke's Bay. They are noted for their fruit intensity, and lately for a style that seems intent on refined elegance rather than power or richness. They have also served to accentuate the value of this Hawke's Bay district's stony soils for growing fine wines, red as well as white.

1987

*12% alc/vol; Cabernet Sauvignon and Merlot; Irongate
Vineyard, Gimblett Road district, Hawke's Bay region.*
Winemaker: Joe Babich
Best drinking: 1995–97

Solid, cherrywood red wine, fragrant, with an intense
heart, and a strong Marmite-vitamin B yeast character
overlaying the mild savoury and fruit qualities. It is
quite charming, if idiosyncratic, wine and the lovely,
intense fruit sweetness of the palate gives it an air of
freshness, and maintains a strong fruit character right
through the wine. Some mild, spicy, savoury characters
on the palate help the complexity, but there is never
quite enough warmth or strength about it to capture
the drinker's attention. Pleasant, charming wine with
interesting features.

1988

*12% alc/vol; Cabernet Sauvignon and Merlot; Irongate
Vineyard, Gimblett Road district, Hawke's Bay region.*
Winemaker: Joe Babich
Best drinking: 1995

Solid, clear mahogany colour, and a meaty aroma,
touched with savoury, mellow oak and a fine freshness,
with a strong Marmite-vitamin B character that shows
up on the palate as well. There is a freshness and vague
intensity about the fruit, but the wine is rather hollow,
with a grainy, dry finish. Pleasant enough to drink, but
it lacks substance and generosity.

1989

*12% alc/vol; Cabernet Sauvignon and Merlot; Irongate
Vineyard, Gimblett Road district, Hawke's Bay region.*
Winemaker: Joe Babich
Best drinking: 1995–2000

Dark, deep, red-mahogany colour, polished and
flickering with deeper hues. The lovely fruit fragrances
are matched with sweet oak, trimmed with mineral
characters, and washed in vitamin B yeastiness. The
palate is lively, sweet with fruit in the middle,
suggesting flavours of blackberries and rich yeast, with
a fine but light tannin backbone and a good finish. The
heart of the wine is an almost fierce fruit intensity, but
the winemaking adornments do not match the fruit
for finesse or length, and the wine survives on the fruit
alone. It is delicious fruit, however, quite succulent in
spite of its intensity, making this wine lovely drinking.

1990

*12.5% alc/vol; Cabernet Sauvignon and Merlot; Irongate
Vineyard, Gimblett Road district, Hawke's Bay region.*
Winemaker: Joe Babich
Best drinking: 1996–2005

Dark young red with blackish depths and a tone of
richness about it. The bouquet is slightly perfumed,
fragrant and fine, with greater depth and less intensity
than previous vintages, and a warm, relaxed nature.
There is intensity in the depths of the palate, however,
a tidy shaft of ripe fruit in harmony with warmth, a nice
feeling of weight and pleasantly furry, vaguely cherry-
flavoured tannins that add to the flavour complexity,
texture and substance of the wine. More finely crafted,
elegant wine, it has lovely balance and a graceful feel
to it, the flavours and fruit intensity supported by
supple, suave textures and slick finishing. Not wine on
a grand scale, but graceful, easy and fine.

1991

*12.5% alc/vol; Cabernet Sauvignon and Merlot; Irongate
Vineyard, Gimblett Road district, Hawke's Bay region.*
Winemaker: Joe Babich
Best drinking: 1999–2006

Dense, dark, purply red, with blackberry and plum
aromas on the nose. Minerals and some perfumed oak
add an extra dimension to its ripeness and abundance,
making for a very stylish bouquet. The palate, too,
exudes style, with lovely, svelte-textured, intense, glossy
fruit, and a touch of yeast to balance it, with flashes of
spicy oak here and there, and the furry grain of tannin,
ripe and mellow. There is warmth here among the fruit
and fluid textures, and signs of real winemaking
elegance to match the grace of the fruit, with intensity
serving the whole wine, rather than being the whole
wine, leaving an impression of flavour and style.

1992

*12.5% alc/vol; Cabernet Sauvignon and Merlot; Irongate
Vineyard, Gimblett Road district, Hawke's Bay region.*
Winemaker: Joe Babich
Best drinking: 1998–2008

Deep, dark, thickish-looking purple-red wine with
flickers of magenta. Hints of nettles on the nose,
among spicy oak, and a vaguely blackberry-
blackcurrant fruit aroma. Mellow, warm and
concentrated with freshness, accentuated by clean

acidity, the fruit is intense and mouth-filling, vaguely sweet and with a chewy substance. The tannins have taste, and the herbaceousness is a nice complexity rather than a distracting feature, complementing the mellow oak and harmonising with the fruit. Good wine, with a lot of interesting bits, depth and momentum, it is heading for a classy future.

BROOKFIELDS CABERNET SAUVIGNON RESERVE

Brookfields were very early in establishing a reputation for serious Hawke's Bay red wine, a reputation they have maintained and enlarged in the decade since their first premium red wine was released. With Te Mata and Ngatarawa, they formed an impressive trio of red wine producers who attracted attention to Hawke's Bay as a suitable winegrowing region for fine red wines based on Cabernet Sauvignon, and they have been followed by a number of other producers who have confirmed and expanded the region's reputation with this variety and its blending partners. Brookfields remains one of the quality leaders, a small, fiercely independent winery focused firmly on making prestige reds from locally grown fruit.

1984

12.5% alc/vol; 100% Cabernet Sauvignon; Werry Vineyard, Tukituki district, Hawke's Bay region; aged in new 500-litre French oak puncheons.
Winemaker: Peter Robertson
Best drinking: 1995–99

A good, even red colour, with just a glimmer of mahogany about it, this wine has a spicy, mellowed fruit nose, with a touch of menthol and cedar. The palate, too, is soft but fresh, with its mellow complexities and layers of sweet fruit just drying out with age, charged with a enlivening acidity that manages to pick the wine up without suppressing its warmer tones. Menthol-mint characters give it an unusual dimension, but this is nice, easy, interesting wine, perhaps lacking in real depth and richness, but very satisfying.

1985

13% alc/vol; 100% Cabernet Sauvignon; Werry Vineyard, Tukituki district, Hawke's Bay region; aged in new and used 500-litre French oak puncheons.
Winemaker: Peter Robertson
Best drinking: 1996–2005

Bright, glossy wine, with a flash of garnet and a very sensual, mellow, animal-like aroma that hints at musk and coffee grounds, urgent and inviting. Suave with juicy fruit, it is paradoxically supple and hard, its slightly coarse finish and abrasive tannins enhancing its sensual, animal qualities. There are some uplifting tones here, too, a freshness and energy that add to the wine's warmth and temptation, and hold up a finish which, for all its roughness, is pleasantly sweet-edged and slightly concentrated. Not exactly elegant wine, or even a classically balanced one, but in the swirl of enthusiasms each feature is countered by the others so that no one ever takes control of the whole wine. Fascinating.

1986

12.5% alc/vol; 100% Cabernet Sauvignon; Werry Vineyard, Tukituki district, Hawke's Bay region; aged in new and used 500-litre French oak puncheons.

Winemaker: Peter Robertson
Best drinking: 1995–96

Deep, dark, red-trimmed verging on tawny brick. Hints of stewed fruit in the bouquet, but fresh, with oaky characters and a distinct whiff of peppermint. Nicely satin-like texture on the palate helps an otherwise lightly flavoured wine, and manages to keep the hard tannins at bay but, in spite of the pleasant warmth and mellow finishing flavours, this hardness is the wine's final word. Clean and lively enough, but a bit simple, light and lacking in depth.

1987

12.5% alc/vol; 100% Cabernet Sauvignon; Werry Vineyard, Tukituki district, Hawke's Bay region; aged in new 500-litre American oak puncheons.
Winemaker: Peter Robertson
Best drinking: 1996–2001

Deep vibrant red from edge to heart, where it plunges into darkness. The nose is all cold tea and sweet bourbon, classically American oak, a rather blunt and superficially attractive characteristic. There is, however, a neat concentration of fresh cassis and strawberry fruit flavours in the palate, which is fresh, direct and clean, the oak just framing, rather than defining it. The length is sufficient, just, with its trim of slightly abrasive tannin helping to extend those lively fruit flavours beyond the palate. A bright, appealing wine, its freshness an ever-present feature, it should keep its zest for a while yet, and could even age to a more mellow type of charm.

1989

12.7% alc/vol; 100% Cabernet Sauvignon; Werry Vineyard, Tukituki district, Hawke's Bay region; aged in new and used French oak barriques.
Winemaker: Peter Robertson
Best drinking: 1998–2014

Blackish red, richly opaque in its depths, but somehow infused with light. The bouquet is equally rich and bright, with aromas of char and coffee, rumours of deep cassis fruit and a clear freshness. This is followed by a mouthful of sweet, big, ripe fruit flavours, long and vibrant, with a wave of perfumed blackberry-cassis character running through, gently spiced with oak. Its very poised, stylish fruit character, enhanced by momentum and depth, never unduly muddled by oak or any other embellishments, finishes with a flash of

bright flavour. This character dominates the wine so much that even the furry, grainy tannins are rendered quietly supportive. A real fruit monster, a little simple for that, but very tasty and impressive.

1990

12.7% alc/vol; 100% Cabernet Sauvignon; Werry Vineyard, Tukituki district, Hawke's Bay region; aged 18 months in new and old French 225-litre barriques.
Winemaker: Peter Robertson
Best drinking: 1997–2005

Dark, ripe red, with a fresh, slightly sappy bouquet with hints of cassis and subtly spicy oak. Fresh, lively, even flashy, packed with bright fruit and with deliciously soft, tender tannins that are beautifully modulated to suit the natural charm of the wine, to give it flavour dimension as well as structural presence. It has warmth, depth and poise to the point of grace, and never allows its inherent freshness or strength to overcome its gentle character. Beautifully crafted wine that has sophistication to match its classy fruit, succulence and a gracefully fine, fruit-flavoured finish; the winemaker has added finesse without undermining these wonderful assets. It is quite delicious drinking even at this young age, but should mature into a very stylish bottle.

1991

12.8% alc/vol; 100% Cabernet Sauvignon; 66% Havelock North district, 34% Ohiti district, Hawke's Bay region; aged 20 months in new and old French 225-litre barriques.
Winemaker: Peter Robertson
Best drinking: 2001–17

Dark, intense cerise-purple red, deeply rich yet bright. The bouquet is thick with still undefined fruit and aromatic oak, with an edge of freshness. The palate is close-grained to the point of thickness, very deep at its heart, and alive with fresh, dark flavours that hint at blackberries and black cherries, even plums, intense but never quite rich. Beautifully constructed, with grainy, substantial, ripe-tasting tannins adding a firm, textural dimension, healthy alcohol warmth and clean acidity. Although still unresolved, this perfumed, fruit-bright wine is already showing signs of class and elegance, its jumble of softness, grain and freshness underpinned by fruit density and a long, sustained finish that echoes the bright fruit. Should become a classic.

BROOKFIELDS CABERNET/MERLOT

Treated by winemaker Peter Robertson as the lesser of his two premium reds, this wine is still a regular high flier, forming with the Cabernet Sauvignon a widely respected duo. It is normally more rustic, convivial, than its pure Cabernet Sauvignon partner.

1986

12.5% alc/vol; 75% Cabernet Sauvignon, 5% Merlot, 20% Cabernet Franc; Cabernet Sauvignon from Tukituki district, Merlot and Cabernet Franc from Bridge Pa district, Hawke's Bay region; aged in 500-litre French oak puncheons.
Winemaker: Peter Robertson
Best drinking: 1995

Darkly mahogany, with vegetal, tawny characters on the nose, and a very faint hint of oak. A paradox of soft and fresh, its pleasant fruit flavours lack depth and substance, with mildly abrasive tannins more an attachment than an integral part of the wine. Simple but nice.

1987

12.3% alc/vol; 70% Cabernet Sauvignon, 15% Merlot, 15% Cabernet Franc; Cabernet Sauvignon from Tukituki district, Merlot and Cabernet Franc from Bridge Pa district,

Hawke's Bay region; aged in new 500-litre French oak puncheons.
Winemaker: Peter Robertson
Best drinking: 1995–97

Fresh, clean and hearty, in colour and in character, this warm-hearted wine has nuances of coffee, chocolate and oak, trimmed with a lively freshness and a faint concentration of cassis. Very supple, agreeable wine, it, too, lacks tannin substance, but its pleasant aftertaste lingers so nicely that it leaves a sense of subtle pleasure and homely comfort. Tidy, moreish wine.

1988

12.2% alc/vol; 70% Cabernet Sauvignon, 15% Merlot, 15% Cabernet Franc; Cabernet Sauvignon from Tukituki district, Merlot and Cabernet Franc from Bridge Pa district, Hawke's Bay region; aged in new 225-litre French oak barriques.
Winemaker: Peter Robertson
Best drinking: 1995

Hearty red-coloured wine, with a mahogany edge and a warm, bottle-aged, composty nose with some fragrant char. Soft, light and mellow in the mouth, it does have a nice edge of freshness and some tidy oak to complement its mild meatiness. A good drink, soft and pleasant.

1989

13% alc/vol; 75% Cabernet Sauvignon, 20% Merlot, 5% Cabernet Franc; Tukituki district, Hawke's Bay region; aged in new and used 225-litre French oak barriques.
Winemaker: Peter Robertson
Best drinking: 1997–2009

This is a big, warm wine, deeply coloured. Its bouquet of animal, chocolate, plum aromas and deep cherry fruit is almost thick with delicious sensuality, and the palate is richer, warmer, with a supple viscosity that is particularly inviting. There is no particular fruit definition, just sweetness and ripeness, and nice supporting tannins, softly grainy, but almost totally subdued by the fruit, which has depth and resonance right to the end, where suddenly there is a neat little collar of oak keeping it company. This is flamboyantly fruity wine, every aspect dominated by ripeness that is concentrated almost to the point of dried fruit, but kept fresh by a flash of acidity. Impressive rather than delicious, the layers of fruit never give ground to any other feature of the wine, leaving it lacking in variety and balancing interest. A very good drink, however, that will gain complexity and interest as it gets older.

1990

12.7% alc/vol; 75% Cabernet Sauvignon, 20% Merlot,
5% Cabernet Franc; Tukituki district, Hawke's Bay region;
aged 12–15 months in new (90%) and used 225-litre
French oak barriques.
Winemaker: Peter Robertson
Best drinking: 1998–2005

Lightish, cerise-red colour, with a very sweet, cherryish nose and lashings of oak aroma. Warm, harmonious oak and fruit palate, with beautifully sweet, mellow flavours, gentle freshness and some lovely soft tannins that invest the wine with an easy, grainy character. This wine is still very young and tense with fruit energy, but the suave oak and extra dimension of tannin give it an excellent balance of textural and flavour features that deliver proportion, making it more complete, more satisfying and interesting than its fruit-driven forebears. This will be very attractive wine in a few years' time, its succulent charms made elegant by good wine craft.

1991

13% alc/vol; 75% Cabernet Sauvignon, 20% Merlot,
5% Cabernet Franc; Tukituki district, Hawke's Bay region;
aged in new and used 225-litre French oak barriques.
Winemaker: Peter Robertson
Best drinking: 2001–11

Deep cerise colours, bright and dark, and a darkly fruited bouquet to match. The nose is fresh and deep, with hints of chocolate and char. The palate is big, with lashings of sweet, not quite precise fruit that has a strong tannin collar from the first, balanced by depth and warmth. Altogether a fresh, lively, very young-feeling wine, with forceful, moderately astringent tannin that builds its momentum and holds a neat bunch of flavours into the finish, leaving a lingering impression of energy and fruit flavour moderated by some gentle oak. Very well made, it promises warm elegance and complexity in the future, and already has a cosmopolitan air about it, in spite of its awkward, angular air of youthfulness.

CHURCH ROAD CABERNET SAUVIGNON

Montana's Hawke's Bay project is based on making international standard red and white wines in the region, from locally grown Chardonnay and Cabernet Sauvignon. To this end, and in the light of their joint winemaking agreement with Deutz in Marlborough, Montana have formed a partnership with the Bordeaux firm of Cordier to help with the Church Road reds. The wines are made in reasonable quantity, are sold at very competitive prices, and have already proved to be serious reds which, in four vintages, have demanded attention. Ultimately Church Road's future will be decided by international customers, who will balance the fruit clarity and value of New Zealand fine wines against the accepted quality standards of Bordeaux, so long as Montana are able to maintain the impressive improvements in red wine production they have achieved in recent vintages.

1990

12.5% alc/vol; 100% Cabernet Sauvignon; Hawke's Bay region; aged in American and French oak.
Winemaker: Tony Prichard
Best drinking: 1995–97

Densely coloured wine, dark plum-red. The bouquet is packed with sweet oak aromas and a faint suggestion of herbaceousness among pretty fruit. There is also pretty fruit on the palate, sweet and bouncy enough to make this a really jolly little number, with plum and currant flavours among the shafts of oak. Finishes neatly, with sweet oak again to the fore, and just enough balance to give it an edge of class, if not the substance of a truly fine wine. Good drinking, though.

1991

12.5% alc/vol; 100% Cabernet Sauvignon; Hawke's Bay region; aged in French oak.
Winemaker: Tony Prichard
Best drinking: 1996–2003

Richly dark, deep colour with polished red highlights. The bouquet has a fine vanilla-oak, plum and blackcurrant complex of aromas, with a faint edge of green beans. The palate is fine, moderately deep, with fruit and suppleness, and some nice, fine, ripish tannins. A solid wine, well made, with some clever touches that hint at elegance here and there, a core of intense fruit and occasional references to oak and charcoal for complexity. Still prickly with youth, it has an even spread to it, good support from the tannin, enough fruit clarity to be identifiably New Zealand in character — and enough fragrance to be Hawke's Bay at heart. Nice wine.

1992

12.5% alc/vol; 100% Cabernet Sauvignon; Hawke's Bay region; aged in French oak.
Winemaker: Tony Prichard
Best drinking: 1997–2003

Dark red and rich, the colour of ripe plums, this wine has a bouquet that is lifted, aromatic, with sweet, vanilla-oak aromas and currenty, herbaceous fruit. Very

neatly balanced, with richer, riper tannins and hints of black cherry flavour, the fruit gradually builds its momentum to a cascade of oak-impregnated flavour that lingers on nicely at the finish. A much more harmonious effort than the previous wines, it is already showing sophistication in spite of its youth, an element of style that matches the intensity and freshness of the fruit, giving interest and texture to its bright flavours. Clever wine that has a promising future.

1993

12.5% alc/vol; 100% Cabernet Sauvignon; Hawke's Bay region; aged in French oak.
Winemaker: Tony Prichard
Best drinking: 1997–2004

Very dark, glossy wine, with a dense, grainy bouquet, oak to the fore, that borders on solidity. This theme continues on the palate, where the close-textured fruit is balanced by a clean freshness, and the flavours of herbs and plums make for an intriguing duality. The graininess and density give the impression of chocolate and, despite the hard edges of youth, there is already a mellowness about this wine that fits the chocolate analogy, although balancing freshness and hints of minerals keep flabbiness at bay. Still extremely young, this wine has a soft burr of tannin that is supportive and friendly enough to suggest that this will mature into a neatly balanced, tasty, interesting wine with a positive, graceful tone.

DELEGAT'S PROPRIETORS RESERVE CABERNET SAUVIGNON

Delegat's made their reputation as fine wine producers with Chardonnay, but the arrival of their Proprietor's Reserve label in the mid-1980s, and their concentration on Hawke's Bay as a source for fruit, saw Cabernet Sauvignon emerge as a permanent part of the company's prestige repertoire. Since then it has been a consistent medal winner in wine competitions, and has built considerable support among restaurateurs for its easy-drinking, early-maturing style.

1986

12% alc/vol; 100% Cabernet Sauvignon; Hawke's Bay region; aged in 225-litre French Nevers oak barriques, 50% used, 50% new.
Winemaker: Brent Marris
Best drinking: 1995–96

Full-coloured, polished, mahogany-looking wine, with

a clear, minerally, leafy-tobacco nose that has fruit hints and an interesting touch of liquorice perfume. Simultaneously sweet fruit and acid at the front of the palate, it does lack warm tannins to fill it out and give it extra dimension, but the fruit is very smart, and it is this lithe succulence that carries the wine, with maturity giving it a frill of flavour complexity. Cautiously made wine, without much craft presence, it depends on its lovely fruit for style and character. Luckily, this is enough to make a very pleasant drink, interesting even if it is rather simple in approach.

1987

12% alc/vol; 85% Cabernet Sauvignon, 10% Merlot, 5% Cabernet Franc; Hawke's Bay region; vintage began 29 April 1987; aged 18 months in 225-litre French Nevers oak barriques, 50% used, 50% new.
Winemaker: Brent Marris
Best drinking: 1995–96

Deeply coloured like mature cherrywood, polished and glossy. The bouquet is slightly leafy, with subtleties of minerals, toast and strangely faded fruit that give an air of delicacy which is apparent in the palate as well. There is a freshness that keeps it interesting, enlivening the slightly green, herby flavours and lightly sweet fruit texture. The edgy, fresh and hardish characteristics are accentuated by some hard tannins, but there are also countering suave oak flavours and textures to give a helpful touch of mildness and some subtlety. In total a lightish, quite pretty, pleasant, slightly angular wine.

1989

13% alc/vol; 85% Cabernet Sauvignon, 10% Merlot, 5% Cabernet Franc; Hawke's Bay region; vintage began 26 April 1989; aged 12 months in 225-litre French Nevers oak barriques, 50% used, 50% new.
Winemaker: Brent Marris
Best drinking: 1995–2000

Healthy-looking wine, its bright, mahogany red seeming as luxurious as expensive furniture. Its nose is also suitably expensive, filled with softly persuasive nuances of coffee, toast, chocolate and ripe cherry-plum aromas. It is further touched up with a spot of spicy oak and light freshness. The palate has the same trim of freshness to lift it, with lots of sweet oak and mellow, mid-palate tannins that build up neatly through the wine to become a substantial background against which the fruit can play out its harmonies.

These are ripe and warm, with a trailing concentration of ripe cherry and blackberry characters that enlivens the thickish impression the wine gives, a character that could be cloying were it not for the tannin and freshness. Although it still tastes very young, it shows no signs of developing an integrated elegance that combines its great variety of facets and characters, a harmony that would make it more than the moreish bottle it now is. More age could improve it.

1990

12.2% alc/vol; 85% Cabernet Sauvignon, 15% Merlot; Hawke's Bay region; vintage began 27 April 1990; 25% of wine finished fermentation in barrel; aged 12 months in 225-litre French Nevers oak barriques, 50% used, 50% new.
Winemaker: Brent Marris
Best drinking: 1995–97

A healthy-looking red of moderately deep colour, just gaining a touch of mahogany at the rim. The bouquet is quite leafy, with a background of pleasantly smoky oak and fresh fruit acidity. Delicate wine with nice fruit feel and flavour, charged with freshness, an interesting dash of herbs and some neatly furry tannin at its heart that holds the flavoury finish together. In spite of its lightness and cherry character, there is a finer balance of parts in this wine, making it more complete and satisfying, in spite of its leanness. Not a wine for long cellaring, it does make a tasty, well-presented interlude.

1991

12% alc/vol; 85% Cabernet Sauvignon, 15% Merlot; Hawke's Bay region; vintage began 23 April 1991; 25% of wine finished fermentation in barrel; aged 12 months in 225-litre French Nevers oak barriques, 50% used, 50% new.
Winemaker: Brent Marris
Best drinking: 1997–2003

Bright, darkish red wine, clear and moderately deep. Its bouquet is a picture of warm clarity, with smokiness, hints of sweet oak and other mellow aromas enhanced by those of ripe, freshly sweet fruit. There is warmth on the palate too, giving the meaty texture of the wine a glow of generosity that combines well with the sweet, ripe fruit flavours and delightfully grainy, lingering texture of ripe, mellow tannins. All this rounds out pleasantly with some neat acid, a good, flavourful finish and a degree of supple tension that is particularly inviting. Although on the light side, there is a feeling of warmth about this wine, as well as a quiet elegance that makes it very easy. Good stuff, balanced, steady, and finely made.

1992

13% alc/vol; 85% Cabernet Sauvignon, 15% Merlot; Hawke's Bay region; vintage began 7 May 1992; 25% of wine finished fermentation in barrel; aged 12 months in French Nevers oak barriques, 50% used, 50% new.
Winemaker: Brent Marris
Best drinking: 1997–2002

Moderate red colour, clear and fresh purple-magenta. This is a delicate but finely tuned wine, with smoky aromas and subtle fruit just touched with leafy aromas and larded with intensity. The palate is fresh, with intriguing hints of orange-like freshness, lightly mellow fruit and sweet, fine oak, with the gentle burr of mellow tannins in support. In spite of its lightness, the balancing act is so well done that this is a very attractive wine, easy and charming, on the edge of elegance.

GOLDWATER ESTATE CABERNET/MERLOT/ FRANC

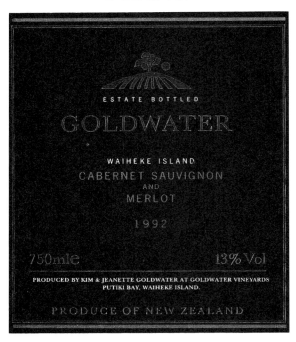

Goldwater Estate were the first to recognise Waiheke Island's potential for fine winemaking and, in 1982, the first to begin realising that potential by making the original Waiheke fine red. Since that wine was released, Waiheke has become something of a *cause célèbre* among a section of the wine-drinking public, especially designer-garbed and arty Aucklanders, with an interest in the exotic and trendy. This aside, the island's red wine reputation is a consequence of Goldwater's efforts to be more than just a cute footnote to the New Zealand fine wine industry, and will continue to be so in the foreseeable future, as they remain the only producer with a serious interest in and commitment to the widest possible fine wine market. The fruit character of the wines is lightly intense, with mild fragrance, and an impression of elegance that begs the support of fine oak.

1982
CABERNET SAUVIGNON

11.5% alc/vol; 100% Cabernet Sauvignon; Waiheke Island district, Auckland region; hand picked on 27 March 1982; aged 22 months in 500-litre French Limousin oak puncheons.
Winemaker: Kim Goldwater
Best drinking: 1995–96

Dark, deep-rimmed mahogany wine with a remarkably fragrant bouquet that sings of old leather and oak furniture, herbs and olives, modulated with sweetness. The palate, too, is a wad of sweetness and grainy tannin shadows that grow as the wine passes, until they take over completely in an austere, dry finish which is almost flavour-free. There is blunt intensity here, like a fruit bonbon, hard and sweet, but lacking in subtlety. For all that there is remarkable fruit energy, enough to keep it drinking well in the middle of its second decade.

1983
CABERNET SAUVIGNON

11.5% alc/vol; 100% Cabernet Sauvignon; Waiheke Island district, Auckland region; hand picked on 2 April 1983; aged in a mixture of year-old and new French Nevers oak 500-litre puncheons.
Winemaker: Kim Goldwater
Best drinking: 1995

Mature mahogany colour, and a similarly aged bouquet, slightly herbaceous, interesting, coffee and old furniture mélange of aromas. Lumpy, sweet, easy, surprisingly refreshing palate, simple but full of zip and life, with a drying, pleasant finish. Good, genial wine, remarkable for its age and context.

1984
CABERNET SAUVIGNON

11.5% alc/vol; 90% Cabernet Sauvignon, 10% Merlot; Waiheke Island district, Auckland region; hand picked on 7 April 1984; aged in new and year-old French Nevers oak 500-litre puncheons.
Winemaker: Kim Goldwater
Best drinking: 1995

Good, mature red, becoming brick-edged and less than

bright with a haze of retained sediment. Earthy, sweaty, mature characters on the nose, with a candy-like sweetness, it smells interesting but not particularly inviting. A mouthful of sweet fruit is not backed up with any depth of fruit flavour or mature complexities, but is good and healthy, if somewhat strung out by austere oak and tannin. Pleasant, older wine that needed more sophisticated winemaking.

1985
CABERNET SAUVIGNON

*11.5% alc/vol; 100% Cabernet Sauvignon; Waiheke Island
district, Auckland region.
Winemaker: Kim Goldwater
Best drinking: 1995–96*

Glossy cherrywood-mahogany colour, bright and deep. The matured, meaty, earthy, soy sauce nose, with hints of cooked broccoli, is warm and pleasing. Nicely weighted, with a clarifying freshness and sweet, tannin-furred fruit flavours that imply currants and other intense dried fruit. Earthiness is the abiding key here, with a tempting, lingering sweetness, and a brisk, dry finish that seems at first to be more austere than it in fact is. Neat wine, with the advantages of mellow bottle age complexities to lift its simple fruit.

1985
CABERNET/MERLOT/FRANC

*12.5% alc/vol; Waiheke Island district, Auckland region.
Winemaker: Kim Goldwater
Best drinking: 1995–97*

Dark tawny-mahogany-coloured wine, with a light, mature bouquet, savoury and lightly fragrant. There is nice sweetness in the mid-palate, but an edge of toughness to this wine. The mature fruit, though, is pleasant, quietly complex and finishing with astringent dryness. The wine seems to be passing away before the fruit, which is incredibly persistent. Nice wine without pretensions.

1987
CABERNET/MERLOT/FRANC

*13.5% alc/vol; Waiheke Island district, Auckland region.
Winemaker: Kim Goldwater
Best drinking: 1997–2010*

Deeply rich, dark colour that is the hue of the best

mahogany. A lovely bouquet of matured oak and sweet, slightly concentrated, fragrant plums and currants, but almost dried, just at the border of fruitcake, without the almonds. The palate has a tangy tension, fresh and lively, one that takes over from the fruit fragrance and pushes it into the background, but the fruit is a persistent presence through the wine, providing an impression of youth, with an undertone of maturity. Suitably deep, with very stern tannins dropping a dry, austere finish that is saved by its pretty frill of fruit sweetness and curranty flavour. A red wine that implies the same sort of fierceness as some whites. This, compounded by its uncompromising tannin, suggests it would perform better with even more bottle age, but it already has impressive complexity.

1988
CABERNET/MERLOT/FRANC

*13.5% alc/vol; 63% Cabernet Sauvignon, 17% Merlot,
20% Cabernet Franc; Waiheke Island district, Auckland
region; hand picked Cabernet Franc and Merlot on 9 April,
Cabernet Sauvignon on 15 April 1988; aged 21 months in
new French Nevers oak 225-litre barriques.
Winemaker: Kim Goldwater
Best drinking: 1995–2005*

Dark, deep, mahogany-coloured wine, bright and dense. Easy, slightly charred bouquet, with a shade of ripe fruit concentration and maturity, but essentially quiet, if not subdued. Nicely light feel in the mouth, its flavours even, steady and enriched by a ripe fruit sweetness that pervades the whole wine. The savoury mellowness of bottle age is beginning to have an effect, but there remains a lively freshness about this wine, which is only mildly modified by faint, fine tannins. Pretty wine, delightfully gracious, interestingly matured, still very much alive, its sweetly meaty flavours and dry finish begging for a rare steak to drink it with.

1989
CABERNET/MERLOT/FRANC

*13% alc/vol; 51% Cabernet Sauvignon, 21% Cabernet
Franc, 28% Merlot; Waiheke Island district, Auckland
region; hand picked, Cabernet Franc and Merlot on
3 April, Cabernet Sauvignon on 11 April 1989;
aged 14 months in new and year-old French Nevers
oak 225-litre barriques.
Winemaker: Kim Goldwater
Best drinking: 1995–2010*

Dark, deep, mahogany-garnished wine with a light bouquet that holds a pattern of maturing ripe fruit, pleasant oak fragrances, against a meaty, earthy backdrop. Savoury in character, its sweetness fading slightly, it has both depth and momentum. Mouth-filling, earthy, sweet flavours build an altogether more generous palate than expected, with warmth, some old furniture oak characters, and a lingering wash of sweetness trimmed with the hearty fur of tannin that keeps the fruit together right through the finish, leaving a lovely shadow of sweetness at the very end. There are ripe plums, currants, tobacco and coffee-tinged spice in there, but harmony, fruit sweetness and reassuring warmth are the abiding features of this wine. It makes a wonderful drink right now, but could easily last another decade.

1990
MERLOT/CABERNET FRANC

13% alc/vol; 45% Merlot, 45% Cabernet Franc, 10% Cabernet Sauvignon press wine; Waiheke Island district, Auckland region; hand picked on 2 April 1990; aged 14 months in 2-year-old French Nevers oak 225-litre barriques.
Winemaker: Kim Goldwater
Best drinking: 1995–98

Plump, glossy, magenta-trimmed wine, and just as plump on the nose, with a soft burr of oak, and some juicy fruit aromas gliding through. Dusky, sexy wine, delightfully mellow and ripe, it has waves of soft, plum-like fruit that wash through the palate like a succulent sea of flavour and charming texture, with an intriguing spice of animal piquancy to lift it from nice to pleasurable. It is made with ease and deft proportions that never impose structural absolutes on sensuality but leave the wine to fade gently like a pleasant memory. A charmer that is always more than just pretty, for it has breadth and depth as well as seductive texture, and the fine grain of crafted excellence. It should continue to intoxicate with style for a few years yet.

1990
CABERNET/MERLOT/FRANC

13% alc/vol; 60% Cabernet Sauvignon, 26% Merlot, 14% Cabernet Franc; Waiheke Island district, Auckland region; hand picked, Cabernet Franc and Merlot on 2 April, Cabernet Sauvignon on 6 April 1990; aged 17 months in French Nevers oak 225-litre barriques, 50% new, 50% used.

Winemaker: Kim Goldwater
Best drinking: 1997–2011

Beautiful wine, its colour a deep, healthy, bright and glossy red, its bouquet a charming harmony of mellow softness, its flavour lightly sweet with fruit, full of fine, gentle flavours, and its long, drying finish a tempting paradox of astringency and sweetness. The fruit, from bouquet to the end of the palate, is an adornment, never the whole show but a mind-catching beauty that runs to the depths as well as enlivening the surface and fragrance of the wine, and is supported at every point by fine-grained oak and a slightly gruff wash of tannin that provides textured dimension as well as a slice of extra, cherry-like flavour. Very, very fine wine, possessing grace as well as beauty, and the pervasive sense of effortless strength and depth that is a characteristic of quality, enriched to the potential of more bottle age to invest its style with the sparkle of complexity.

1991
CABERNET SAUVIGNON AND MERLOT

13% alc/vol; 57% Cabernet Sauvignon, 35% Merlot, 8% Cabernet Franc; Waiheke Island district, Auckland region; hand picked, Merlot and Cabernet Franc on 12 April, Cabernet Sauvignon on 13 April; aged 16 months in new and year-old French Nevers oak 225-litre barriques.
Winemaker: Kim Goldwater
Best drinking: 1998–2008

Deep, dark-coloured wine, bright but so dense that it is almost opaque, it is just losing its cerise hues for more conservative reds, but as yet no mahogany. A strangely earthy, soy sauce note in the bouquet, with an almost Italian concentration deep within its slightly smoky body that has suggestions of damp old-fashioned roses. Quite masculine in feel, with an abrasive edge and a tarry intensity that reinforce the Italian similarity. Intriguing wine, full of vigour but no longer youthful, its intensity, stroppy tannins and earthy tones keep tempting you back to the glass, and it almost demands food to complete its underlying harmonies. Not a wine for the faint-hearted, but it has a certain swagger that is very appealing.

1992
CABERNET SAUVIGNON AND MERLOT

*13% alc/vol; 55% Cabernet Sauvignon, 34% Merlot,
11% Cabernet Franc; Waiheke Island, Auckland district;
hand picked, Merlot and Cabernet Franc on 22 April,
Cabernet Sauvignon on 30 April 1992; aged 15 months
in new French Nevers oak 225-litre chateau barriques.*
Winemaker: Kim Goldwater
Best drinking: 1999–2015

Dark, blackish, magenta and purple wine, its bouquet
shot with bright fruit notes and a charming, soft
fragrance, its palate warm, with a gloss of intense,
bright fruit flavour and quite clipped tannin muscle.
It seems a little irascible at being disturbed so young,
but has a lingering sweetness from its ripe fruit origins
that suggests it will calm down with some bottle age,
comforted by clever, grainy tannins and a good
measure of expensive-tasting, lingering oak. Classy
wine with a real future, it has more presence than most
of the earlier vintages, and very impressive fruit and
winemaking embellishments, but does not sacrifice its
attractive edge for any of this. Wine to keep for a very
special occasion.

1993
CABERNET SAUVIGNON AND MERLOT

*13% alc/vol; hand picked, Merlot, Cabernet Franc and
some Cabernet Sauvignon on 2 and 3 April, balance of
Cabernet Sauvignon on 7 April 1993; aged 13 months in
new French Nevers oak 225-litre chateau barriques.*
Winemaker: Kim Goldwater
Best drinking: 1998–2011

Deep, almost opaque, glossy red, flickering cerise-
purple, lush, sensual-looking. Fresh-edged fruit on the
nose, with layers of very sophisticated oak that speaks
of mellow spiciness, and notes of red berries, but the
essence is freshness. Nice, fruit-filled, gently tannic at
first and, while the tannin builds, so does the fruit
momentum, giving a certain fruit richness to the
finish, which is neatly packaged with tannin and some
fine oak again asserting itself. Lively wine, with cut and
carry, the appropriate measures of oak and tannin and
vibrant acidity, it should live and grow for many years
yet, building a patina of complexity on its already
impressive characters.

KUMEU RIVER MERLOT/CABERNET

These have never been blockbuster wines, nor
serious contenders for awards in the upfront
world of wine competitions, but as red wines
with subtlety and poise they have few peers in
New Zealand. They have established Michael
Brajkovich, Auckland and Merlot as significant
factors in the quest for red wine quality in this
country. Since the attention-grabbing 1983 and
1984 Merlots, the wine has evolved into a
Cabernet-supported, Merlot-based wine that is
fashioned around harmony. As such it has built
a reputation of red wine charm for Kumeu
River. Often reserved, but rarely less than fine,
these wines are quietly confident alongside the
grand statements of richness made by the same
producer's Chardonnay and Sauvignon.

1983
MERLOT

*11.5% alc/vol; 100% Merlot; Kumeu district,
Auckland region.*

Winemaker: Michael Brajkovich
Best drinking: 1995–96

Good, solid, mahogany-coloured wine with a nice gloss to it. The bouquet is built on an underlying intensity of concentrated, ripe fruit made fragrant with minerals and coffee and a warm, inviting ripeness that, in spite of its mellow tones, retains a clean freshness. There is also a freshness about the sweet-feeling fruit that forms the substance of the palate, keeping it quite lively until it starts to show the dryness of bottle age in its finish, which leaves behind an austere memory of an otherwise very tasty wine. The heart of mild intensity remains, however, providing a basis on which the nicely formed subtleties of bottle age flavour have been established, enough to fend off some of the rather tough tannic characters, and to show how beautifully Auckland-grown Merlot can age. Still a nice drink, interesting and pretty in parts.

1984

11% alc/vol; 100% Merlot; Kumeu district,
Auckland region.
Winemaker: Michael Brajkovich
Best drinking: 1995

Ripe, mahogany-red wine, just turning tawny at the rim, with a sweetly spiced oak- and cassis-invested bouquet that has an unusual suggestion of bubblegum among its various fragrances. Fruit-sweet and blatantly pronouncing its bottle-aged nature, this mature wine still has fruit but has lost some of its warmth, fading quite quickly after the first charge of matured fruit and supple texture. Subtle flavour patterns keep it interesting, but it is more of an artefact than a delicious drink.

1985
CABERNET/MERLOT

12.3% alc/vol; 80% Cabernet Sauvignon, 20% Merlot;
Kumeu district, Auckland region; aged for 12 months in
225-litre French oak barriques.
Winemaker: Michael Brajkovich
Best drinking: 1995–98

With a colour reminiscent of expensive old cherry-wood furniture, and aromas of tobacco, leather, vanilla and ripe hay, there is an air of gentleman's club about this wine, of warmth, tradition and a strong sense of propriety. In spite of this opening, the palate is more

indulgent with a wash of sweet fruit flavour, some softly supple substance in the middle that is quite delicious and an extravagance of cedar, blackberry and tobacco that lingers into the mildly austere finish. A very good, harmonious wine with considerable charm and succulence that is couched in such tender terms as to be almost gentle, if it were not for the slightly stern tannins. Although never big, its heart of mildly concentrated cassis-coffee characters supports such a cast of flavour nuances that it is transformed into an entrancing, extremely sippable bottle.

1986
MERLOT/CABERNET

12% alc/vol; 70% Merlot, 25% Cabernet Sauvignon,
5% Cabernet Franc; Kumeu district, Auckland region;
hand harvested 15–23 April 1986; aged for 12 months in
225-litre French oak barriques, 15% new.
Winemaker: Michael Brajkovich
Best drinking: 1995

Rich mahogany-coloured wine with a beautifully fragrant bouquet that is almost perfumed, and would be if its aromas of cinnamon-nutmeg spice, sweetly subtle fruit, coffee and chocolate aromas were not so savoury in character. Plump in the mouth, just juicy, with an astringent tannin edge and quite fresh acid, this is a clean, clear wine, with warmth in the middle, but it fades away rather quickly to a fresh, simple finish. Nice but light, it has a limited future, but remains a pleasant drink.

1987

12.5% alc/vol; 70% Merlot, 25% Cabernet Sauvignon,
5% Cabernet Franc; Kumeu district, Auckland region; aged
in 225-litre French oak barriques, 15% new, 85% used.
Winemaker: Michael Brajkovich
Best drinking: 1996–2006

Another picture of immediate loveliness, its deep red colour just thickened to darkness at the centre of the glass, and a lilting fragrance that is full of charm and soft, ripe berries, with just a hint of coffee and toast to give it a savoury balance. With sweet fruit on the palate, the prick of minerals, supple tone, a heart of warmth and moderate concentration, and some fine, grainy tannins, it is quite complete, with a feeling of soft tension that enhances its aura of finesse. The impression is of beautiful craft, each flavour and structural nuance neatly dovetailed with others to give a seamless grace to the whole passage of the wine, leaving behind perfectly modulated shadows of furry tannin grain, oak and a fading concentration of sweetish fruit. Super wine, an elegant construction of fragrance, flavour and structural essentials that has subtlety to balance its warmth and strength, and an effortless poise that is the mark of an aristocrat.

1989
CABERNET/MERLOT

12.5% alc/vol; 20% Merlot, 40% Cabernet Sauvignon, 40% Cabernet Franc; Kumeu district, Auckland region; aged 24 months in French Alliers oak barriques, 15% new, 85% used.
Winemaker: Michael Brajkovich
Best drinking: 1996–99

Light cherrywood, tawny-edged colour, with a coffee and toast bouquet. A sweet kernel of intense fruit at the front of the palate, with fruit flavour and quiet warmth in the middle, this is a rather tense wine, well modulated and suitably fresh-edged with a gentle, furry grain of tannin, but it has an air of toughness about it that does not suit the natural subtlety of the style. Quite angular, with a lingering dryness and gentle flavour at the finish, it tastes young enough to offer hope for growth in the future.

1990
MERLOT/CABERNET

12.5% alc/vol; 70% Merlot, 30% Cabernet Sauvignon; Kumeu district, Auckland region; harvested 17–24 April 1990; aged 24 months in 225-litre French oak barriques.
Winemaker: Michael Brajkovich
Best drinking: 1996–2003

Moderately deep red wine that looks warm and inviting, an impression confirmed by its fresh, clear, mineral-edged bouquet, charged with fragrances of coffee and violets and more than a hint of chocolate. A very supple, appealing palate, with Christmas plum, coffee and chocolate flavours, warm, fresh and clean, with lovely soft, ripe-tasting tannins that give depth and dimension; they grow as the wine progresses and finally dominate the finish with an austere, youthful vigour. Firm and young, with a wash of warmth and full of adolescent fruit that is yet to show the beauty of its subtle potential, it already has the sort of poise expected of fine wine, and should develop nicely into a wine of beauty and grace.

1991

12.5% alc/vol; 60% Merlot, 10% Cabernet Sauvignon, 30% Cabernet Franc; Kumeu district, Auckland region; harvested 19 April–2 May 1991; aged 24 months in 225-litre French oak barriques.
Winemaker: Michael Brajkovich
Best drinking: 1997–2007

Clear, moderately deep red, with a fine, grainy oak bouquet filled with aromas of mulberry, coffee and Christmas plums at their juicy, ripe best. The palate is similarly oaky, packed with a filling of fresh, warm fruit, coffee and cinnamon flavours that maintain their presence right through the palate, welling up at the finish to complement the grainy, ripe tannins. Round, poised wine, with a sweet fruit heart, a clean edge of fresh acidity and warm, generous length, this is shaping up as a very classy act indeed. This is a wine that will not only go the distance, but will do so with a grace that is as much a feature of its textural qualities as it is of fragrance and flavour. Truly elegant and harmonious, this is already a lovely bottle.

MATUA VALLEY CABERNET SAUVIGNON

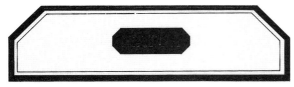

Waimauku
CABERNET SAUVIGNON
1993
PRODUCE OF NEW ZEALAND
PRODUCED & BOTTLED BY
MATUA VALLEY WINES LIMITED, WAIKOUKOU ROAD, WAIMAUKU
ℓ750mls   13.0% Vol

Matua Valley first made their winemaking reputation with a number of noticeable red wines in the early 1970s, and the 1985 Cabernet Sauvignon marked a return for the company to red wine respectability, winning critical approval as well as competition medals and customer support. Since then they have maintained a reputation for good, solid Cabernets with a sequence of successful wines based primarily on grapes from the Hawke's Bay region, and have established Matua Valley as one of the better red wine producers in the country.

1985

12.5% alc/vol; Cabernet Sauvignon.
Winemaker: John Belsham
Best drinking: 1995–1997

Deep, dark mahogany in colour, with an unusual whiff of tomato sauce on the nose and amid fragments of canned peas in a bouquet that is fresh and clear. From the beginning this wine has a lovely feel to it, with very nice fruit flavours, not intense but substantial, and tinged with green herbs that have a bean character

about them. The hard-edged tannin at the finish does not eliminate the soft, warm feeling provided by the convivial flavours and mellow complexities, nor the charm of its essentially sweet fruit character. Nice wine, almost fine, always satisfying.

1986

12.5% alc/vol; Cabernet Sauvignon.
Winemaker: John Belsham
Best drinking: 1995–1998

Very dark, deep-coloured wine that is as dense as bitter chocolate with flashes of seasoned mahogany showing through. The nose is rich with char, cassis-like blackcurrant aromas and herbs that have the smell of ripe tobacco, characteristics that rear up in the palate as well, underscored by sweet, silky textures of ripe fruit, and moderate, thin-edged tannin burr that compete with fresh acidity at the edge. Nicely weighted wine, its air of freshness keeping up a tension between texture and flavour, but the finish is a murky jumble of flavours and austere tannins that leave a less than classy impression. Pleasant drinking, with some lovely moments of delicious fruit.

1987

12.5% alc/vol; Cabernet Sauvignon; Dartmoor Valley district, Hawke's Bay region.
Winemaker: Mark Robertson
Best drinking: 1996–2001

Dark and very deep, mahogany-trimmed wine, with a bouquet that has lashings of charry oak and the mellow ripeness of bottle age showing through, embellished in places by a glimmer of ripe blackcurrants. Very sensual feeling, with its satin-like texture loaded with warmth and lush fruit flavours that are strung with bottle age complexities and those bright flashes of blackcurrant flavour. Nice, gripping, quite meaty-feeling tannins give good support, along with a fresh, fine acidity, aspects that fill out the wine and yet elongate it at the same time, qualities of substance and elegance that produce an impression of real class. Balance and finish are nicely made, conveying a sense of fine craftsmanship, and even the slight herby tang that persists throughout is never off-key.

Long, smart, flavourful wine, still holding depths that age could turn to greater complexity.

1989

11.5% alc/vol; Cabernet Sauvignon; Dartmoor Valley
district, Hawke's Bay region.
Winemaker: Mark Robertson
Best drinking: 1995–97

This is a dense wine in spite of its moment of fragrance, with very dark, deep, almost inky colour and a bouquet stuffed with fragrant fruit that is lined with charred oak and a telling note of leafy green. Greenness also disturbs the palate somewhat, although it is a green flavour rather than a texture, for the meatiness of its ripe fruit qualities sustains the impression of density. Good wine, it lacks proportion, a balance that would make it more than just a collection of various flavours.

1990

12.5% alc/vol; Cabernet Sauvignon; Dartmoor Valley
district, Hawke's Bay region.
Winemaker: Mark Robertson
Best drinking: 1996–2004

Deep, healthy-looking red with a hint of mahogany at the rim and some darker depths about it. Nice aromas of cassis and redcurrant abound, with subtleties of smoky, charred oak and a sense of easy, fresh clarity that are repeated in the palate, where blackcurrant fruit asserts itself among a pattern of oak and leafy herbaceousness. The softness and juicy texture prevent the wine from being diminished by this green aspect, which becomes a balanced part of the whole, with other 'hard' characters such as acid and nicely furry tannins complementing its sweet, soft feel. Set up to be a real charmer when all its parts fall into harmony and are enhanced by some of the complexity that bottle age can deliver.

1991

13% alc/vol; Cabernet Sauvignon; Dartmoor Valley
district, Hawke's Bay region.
Winemaker: Mark Robertson
Best drinking: 1998–2005

Very dark, deep purply red, with quite meaty, tomato leaf aromas, shot with hints of cassis-blackcurrant concentration and clear wafts of cedar and oak. Fresh moments of cassis-like flavours also fill in the palate, ripe enough to give it depth as well as brightness, but the dominant impression is of a facade of flavour without tannin to back it up, right to the moderately rich, chocolate-like finish that lingers softly with nuances of warm flavour. There is a shaft of greenness through the wine as well, a disconcerting tang that is always noticeable, disturbing the sweet fruit gloss. Interesting, at moments impressive, always enjoyable in spite of its awkwardness, if it mellows and harmonises with more age, the fruit apparent in its depths should get a chance to put on a quality performance. Until then, though, the jury is still out on this wine.

1992

13% alc/vol; Cabernet Sauvignon; Dartmoor Valley
district, Hawke's Bay region.
Winemaker: Mark Robertson
Best drinking: 1997–2005

Rich, ripe colour that is red and purple at once, with lights flashing up from its very dark depths. The nose, fragrant and spicy, hints at concentrated, fresh fruit, but is mostly a backdrop for that appealing, spicy oak. The rich intensity of the fruit gets more chance in the palate, where its concentration is again apparent, freshened with acidity to a point of lively incisiveness that is here supported by the oak and a solid, ripe-feeling tannin that appears as a substantial counterpoint to the lovely fragrance. Greenness is here, too, but neatly subdued by other characters to a supplementary role, although it shines through at the end rather more. Good wine, hard-edged at present, with fragrance and concentration its predominant features, it has a promising future and should become pretty, if never really charming.

NGATARAWA GLAZEBROOK CABERNET/MERLOT

From it first vintage this wine promised to become a very classy act, depending on depth of fruit and winemaking balance to make its mark. These are not factors to attract attention in a country where the early spectacle of white wine fragrance is so highly esteemed, and Glazebrook has never had the critical support that its quiet class suggests it should. These are wines that prefer to retire in rowdy company rather than compete by shouting how fruity they are and, in spite of being persistently ignored by critics, winemaker Alwyn Corban has continued to make them this way: deep, carefully formed and reserved, wines that perform best after a number of years in the bottle. Wine drinkers have gradually come to respect the sophistication and quiet elegance of these wines, and now even a few critics have begun to appreciate their quality.

1985

12.5% alc/vol; 90% Cabernet Sauvignon, 10% Merlot;
Ngatarawa district, Hawke's Bay region.
Winemaker: Alwyn Corban
Best drinking: 1995–96

Moderate-coloured, macrocarpa-scented, spicy, fragrant, delightful wine, its tender character permeating every aspect, but never flattening out the suave, rippling effect created by a swarm of flavour nuances and counter-balancing soft and fresh textures. If anything, it lacks firm oak and some gruff tannin to give it dimension, especially at the finish, where it falls a bit short, but its easy, charming style is almost enough to carry it. Very pretty, it seems to be at its best right now, showing the benefit of bottle age on attractive fruit.

1986

13% alc/vol; 90% Cabernet Sauvignon, 10% Merlot;
Ngatarawa district, Hawke's Bay region.
Winemaker: Alwyn Corban
Best drinking: 1995–2000

Dark, deep, glossy mahogany red wine, with a very gamy bouquet that suggests venison and spices, cinnamon, anise and the warm fruit aromas of plums. There is still a keen edge of freshness to the palate, an aspect that is beginning to be softened by deep flavour and the harmonising characters of bottle age, without diminishing the rolling impression given by sweet and lively fruit, flavours that are stretched out into a lingering finish by some lovely, soft, husky tannins and a moderate chime of oak. Deep and clear, it appears very young still, enough to expect considerable developments with more bottle age, for which a little more oak and tannin would have been advantageous, but it promises to remain a melodious, neatly balanced charmer for many years yet.

1989

13% alc/vol; 85% Cabernet Sauvignon, 11% Merlot, 4%
Cabernet Franc; Ngatarawa district, Hawke's Bay region.
Winemaker: Alwyn Corban
Best drinking: 1997–2016

Dense colour, with some reddening at the rim, but otherwise it looks like an infant—solid to the point of being opaque. Neither does the bouquet give any sign of maturity, with earthy aromas that are deeply embedded with blackcurrant fruit and some fine, sweetly gentle oak. Quietly classy, it has very impressive depth to it, with aspects of complexity half buried therein, inviting further investigation, but never giving anything away other than substance and very close-grained texture. The palate too, is quiet, intense, running very deep and broad with a edge of liveliness that gives it a spark, together with a flicker of minerals. There is liquorice and some fragrant macrocarpa in there among the intensity and close texture, characters that linger even after the fresh, clean edge has made its presence felt at the finish, kept clinging with flavours of fruit and oak by softly definite, staunch tannins that seem to enclose the sweet heart of this remarkable wine. The whole thing has an assured essence of class, of poise and elegance, that is made without ever grandstanding, a feature carefully crafted out of the wine's many assets without a single part dominating, or even standing out from the others. Very fine wine indeed.

1990

13% alc/vol; Ngatarawa district, Hawke's Bay region.
Winemaker: Alwyn Corban
Best drinking: 1998–2005

Solidly magenta-red with dark, almost oily depths, this wine has a macrocarpa-like wood fragrance about it that seems to be a particular characteristic of this style—a perfumed fragrance that is almost resinous, complemented here by chocolate and coffee aromas and a fine tang of berryfruit. The palate, too, is fine and tense, with keen, bright flavours and a very fresh dimension given extra energy by some frisky tannins. This characteristic imparts an overall nerviness to the wine, but there is enough deeply ingrained sweet berryfruit and fine oak here to suggest that it should be long and elegant when it has matured past this lively stage. Certainly the nature of both oak and riper tannins suggests that the structure is there, and the reserved nature of the fruit is an aspect of this wine that early vintages have matured to delicious harmony. Looks to be one worth waiting for.

1991

13% alc/vol; 80% Cabernet Sauvignon, 15% Merlot, 5% Cabernet Franc; Ngatarawa district, Hawke's Bay region.
Winemaker: Alwyn Corban
Best drinking: 2000–2016

Very purple-red, deep and dark, this wine has a ripe plums and spice bouquet that is reminiscent of Christmas pudding, without the brandy. It also has that hallmark whiff of macrocarpa wood that must be a consequence of the Glazebrook blend of oak and fruit grown on the Ngatarawa site. The palate is fresh and fluid, with noticeable oak finely tuned to fit in with texture and flavour, holding on through fresh, sweet fruit flavours that are deeply intense, into a tail that is charged with ripe, black cherry-flavoured tannins and a lingering trace of concentrated blackcurrant fruit. Appropriately for a winery based in an old racing stable, this wine has the rippling sinuous character of a thoroughbred, sleek and powerful, but with the quiet self-assurance of a champion. It should evolve into a wine of fragrant, effortless elegance.

1992

13% alc/vol; 50% Cabernet Sauvignon, 40% Merlot, 10% Malbec; Ngatarawa district, Hawke's Bay region.
Winemaker: Alwyn Corban
Best drinking: 1996–2000

Dark, blackish purple-red and very deep, this is a powerfully aromatic wine, its nose laced with cinnamon and almost florid, deep fruit that is curranty and plum-like, a blend that evokes ideas of Christmas pudding, although less obviously than the previous vintage. The lustrous palate has a fresh, fruit juice character, fine and delicious, with the liveliness of acidity masking its true depths, but both flavour clarity and warmth manage to show through, investing resonant cherry-plum flavours that linger alongside firm, grainy, softly rich tannins. Somewhere in this deep pool of flavours and texture there is oak, but it is felt rather than tasted, not making its flavour noticeable until the very end, where it fits in neatly next to fruit and husky tannins. Definitely wine with a future, its present flashy freshness should moderate with time, to be replaced by savoury-sweet fragrance from the solid investment in ripe fruit.

STONECROFT CABERNET SAUVIGNON/ CABERNET/MERLOT

This small Hawke's Bay winery has the most consistent record so far of those making wines from the acclaimed, deep, stony soils of the Gimblett-Mere Road area west of Hastings. Known primarily as the winery that pioneered Syrah in the fine wine era, its Cabernet-based reds have had less media support but have consistently proven to be among the most deeply flavoured, powerful reds from New Zealand.

1987
CABERNET SAUVIGNON

12.5% alc/vol; 100% Cabernet Sauvignon; Mere Road district, Hawke's Bay region; hand harvested 9 April 1987; aged for 18 months in 500-litre used oak puncheons. Winemaker: Alan Limmer Best drinking: 1995–2002

Ripe-looking, full, deeply mahogany wine with a most unusual bouquet that has strong suggestions of smoked trout on the nose, backed by dense, ripe fruit that verges on the concentration of dried fruit. The concentrated fruit is neatly contained between iodine-like oak on the palate, too, giving the impression of an exotic wine sandwich, with moderate depth balancing its fresh edge. Intriguing and just a bit simple, but the lovely fruit is very seductive, its suave nature brusquely tempered by a rough, tough grip of tannin that keeps the drinker interested.

1988

13% alc/vol; 100% Cabernet Sauvignon; Mere Road district, Hawke's Bay region; hand harvested 27 March 1988; aged for 18 months in 500-litre French Nevers oak puncheons, 50% new. Winemaker: Alan Limmer Best drinking: 1996–2000

Dark and soft, from its very pretty, garnet tones to the flavourful finish, this is attractive wine, decorated with hints of soft violet fragrances among the bright, sweet fruit flavours and brisk collar of spiced oak. Mellow, vaguely dusty and very nice to know, it has warmth enough to counter little bits of brisk, green herbs and fairly tough tannin. It emerges as a real charmer, sweetly tempered and convivial so that it is very satisfying without ever being truly classy.

1989

13.5% alc/vol; 100% Cabernet Sauvignon; Mere Road district, Hawke's Bay region; hand harvested on 27 April 1989; aged for 21 months in 500-litre French Nevers oak puncheons, 70% new. Winemaker: Alan Limmer Best drinking: 1999–2009

Dark, opaque red, garnet at the rim of its glossy body, with delicious aromas of coffee and spicy herbs pervading the ripe, plum-like fragrances that make up the substance of the bouquet. Flavours of plums and blackberries immediately make their presence felt on the palate, gushing fresh and forward, but tempered with bold tannins that have substance as well as a rough presence, and a faint abrasion of herbal green. Moderate length is helped by the tannins, which maintain a warm, fairly rich texture, as well as some of the fragrant flavours, on into the aftertaste, but it is essentially a hard finish to an otherwise buoyant wine.

Overall the impression is of strength and deep, restrained power, features that will help this wine evolve further with bottle age, to a stage when it should unleash an abundance of flavour nuances derived from its lively fruit.

1990

13% alc/vol; 85% Cabernet Sauvignon, 15% Merlot;
Mere Road district, Hawke's Bay region; hand harvested
15 April 1990; aged for 21 months in 500-litre puncheons,
10% American oak, 90% French Nevers oak, 50% new.
Winemaker: Alan Limmer
Best drinking: 1997–2010

Dark, black-tinged, deep plum-coloured wine with a richly fragrant bouquet that has a slightly smelly oak and coffee aroma, but is essentially ripe and mellow in spite of its sprightly freshness. In the mouth sweet, ripe fruit takes over with a deep, warm flood that gently fills every corner with glowing flavours supported by real strength and ramrod tannins that have substance as well as texture, giving the wine extra dimension and weight, as well as momentum. At every stage there is a jewel-like garnet quality about this wine, from the red flashes of colour, to fruit flavours that shine from the dark, tannin-lined depths, and even the firm, furry tannin-trimmed finish that is brightened by an edge of acid. Paradoxically, the strength is matched by a lightness that implies ease, the effortless balance of elegance. Very fine fruit made into an equally fine wine with years of bottle age potential, it already tastes like a real treasure.

1991

13% alc/vol; 85% Cabernet Sauvignon, 15% Merlot;
Mere Road district, Hawke's Bay region; hand harvested
14 April 1991; aged for 21 months in 500-litre puncheons,
10% American oak, 90% French Nevers oak, 50% new.
Winemaker: Alan Limmer
Best drinking: 2001–2016

There is so much deep, ravishing fruit in this wine that it tastes immortal, even in its aggressive youth. Bright and glossy, with magenta flashes lighting its deep colour, it has a superbly tempting bouquet filled with aromas of lush, ripe berryfruit, and expensive, spicy oak enlivened with fresh energy. The mouthful of sweet fruit it then delivers is deep and dense, hinting at chocolate and blackberries, with a very soft, strokable feel that suggests satin and velvet, before it is ruffled

by the sprightly abrasions of ripe, strong tannins that never stoop to hardness. There is oak on hand as a companion, adding to the wine's warmth and texture, partnered by other mellow complexities, even a touch of herbs, while among all the angles of tannin, alcohol, acid and the clutter of flavours there is a sense of elegance, of long, lingering wine of fine texture, enhanced by fragrance. Has the promise of a spectacular bouquet with more time in bottle, and myriad flavour patterns to match.

1992

13% alc/vol; 85% Cabernet Sauvignon, 15% Merlot;
Mere Road district, Hawke's Bay region; hand harvested
15 April 1992; aged for 21 months in 350-litre French
Nevers oak hogsheads, 50% new.
Winemaker: Alan Limmer
Best drinking: 1999–2007

Deep, opaque, magenta-plum colours show off the youth of this wine, with its high-toned aromas of raspberry and plum fruit tinted with cinnamon spice and oak and deepened by concentration. The palate has a lovely robe of blackberry fruit flavours, glossy and suave, with an attractive hints of herbs, mint and oak subtleties all layered like some expensive pastry. Essentially this is a deep, steady, very fine-textured wine, well filled out with mouth-filling tannins of good character, and finished with vigour and lingering fruit-oak flavours in good style. Very deftly made wine, its concentration a major part of its appeal, it has balance, warmth and flair, as well as an abundance of beautiful fruit flavour on which to base its future success. Wine for the cellar, for at least the next five years.

TE MATA AWATEA

This was originally a straight Cabernet Sauvignon from the Awatea Vineyard, planted on deep, stony 'red metal' soils on a terrace to the west of the Te Mata winery, a site that was for many years a supplier of grapes for Vidals' historic red wines. Awatea Vineyard was completely replanted during the early 1980s, with the result that there was no 1984 wine under this label. Now it is the second red wine of Te Mata Estate but, in spite of this status, few red wines in the country can match it for fragrance and finesse.

1982

*13% alc/vol; Cabernet Sauvignon; Te Mata district,
Hawke's Bay region; hand picked 14–19 April 1982.
Winemaker: Michael Bennett
Best drinking: 1995–2000*

Deep, dark, cherrywood-coloured wine, bright and clear, with a freshly aromatic bouquet that is fragrant with delightful cedar characters and a fine substance of sweet, age-matured blackcurrants and ripe oak. Chunky fruit flavours are immediately noticeable on the palate, which still has a youthful sweetness that harmonises with the sturdy but momentary oak, with nuances that peel off into other subtly different flavours as the wine progresses. A lumpy, occasionally coarse

tannin runs here and there across the background of fruit, complementing the warm, genial nature of this wine, and giving it a grainy, mildly abrasive, dry finish that carries echoes of sweet fruit. In spite of its age, there is still plenty of life here, and its mellow charms offer very toothsome, quietly satisfying drinking.

1983

*12.5% alc/vol; Cabernet Sauvignon; Te Mata district,
Hawke's Bay region; hand picked 7–12 April 1983.
Winemaker: Michael Bennett
Best drinking: 1996–2004*

Deep, very dark red, shiny and touched with bits of black. The fresh cedar and blackcurrant nose is fragrant but quite dense in character, with a touch of mint in the background, and a notion of close-grained, fine texture that is repeated in the texture of the palate, where sweet fruit, oak and a hardish tannin are crammed together to a point of unusual density. Very young-seeming wine, permeated by an air of vigorous, deep fruit and the hard edge of tannin, its compressed nature giving it a focus without any appearance of concentration. The finish, too, is very close-grained, solid and dry. The wine finishes well but not particularly long, although the fruit flavours that have until now been under pressure from the tougher features begin to assert some delicious, berryish characters which inject a final tone of charm to an otherwise uncompromising wine. Still seems to need more cellar time.

1985

*12.5% alc/vol; Cabernet Sauvignon; Te Mata district,
Hawke's Bay region; hand picked 11–12 April 1985.
Winemaker: Peter Cowley
Best drinking: 1995–2000*

This wine is the dark, glossy colour of rosewood furniture, fragrant and minerally on the nose, together with a hint of silage, and lashings of blackcurrant-blackberry aromas imparting a glorious succulence to the bouquet. The trim of oak aroma introduces the fine oak character that stands guard over the lovely, fresh sweetness of fruit flavours on the palate, which is not big, but has a very persuasive presence that stays with the drinker long after the final swallow, leaving an impression of ripe, sweet fruit to the very end. In spite of this fruit charm, this is not simple wine. Its grainy tannins give textural depth and contribute to length as well as substance on the palate that serves to frame the concentrated fruit flavours in the mid-palate. It seems to be in perfect shape right now, warm and mature, yet with a touch of vigour that gives it a youthful glint, a counterpoint of freshness and maturity that is in harmony with the sweet-austere relationship of tannin and fruit. Begs for the company of a big steak.

1986

12.5% alc/vol; Cabernet Sauvignon, Merlot, Cabernet Franc; Te Mata district, Hawke's Bay region; hand picked 2 and 11 April 1986.
Winemaker: Peter Cowley
Best drinking: 1995–97

Mellow, bright mahogany colour, with elements of silage and mint on the nose, complemented by smoky oak and an aromatic, essency blackcurrant fruit. Attractive, mellow wine, deftly balanced and showing the complex charms of bottle age in harmony with a touch of remaining blackcurrant fruit and some savoury, herbal tones among the charred oak. Warm to the end, where a brusque, mildly fruit-flavoured tannic tang carries the wine on. Very pleasing, sophisticated and in need of drinking while it still has some of the charm of fruit left.

1987

12.5% alc/vol; Cabernet Sauvignon, Merlot, Cabernet Franc; Te Mata district, Hawke's Bay region; hand picked 3 April 1987.
Winemaker: Peter Cowley
Best drinking: 1995–2002

This superbly elegant wine is gracious in colour, bouquet and taste, a picture of fine red wine fruit and skilled winemaking delivered with finesse. Healthy-looking, its moderately deep colour alive with dark, glossy, mahogany tones, it is tempting wine from the start, and the bouquet, lovely with fragrances of fine fruit, oak spice and a trace of mint, completes a very tempting, gracious introduction. And the palate delivers. Elegant, with high-toned, sweetly ripe fruit and classy oak to the fore, it has depth and substance in support, plus the assets of steadily building tannins that have dimension and gravelly texture as well as a light touch of cherry flavour which comes through at the finish and lingers with a distinct aromatic presence. Fine-grained, close-textured wine, with svelte fruit which has yet to evolve a full range of complexity, but

has such even length that it is never less than elegant. Has all the appearance and poise of a thoroughbred, a wine that delivers the pure clarity of New Zealand-grown fruit with cosmopolitan elegance.

1988

12% alc/vol; Cabernet Sauvignon, Merlot, Cabernet Franc; Te Mata district, Hawke's Bay region; hand picked 12–13 April 1988.
Winemaker: Peter Cowley
Best drinking: 1995

Solid red colour, with just hints of mahogany creeping in, this wine is herbal and oaky, quite light, with a fruity, pleasing palate that is easily balanced with tannin and acidity. Finishing light, its balance implying charm, it is attractive wine without any great presence or momentum, but enough to be a pleasant dalliance between grander wines.

1989

12.5% alc/vol; Cabernet Sauvignon, Merlot, Cabernet Franc; Te Mata district, Hawke's Bay region; hand picked 10–28 March 1989.
Winemaker: Peter Cowley
Best drinking: 1998–2010

Dark, glossy, deep plum-coloured wine, rich to look at and to smell, its beautiful fragrance laden with sweet-spicy oak aromas and a finesse of berryish fruit tinged with herbs. In spice of its lifted beauty there is depth and substance here as well, a rich mellowness that is particularly inviting. The palate is fresh and clear with moderately intense, juicy fruit flavours that sweep through your mouth, supported by mild tannins which gradually build through the wine to a finishing crescendo of fur and gravel. This relationship between fruit and tannin is a fascinating one that changes as the wine passes, beginning with svelte fruit supported by tannin grip, but gradually evolving into a warm burr of tannin backed by some sweetly charming fruit flavours, a transforming juxtaposition that keeps the wine alive without relying simply on lush fruit.

Very fine, delightfully proportioned so that it never seems overworked, its edge of intensity gives it a sense of fruit quality to match its winemaking sophistication and those lovely tannic riches. In spite of this, it is still in need of some more flavour complexities to give it a final flourish of quality, but it is so youthful that these should develop with more time in the bottle. Certainly, it seems likely to be some years before the close-grained density of the middle palate begins to open up some of its flavour treasures.

1990

12.5% alc/vol; Cabernet Sauvignon, Merlot, Cabernet Franc; Te Mata district, Hawke's Bay region; hand picked 28 March–27 April 1990.
Winemaker: Peter Cowley
Best drinking: 1997–2006

Solid, healthy, ripe, moderately deep red wine with a beautifully fragrant, sweet fruit and musky, suave oak bouquet, it is the epitome of elegance. The palate, too, is quite beautiful, softly delicious with fruit and a gentle touch of herbs. Its succulence is immediately persuasive, but gradually gives way to a swelling tannin structure that takes the wine on into an equally beautiful, fruit-lined finish. This tannin provides the wine with a quietly assertive substance that underpins the warmth and fruit without becoming rough or coarse, giving the wine presence as well as taste. The blackcurrant fruit flavours, however, get into every nook and cranny of the wine, like a light illuminating every corner, imparting a sparkle and completing a picture that is a complexity of textures — fresh, smooth, gruff in places, lifted in others, then fine and close, almost reserved. With the little whirlwinds of flavour kicked up by oak and lively fruit, the wine is never still, never dull, yet retains its charm and poise in every situation. Delicious, delightful, elegant, approachable, but made to last.

1991

13% alc/vol; Cabernet Sauvignon, Merlot, Cabernet Franc; Te Mata district, Hawke's Bay region; hand picked 8–27 April 1991.
Winemaker: Peter Cowley
Best drinking: 1997–2012

Dark, red, glossy red wine, fairly deep and very attractive to the eye and the nose — its bouquet is a beautiful blend of fragrant oak, and pretty, sweetly ripe fruit that sings of blackcurrants and a seasoning of herbs. The soft, tender, succulently perfumed palate is fine and laden with ripe, soft, summery fruit to the point of mouth-watering succulence, while retaining an almost fierce clarity of flavour. There is a heart of concentration to the fruit that the oak and tannin support, giving real depth to the wine, as well as the

textural substance that high-quality reds demand. Fruit is the core of the matter here, a sweet brilliance that is undeniable, but the winemaking has not left it to its own devices, harmonising suitable strong elements of grainy oak and richly flavoured, furry tannins into it. In spite of this, there is an air of ease, of suave silky sophistication lined with mint as well as oaky pleasantries, that almost insists you drink it now, and damn waiting for bottle age to add the wonderful subtleties it undoubtedly will.

1992

12.5% alc/vol; Cabernet Sauvignon, Merlot, Cabernet Franc; Te Mata district, Hawke's Bay region; hand picked 10–30 April 1992.
Winemaker: Peter Cowley
Best drinking: 1997–2001

Dark, deeply magenta-coloured wine, fresh with aromas of mint, herbs and oak, with a faint trace of blackberries making fragrance an essential part of its obvious charm. Fresh and mellow at once on the palate, with sweet fruit flavours and some pleasing concentration that comes back at the finish in a tasty flavour which is framed with softly grainy tannin. Well shaped and showing off its young flavours, it has an attractive touch of warmth to match its pretty fruit and mellow subtleties.

TE MATA COLERAINE

This one wine changed the direction of the New Zealand wine industry by establishing that the country was capable of growing fine red wine. When the 1982 wine was released, Te Mata Estate had already won the trophy for the top red wine in New Zealand with its 1980 Cabernet Sauvignon, but the 1982 Coleraine did more than just win prizes; it proved unequivocally that red wine with colour, depth of flavour, sophisticated palate structure and longevity could be made in New Zealand.

Subsequently, Coleraine has remained the leading example of red winemaking in the country, with a string of wines that have never been less than accomplished, and have always been as good as any particular vintage has allowed. Indeed, no one wine has so dominated any fine wine category. Also, the capacity for age attributed to these wines in their youth has so far proven to be correct.

Not prepared to take their success for granted, Te Mata have always sought to improve and refine their winemaking, to the point of extensive vineyard replanting and, after years of research, the construction of a highly

sophisticated specialised red wine fermentation centre. Since 1989 Te Mata have produced a tiered group of red wines, with Coleraine at the summit, followed by Awatea, supported by a generic Cabernet/Merlot, rather than produce wines according to the vineyard source of their fruit, as was the case initially.

Coleraine was originally made from grapes grown in the vineyard surrounding the house of proprietors John and Wendy Buck.

1982

13.5% alc/vol; Cabernet Sauvignon, Merlot, Cabernet Franc; Te Mata district, Hawke's Bay region; hand picked 14–19 April 1982.
Winemaker: Michael Bennett
Best drinking: 1997–2003

Dark, bright, cherrywood-mahogany colour, rich and glossy. The bouquet is fragrant to the point of being perfumed, with fruitcake and vanilla-oak aromas that are rich, with some warm, leafy maturities. The palate is still fresh and lively, with a lilting acidity and even, sweet fruit flavours and texture right through to the end, filled all the way with varying moments of spice, mellow richness, warmth. Grainy, slightly tough tannins keep the fruit company, and show up astringent at the end, but supported at that point by mellow fruit characters that have managed to retain a note of perfumed freshness. This is a big, solid, rather brash wine, with chunks of oak among quite dazzling, ripe, deeply flavoured fruit, giving off an air of warm conviviality that is particularly satisfying. It is fruit that is embedded in every part of the wine, and at the finish rides the tannin and warm alcohol to a friendly, furry departure that always suggests another sip, another glass. Still hearty, lustrous stuff, with a promise of some years yet, it remains a memorable wine more than a decade after it was made.

1983

13% alc/vol; Cabernet Sauvignon, Merlot, Cabernet Franc; Te Mata district, Hawke's Bay region; hand picked 7–12 April 1983.
Winemaker: Michael Bennett
Best drinking: 1995–2001

Dark, deep, dense colours that suggest very ripe plums

among the blackish hues. With herby, ripely mint-tinged aromas among the fragrant oak and meaty, lively fruit, it has a distinctly solid feel about its bouquet, with moments of intensity and lightness alternating within it. Fresh and slick on the palate, with deep, close, sweetish fruit flavour that feels smooth and long, infested with oak and hard-edged, grainy tannins that finish rather abruptly. Good, hearty, dense wine, with real warmth in the middle and an air of casual rusticity that is almost charming, kept honest by its solid flavour depths. Substantial stuff, mostly body, but with some nice fragrant decorations and the promise of more complexity and fining down with some extra bottle age.

1984

12% alc/vol; Cabernet Sauvignon, Merlot, Cabernet Franc; Te Mata district, Hawke's Bay region; hand picked 16–17 April 1984.
Winemaker: Peter Cowley
Best drinking: 1995–96

Darkly coloured wine with a bouquet that is a harmony of herbal, spicy characters and bright moments of dried fruit intensity. Raisin-like intensity is a noticeable palate character as well, adding a dimension of fruit intensity to its otherwise herbal flavours, riding in the supple, refreshing body of the wine in the company of soft, meandering tannins. Warm and pleasant wine, easy to drink, delicately harmonious and filled out by the mild intensity of the fruit, it finishes with a soft touch and a gentle echo of herbal fruit.

1985

13% alc/vol; Cabernet Sauvignon, Merlot, Cabernet Franc; Te Mata district, Hawke's Bay region; hand picked 10–11 April 1985;
Winemaker: Peter Cowley
Best drinking: 1995–2005

Darkly glistening with a mahogany sheen, this deep wine is heady with sweet oak and dense fruit that is almost impregnable on the nose and palate. Less than fragrant, the closely packed fruit aromas have a solid substance to them, cast in mellow, warming tones among the oak. They are just as close to taste, as dense as the finest, darkest chocolate, enlivened by warmth and a feeling of bright clarity delivered by a stream of clean acidity that runs right through the palate and out into a mildly astringent, grainy tannin finish. The solid dimension does fade somewhat as the wine passes

through, but the finish is tough and full of enough flavour to compensate and leave the impression of depth and serious intent. There are some fascinating nuances just beginning to emerge, subtleties of spice and minerals among the ripe, curranty fruit and, in spite of its thick impression, there is a firm tone of finesse throughout. Not quite elegant, but definitely classy, it promises to offer tasty rewards to those who cellar it for a good few years yet.

1986

13% alc/vol; Cabernet Sauvignon, Merlot, Cabernet Franc; Te Mata district, Hawke's Bay region; hand picked 18 April 1986.
Winemaker: Peter Cowley
Best drinking: 1995–98

The colour of freshly polished, old mahogany this is immediately pretty wine, and the nose is even more inviting, slightly oak, mellow, with a sweetish herbal character and some hints of minerals among the glimmers of fresh berries. It seems lighter than the warmth at its heart implies, but the flavours of fruit, oak and winemaking components are so neatly balanced that it is a lightness of touch rather than of character, a clever piece of wine craft. The fresh clarity of the vaguely sweet fruit flavours is tinged with smoky oak and coffee to a fine complexity that has a suave texture and a lingering, lightly stylish finish that is all grace and balance, with a drying, flavour-fresh tail. A clean, lively wine in spite of its mellow tones, it simply glows with flavour and an entrancing perfume that permeates every characteristic. Particularly yummy, sufficiently classy, delightfully fine.

1987

12.5% alc/vol; Cabernet Sauvignon, Merlot, Cabernet Franc; Te Mata district, Hawke's Bay region; hand picked 14 April 1987.
Winemaker: Peter Cowley
Best drinking: 1996–2002

Deep, ripe mahogany colour and a very attractive, fragrant bouquet that opens up like lace set this wine up as a star, and it is. There are sappy moments on the nose, but they are reduced to interesting counterpoints in a bouquet that is lavish with beautiful delicacies of cedary oak, fine fruit, hints of pine and dried flowers in a display that is as finely textured as it is expansive. This finesse is immediately apparent on the palate as well, where the freshness and depth of fruit flavour never become assertive, keeping in tune with the harmonies of oak and ripe, fine tannins in a lovely balance that seems to hold, whatever the predominant feature. At the beginning this is a kernel of sweetly flavoured fruit concentration which in the middle gives way to mouth-filling warmth and texture, shot with the cherry flavours of ripe tannin that gradually take over as their gruff graininess emerges in a dry, lingering finish. This changing character is like a ripple of textures through the wine, each beautifully morticed into the other in a seamless movement from fore-palate to finish that is simple lovely. Superb wine, gracefully proportioned, effortlessly fine, it is still showing a youthful compactness and fresh edge that hints at more lacy flavour embellishments yet to come.

1988

12.5% alc/vol; Cabernet Sauvignon, Merlot, Cabernet Franc; Te Mata district, Hawke's Bay region; hand picked 13–14 April 1988.
Winemaker: Peter Cowley
Best drinking: 1995

Healthy, lightish mahogany colour, with red flashes, and a light bouquet that is clean, clear and faintly herbal, with a sliver of nice oak. Light with pleasant, pretty flavours and a measure of freshness and comfortable length, it has no exact faults, but nor does it have any particularly positive characteristics. It is simply, easily pleasant, well shaped and balanced, more a wine of subtle textures than flavour. Pretty, tender red for drinking now.

1989

12.5% alc/vol; Cabernet Sauvignon, Merlot, Cabernet Franc; Te Mata district, Hawke's Bay region; hand picked 21–23 April 1989.
Winemaker: Peter Cowley
Best drinking: 1998–2014

Pretty-looking wine, darkly coloured and showing off flashes of cerise and magenta, it has a very fine, deep bouquet that is alive with the sweet perfume of ripe fruit and oak, bright but not fruity, a robe of aroma that is enhanced by nuances of smoke and minerals and a subtle, spicy fragrance. The palate is filled with seductive depths of ripe, glossy, satin-like fruit that is sweet in character, welling up in a cascading clamour of flavours which are bright and mellow and fresh in

turn, shot with the savoury spice of oak. This is all supported by a healthy cut of acid, warmth and a great furry shaft of tannin that embraces the fruit while it builds to a long, resonant finish of lifted astringency and gently tapering, lingering, fruit flavours. Everything is here—fragrance, ripe fruit, intensity, depth, momentum, oak and ripe, strong tannins—but no feature asserts itself over the others in a wine that is, above all, harmonious. In spite of that there is real and effortless fruit power behind it, which is inevitably the driving force of the wine, giving it its heart of clarity and warmth against which the other aspects can weave their beautiful patterns of texture and flavour. It is still very tight, almost dense, still sinewy, but has enough juice to be immensely pleasurable right now, without suggesting that it will not grow and flourish with a lot more bottle age. Splendid stuff with an air of grandeur.

1990

12% alc/vol; Cabernet Sauvignon, Merlot, Cabernet Franc; Te Mata district, Hawke's Bay region; hand picked 28 March–27 April 1990.
Winemaker: Peter Cowley
Best drinking: 1998–2006

Very deep, richly coloured wine with hints of cerise and a faintly purple glow at the rim, it opens beautifully into a fragrant, suave, sexy perfume that is sweet with fruit aromas and glittering fragrant nuances. There are blackcurrants here, and hints of violets, chocolate, coffee, even some delectably ripe plums in the background, where the texture is dense and fine. There is fine density in the palate as well, a close-grained background to the sweet, svelte fruit texture that is immediately impressive as it spreads a patina of ripe, plum-impregnated flavours around your mouth. This is backed by warmth and tender, pervasive tannins that are never assertive but provide a steady, background burr to the easy face of the wine, assisting the spread and fragrance of fruit and its oak embellishments. The finish is graceful, long, gentle, but never weak, accentuating gracefulness. Never less than delicious, this is fine wine at its charming best, elegant, ethereal rather than muscle-bound, but strong enough to carry itself with poise. It should develop into a really lovely wine once the fruit develops some bottle age complexities.

1991

13% alc/vol; Cabernet Sauvignon, Merlot, Cabernet Franc; Te Mata district, Hawke's Bay region; hand picked 8–27 April 1991.
Winemaker: Peter Cowley
Best drinking: 2000–2021

From the first this is most impressive wine, its dark, very deep, cerise-trimmed, almost blackened red promising depths and substance that are subsequently delivered with consummate style and elegance. The bouquet is full and deep, with a blackberry intensity which has a thick meatiness about it, mingled with wafts of spice and very finely textured oak, but has such life that it conveys an impression of virility and clarity. A great, sweet body of flavour sweeps across the palate, carrying too much flavour and texture to be easily isolated and contained, its richness verging on creamy, with a silky-satin tension giving it a sensuality that lifts the flavours up from their deep heart. Backing all this is some fine, firm oak and an immense framework of gravelly, softly abrasive, black cherry-flavoured tannins that give the wine the substance it needs to support such glamorous, wide-ranging fruit. Although it has the Coleraine keynote of freshness that imparts a lively fruit clarity, there is more chunky chocolatey, ripe, plum-like warmth here, fat characteristics that could push it out of proportion, but they never do, even at this young age.

Still a baby, it is already an impressive drink, but the future promises something spectacular, when all that fruit is resolved into a myriad of flavour subtleties and nuances, adding to the dazzle of the palate, and giving even more flavour and lingering elegance to the long, tasty finish. In spite of its stature, however, this remains an exquisitely delicious wine, giving everything to the drinker from fragrance, to flavour and texture, to memorable finish. Fine and fabulous.

VIDAL RESERVE CABERNET SAUVIGNON

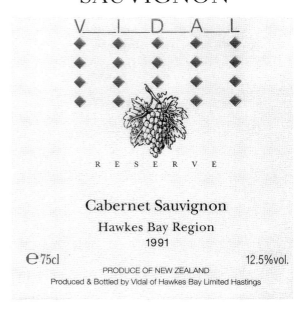

VIDAL

R E S E R V E

Cabernet Sauvignon

Hawkes Bay Region
1991

℮ 75cl   12.5%vol.

PRODUCE OF NEW ZEALAND
Produced & Bottled by Vidal of Hawkes Bay Limited Hastings

The prestige label under the Vidals part of the Villa Maria group, these Reserve reds, both straight Cabernet Sauvignon and the Cabernet/ Merlot blend, are arguably the finest of this company's highly regarded red wines, with illustrious competition records and widespread critical acclaim.

1987

12.1% alc/vol; 100% Cabernet Sauvignon; Hawke's Bay region; harvested 29 April 1987; aged for 18 months in 225-litre French oak barriques.
Winemaker: Kate Radburnd
Best drinking: 1995–98

Deep, ripe, rich mahogany colour, with a beautiful fragrance to the point of being perfumed, set with delicious oak and filled from the centre with nuances of aniseed and liquorice, a trace of violets and flashes of cassis-bright fruit. A very plausible wine, dry and deep with fruit-based flavours, bright tones and only a faint jar of green tannin, it persuades your senses with a silky stream of complexities that conclude with a long, aromatic finish dripping charm and elegance. Almost all the components of classy red wine are here, from ripe fruit to expensive oak, beautifully crafted into an elongated, easy shape that swoops onto your palate and carries it away. Fussy tasters may quibble about a general lightness that leaves the wine just short of warmth, and slightly coarse, one-dimensional tannins, but these are afterthoughts, only found if there is a suspension of pleasure. Altogether a poised, graceful wine that is as long as any enthusiast could expect, with beautifully integrated flavours and an ethereal spirit of lightness.

1989

12% alc/vol; 100% Cabernet Sauvignon; Hawke's Bay region; harvested 5 April 1989; aged for 18 months in 225-litre French oak barriques.
Winemaker: Kate Radburnd
Best drinking: 1995–98

Dark, deep red with a mahogany edge to it and a smoky oak bouquet that hides some slightly vegetal meatiness underneath its fragrant high points. The warm and fruit-laden palate is still fresh, with some lovely tannins that build up through the wine to a peak of gruff graininess which holds the almost solid fruit flavours through into a long, tasty finish. There is quiet warmth in the middle, and a chocolate-like texture, but these are fighting with a green character that persists throughout, and an intrusive acidity that seems out of kilter with the warmer tones at the wine's heart. Clean, fresh and tasty.

1991

12.5% alc/vol; 100% Cabernet Sauvignon; Hawke's Bay region; aged for 20 months in 225-litre French oak barriques.
Winemaker: Elise Montgomery
Best drinking: 1997–2001

Dark, deep, cerise-edged red wine with a darkly oaky nose, rich with aromas of stewed plums and a resilient meatiness that is fringed with green. Chocolate-textured wine, backed with clean freshness and lively, firm, ripely juicy fruit flavours that give it an excellent fruit dimension from beginning to end, neatly complemented by smoky, fine-grained oak. A very steady wine, strangely loose in character, but its lovely fruit keeps it up in the high-class category—fruit

flavours, aromas and texture that speak of good grapes, with the extra gloss of smart, rich oak. It still seems very young, and would benefit from a few more years of bottle age to allow the extra dimension of flavour complexity to tart up the fruit.

VIDAL RESERVE CABERNET/MERLOT

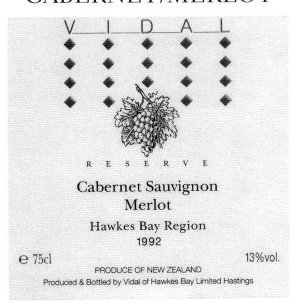

The companion wine to the above, this has an only slightly shorter list of awards and trophies. The 1987 wine is the most decorated of all New Zealand's red wines, having won Wine of the Year at the International Smallmakers Competition in Sydney, as well as gold medals in London, Sydney, Hobart, California, and twice in the Air New Zealand Wine Awards.

1987

12.4% alc/vol; 85% Cabernet Sauvignon, 15% Merlot; Hawke's Bay region; harvested 29 April 1987; aged for 19 months in 225-litre French oak barriques.
Winemaker: Kate Radburnd
Best drinking: 1995–99

Bright, moderately deep, tawny-tinged mahogany with a distinctive whiff of oak furniture on the nose, some toast-like subtleties and a charming concoction of lively soft fruit, vanilla and mild spice fragrances. Very soft and sweetly charming on the palate, suave to the point of seductiveness, with a deep well of fruit clarity that is like cassis in the intensity of blackcurrant freshness and flavour, kept company by a latticework of sophisticated oak which supports the undeniable elegance of this wine. It is fruit flavour and oak right through, warmed up nicely and enriched by some cosy textures in the middle, and a finish that keeps all that delicious ripe fruit in full view. Superbly elegant wine, fruit and oak beautifully crafted together, still tasting fresh but enjoying the advantages of bottle age that give it a cosmopolitan edge. A natural beauty, dressed with style.

1989

12.5% alc/vol; 64% Cabernet Sauvignon, 36% Merlot; Hawke's Bay region; harvested 5 April 1989; aged for 18 months in 225-litre French and German oak barriques.
Winemaker: Kate Radburnd
Best drinking: 1996–99

Jolly red mahogany-coloured wine, with a charred, smoky herbaceousness on a nose that is solid, yet shows a brisk mineral note. Very supple, sweetly flavoured, ripe, mellow palate that is piled with lovely fruit in layers and layers of juicy flavour, smooth texture, complemented by traces of fine oak and a supportive green-mineral edge. Very attractive wine, with so much lovely fruit that you almost forget anything else in it, even as you taste, but there is some nicely grainy tannin, soft-edged and lingering. At the end, though, there is an assertive greenness that pushes even this fruit into the background. After the gushing softness of the palate, this hardness is a discordant note in an otherwise attractive wine, but it is the memories of the fruit that linger in spite of this.

1990

13% alc/vol; 57% Cabernet Sauvignon, 43% Merlot; Hawke's Bay region; aged for 20 months in French oak barrels, following completion of fermentation in barrel.
Winemaker: Kate Radburnd
Best drinking: 1997–2001

Dark, deep garnet-mahogany, glowing rich colour introduces this very fleshy, ripe, supple-feeling wine

that seems to be more about texture than flavour, but has enough to suggest that some more time could unleash sufficient complexity to turn it into a winner. There is deep, somewhat restrained, ripe, mellow fruit on the nose, masked somewhat by charred oak and a tang of minerals. Very warm-hearted wine, set off by a fresh character which implies rather than tastes of specific fruit, but has a very nice, spicy oak touch to it and some gently grainy, quietly building tannin leading to a lingering finish that shows of the oak again, and that undercurrent of subtle fruit. Deep and tightly knit, the promise seems to be there in its depth and tidy construction.

1991

13% alc/vol; Hawke's Bay region; aged for 20 months in 225-litre French oak barriques.
Winemaker: Elise Montgomerie
Best drinking: 1996–99

Very dark, ripe cherry-coloured wine, chocolatey on the nose with a fruit centre like something from a confectioner but without the heady sweetness. Concentrated and intense at the centre, suave, fresh and mellow at once on the palate, it has spotty tannins that are angular but deep, and hold everything together to a charming, fruit-tinged finish. Warm and festive wine, a touch simple but showing off its lovely fruit, suggesting that with a bit more time, it could gain in complexity and attain the sophistication needed by truly fine wine.

1992

13% alc/vol; 52% Cabernet Sauvignon, 48% Merlot; Hawke's Bay region; aged for 18 months in 225-litre French oak barriques.
Winemaker: Elise Montgomerie
Best drinking: 1996–98

Deep, rosy, magenta-coloured wine, it tastes as youthfully attractive as it looks, with a chocolate-textured and flavoured neatness and density that is rather intriguing. Cherry chocolates on the nose, infused with oak, and lashings of sweet fruit on the palate give it a bouncy, scrumptious character, focused by a concentrated heart that is moderate in depth and length. Tannins have a strange adolescent angularity, moderated somewhat by the aromatic fruit character that rides right through the wine. A very attractive, forward, pretty young thing.

VILLA MARIA RESERVE CABERNET SAUVIGNON

Villa Maria's reputation for high-quality reds was made through the later vintages of the 1980s with a succession of impressive Reserve label, award-winning wines, based on ripe, bright fruit flavours and extravagant oak treatment. They have been on stage collecting medals and trophies so frequently that it could fairly be said that Villa Maria have set the competition standard for red wines in New Zealand.

1987

12% alc/vol; 100% Cabernet Sauvignon; Ihumatao district, Auckland region; aged for 14 months in new 225-litre French and German oak barriques.
Winemaker: Kym Milne
Best drinking: 1995–98

Dark, just becoming mahogany, with a solid bouquet that has heart, but is not lively. Very deep flavours of fruit, with a surface trimmed by oak, some warm substance, and herby edges. Pleasant tannins, ripish, show up at the finish, and have a presence, although not a flavour, in the middle of the wine, but there is a lack of resonance in this rather stolid wine. Fresh, but neither bright nor warm enough to be either lively or substantial. Good, honest fruit-based wine.

1989

12.5% alc/vol; 100% Cabernet Sauvignon; Hawke's Bay region; aged for 18 months in new 225-litre French and American oak barriques.
Winemaker: Kym Milne
Best drinking: 1995–99

Deep, dark mahogany filtered colour, glossy, with herbaceousness on the nose and layers of oak through which suggestions of warm fruit protrude. Sweet fruit flavour by the bucketful on the palate, lashings of sweet-savoury oak and a frisk of green on the palate, with the green pushing its way forward at the finish. Clear, clean, jolly, fruity wine, it has a feeling of simple luxury in the succulence of its fruit, and a touch of class in its expensive oak.

1990

12.5% alc/vol; 100% Cabernet Sauvignon; Hawke's Bay region; aged for 16 months in new and used 225-litre French oak barriques.
Winemaker: Kym Milne
Best drinking: 1995–97

Dark, deep, plum-tinged, with an unusual character in its aromatic bouquet, alongside some clever oak and mild suggestions of ripe, berryish fruit. Sweet fruit surges through the palate, fresh and fragrant, lined with oak and nicely balanced by lively acidity. Good, friendly, fruit-flavoured wine that is unusually perfumed right through, it has a lot of charm.

1991

13% alc/vol; 100% Cabernet Sauvignon; Hawke's Bay region; aged for 16 months in new and used 225-litre French oak barriques.
Winemaker: Kym Milne
Best drinking: 1995–98

Again very deep, dark and coloured like ripe summer plums, this wine has a nose that shows a reserve which has not been typical so far, dark and deep with blackberry fruit hints but without any obvious extravagances other than a brisk seasoning of sawdusty oak. Blackberries are a definite presence on the palate, which is much livelier with fruit freshness and a glossy, ripe tension that produces a sense of length and elegance at the heart of the wine. There is noticeable warmth here, too, but it is restrained by the freshness of acidity provided by the fruit flavours. An almost classy wine, lovely in its fruit charm, with an expensive twist of oak, it is a delicious drink.

VILLA MARIA RESERVE CABERNET/MERLOT

The other of the Villa Maria prize-winning giants, this, too, is a fruit-based, oak-embellished wine of impressive colour and flavour.

1987

12% alc/vol; 80% Cabernet Sauvignon, 20% Merlot;
80% Hawke's Bay region, 20% Ihumatao district; harvested
in Auckland 13 April, Hawke's Bay 4 and 23 April 1987;
aged for 14 months in 225-litre French and German
oak barriques.

Winemaker: Kym Milne
Best drinking: 1995–98

Lovely dark, ripe colour, with sweet, bottle age mature, cassis-like fruit lifted by a freshness of fragrance that is oak-lined and shows an interesting beetroot aroma complexity. The palate is beautifully supple, with a heart of freshness and a lift that almost tingles with life among the bright fruit flavours which have a mellow, mature, vaguely plumlike character about them. Brisk tannins surround this core of light, delicious flavour, adding to the impression of liveliness, but imposing a rather astringent, tough finish on an otherwise delightful wine.

1989

11.5% alc/vol; 68% Cabernet Sauvignon, 32% Merlot;
Hawke's Bay region; harvested 20 and 29 March 1989;
aged for 16 months in 225-litre French and German
oak barriques.
Winemaker: Kym Milne
Best drinking: 1995–96

Dark, healthy-looking red wine with a sweet, tobacco-lined, fragrant bouquet that has oak and cassis fruit characters. A fresh and fruity mouthful, mellowed and made more interesting by the effects of bottle age, but kept lively by its juicy dimension, and a lively acidity that give it a white wine feel in spite of its colour. Lively, talented wine, its fruit and oak nature full of delicious invitation.

1990

12% alc/vol; 85% Cabernet Sauvignon, 15% Merlot; 85%
Marlborough region, 15% Hawke's Bay region; aged for 20
months in new year-old 225-litre French oak barriques.
Winemaker: Kym Milne
Best drinking: 1995–96

Dark, deeply coloured wine, with an enticing, almost rich, chocolate inflection to its smoky oaked, herby nose that is dark with promise and already pretty with sweet, aromatic nuances. Nicely weighted, supple, fresh palate, with fruit flavours and mild, attractive tannins that swell to an abrasive, dry, somewhat austere but flavoury, finish that is crisped up with acid. Its lovely fruit made angular by structural components, this remains a very pleasing drink.

1991

13% alc/vol; 78% Cabernet Sauvignon, 22% Merlot;
Hawke's Bay region; harvested 25 April 1991; aged for
16 months in new and year-old 225-litre French and
German oak barriques.
Winemaker: Kym Milne
Best drinking: 1996–2001

Darkish red, still showing its magenta-tinged youth. Blackcurranty, berryish aromas on the nose are building a smart bouquet with the help of some fragrant oak. A generally quiet, pretty, light and supple palate, it is very fresh with attractive fruit and a pleasant tang of acidity, some shafts of oak giving it a structural presence beyond the acid. Mild tannins help through to the finish, keeping the flavour lingering without disturbing the pretty fruit. There is elegance here, charm, and a sense of proportion that delivers grace, with depth and warmth enough to suggest some good drinking in the future.

1992
MERLOT/CABERNET FRANC

13% alc/vol; 78% Merlot, 22% Cabernet Franc; Hawke's
Bay region; aged for 15 months in new and used 225-litre
French and German oak barriques.
Winemaker: Kym Milne
Best drinking: 1995

Moderate to light red, tinged with a plum-like purple, this light, fragrant wine is slightly herby, well oaked, with the tang of redcurrants on both bouquet and palate. Smooth and fresh, its redcurrant character supported by other berry flavours and lovely oak, it has a quiet charm that is a result of its pervasive mildness. A very pleasant glass.

PINOT NOIR

PINOT NOIR WAS CERTAINLY IN NEW ZEALAND VERY EARLY; IT MAY EVEN HAVE been brought across by Busby in the first importation of winemaking grapes in the early 1830s. The first government viticulturist, Romeo Bragato, commented on it favourably when observing vineyards during the 1890s, and he made successful wine with it at his experimental winery at Te Kauwhata.

By the turn of the century it was growing in both Hawke's Bay and the Wairarapa, where it was being used to make reasonable quality, light red wine, and it has been a part of the Mission Vineyards in Hawke's Bay since at least the end of the 1880s. It never stood out as a most exciting variety at the time, and nor were the winemaking skills of those pioneers quite up to transforming Pinot Noir into the sort of wine that would turn heads.

In the fine wine era it has been a late starter, primarily because there was limited success with it in the establishment years of the 1960s and 1970s, when it was treated by many winemakers as another version of Cabernet Sauvignon and vinified accordingly. During those years Pinot Noir was invariably overcropped, allowed to grow too vigorously, and made with little regard for its delicacy or fragile softness as a wine.

It is only since the development of Martinborough in the Wairarapa, with its group of dedicated Pinot Noir winemakers, that progress has been made towards refining viticultural techniques to grow the variety and its many clones successfully in New Zealand. In parallel, winemakers have also made great advances in developing winemaking processes that will use these grapes to best advantage, and at last a truly fine tradition of New Zealand Pinot Noir is beginning to take shape.

The process has involved winemakers travelling to California, Oregon and Burgundy to gather experience in growing, and making wine from, Pinot Noir. These and countless trials with trellising systems, crop load and the meticulous detail of various clones' performance according to rootstock, soil type and climate, have brought significant progress. Added to this has been accumulated experience in the critical field of oak aging, combined with sophisticated fermentation skills, all of which have been shared widely through New Zealand's winemaking community.

This sharing is as responsible as any factor for the dramatic improvement in the overall quality of New Zealand Pinot Noir, for it is not just the number of fine Pinot Noirs that have grown in recent years, but the general standard of all Pinot Noirs. The annual Pinot Noir conference, where winemakers taste, criticise and share their experiences, has become a catalyst for excellence, spreading enthusiasm as well as technology to every corner of the New Zealand industry.

There are currently more than 20 clones of Pinot Noir in New Zealand, of which the one known as Gamay Beaujolais and another called Bachtobel were the most commonly planted in the establishment period. Comte Odart and Reveney are the oldest surviving clones from the pioneer era, and Pommard (UCD5), AM 10/5 and 2/10 are currently favourites among the élite Pinot Noir producers, along with the 'Abel' clone which, legend has it, came from a Grand Cru vineyard in the Vosne-Romanée district of Burgundy during the 1960s.

Pinot Noir is a major component of the fine wine industry in New Zealand, with over 7 per cent of the total vineyard area, and significantly more of that portion dedicated to fine wine production. Most of this is used for the production of sparkling wine; Marlborough has the largest proportion, followed by Hawke's Bay. The vineyards of Wairarapa, Nelson and Central Otago provide Pinot Noir almost exclusively for red wine production, however, and in these regions can be found the élite producers who have established the strong culture of quality for this variety.

ATA RANGI
PINOT NOIR

Ata Rangi is a pioneer of premium Pinot Noir wine in New Zealand, one of the Martinborough originals who recognised this Wairarapa district's potential for growing Pinot Noir grapes. Early on, owner Clive Paton secured supplies of the so-called Abel clone from the Auckland vineyard of Malcolm Abel, and his wine has subsequently been based primarily on this, although he has recently followed the mixed clone ideas and planted Pommard and 10/5 among others.

A consistent trophy winner in local wine competitions, the seductive, perfumed Ata Rangi style, tempered as it is by the fierce competition with its Martinborough contemporaries, continues to lead the way for Pinot Noir hopefuls throughout New Zealand.

1986

14.4% alc/vol; 98% Pinot Noir, Abel clone, 2% Cabernet Sauvignon; Martinborough district, Wairarapa region; 14–16 months in French oak, 25% new, 75% old.
Winemaker: Clive Paton
Best drinking: 1995–97

A rich, glossy mahogany, this wine still has good depth of colour. The bouquet is faintly aromatic, savoury, with a note that suggests prunes, caramel, even tar, all of which is confounded by a sweet, light palate that is rather pretty and fresh. A tidy wine, a bit rough at the finish, but with lively acidity still and a faint herbal note all tempered by attractive bottle age complexity.

1987

13% alc/vol; 100% Pinot Noir, Abel clone; Martinborough district, Wairarapa region; 14–16 months in French oak, 25% new, 75% old.
Winemaker: Clive Paton
Best drinking: 1995–98

Moderately deep, light mahogany-coloured wine with a dusty, mineral nose that shows traces of tomato sauce character. It is anything but a dusty mouthful, however, having a hearty dash of fruit sweetness and some pretty, savoury complexities that are quite delicate. There is a feeling of freshness about it, and some slightly awkward tannins that leave the finish rather dishevelled, but it is delightful in the middle, delicate and suave as Pinot Noir should be.

1988

13% alc/vol; 100% Pinot Noir, Abel clone; Martinborough district, Wairarapa region; 14–16 months in French oak, 25% new, 75% old.
Winemaker: Clive Paton
Best drinking: 1995–96

Lightish colour, with a tawny edge and a complex bouquet that is a collection of dusty, herbal, savoury notes which at times suggests dried mushrooms. Mellow oak and sweet fruit in the mouth, complex still and quite fragrant, it makes mention of mushrooms and sage in a rather eloquent collection of flavours that mix well the savoury and chewy fruit characters. As with the earlier vintages, the best part of this wine is in the middle, but it is a very good middle indeed, and one that invites you back for its special performance, which ends on a light, slightly austere note, without any of the sweet fruit flavours that charm in the middle.

1989

13% alc/vol; 100% Pinot Noir, Abel clone; Martinborough district, Wairarapa region; 14–16 months in French oak, 25% new, 75% old.
Winemaker: Clive Paton
Best drinking: 1995–99

There is still some purple lingering at the edge of this glossy, mahogany-hued wine. Purple, with a hint of the famous horse manure nose that some Burgundies boast, rich and fragrant with mushrooms and minerals to keep it company. Chunky wine, with sweet fruit flavour concentrated in its heart and a rather tough demeanour, but the tannins are more sophisticated than in the earlier vintages, in better harmony with the whole wine, and the finish is longer, more satisfying, with fruit flavour and traces of mushroom and oak. A tasty, pleasing wine of good character.

1989
'RESERVE'

13% alc/vol; 100% Pinot Noir, Abel clone; Martinborough district, Wairarapa region; 14–16 months in French oak, 50% new, 50% old.
Winemaker: Clive Paton
Best drinking: 1995–2000

Concentrated fruit aromas and full, aromatic oak make an instant impact for this hearty red-purple wine. Oak and cherries that just roll on into the palate, which is quite graceful in spite of its bold fragrance, flavours moderated by nuances of mushrooms and spice, and buoyed by a steady texture that has grainy tannin and sweet fruit in partnership. This tannin also gives the finish length and a gravelly feel that extends the sweet fruit flavours and aromas to the very end. Fresh without being too clean and crisp, this is a wine that makes its texture work for it, supporting and enhancing the flavours of fruit, oak and bottle age complexity.

1990

13% alc/vol; 100% Pinot Noir, 70–80% Abel clone, balance Pommard, 10/5 and some others; Martinborough district, Wairarapa region; hand picked 25 March–4 April 1990; 14–16 months in French oak, 50% new, 50% old.
Winemaker: Clive Paton
Best drinking: 1995–97

Healthy-looking wine, shiny red with hints of mahogany, it has a lovely perfumed, fragrant bouquet that is very attractive and wholesome, with a dab of manure and smoke for interest and great depths of sweet, frothy fruit aroma. A mouthful of sweet, suave wine follows, not fruity but full of fruit feel and a supple silkiness that is almost slick, smooth, soft. Quite delicious, sexy stuff that feels as it tastes: a duet of sensations each with its own subtleties and mouth-watering succulence. Beautiful for red wine, rather soft and gentle at the end, but the flavour lingers as a sweet memory, complete with fading perfume and a slight twist of greenness that suggests it could improve with a little more bottle age.

1991

13% alc/vol; 100% Pinot Noir, 70–80% Abel clone, balance Pommard, 10/5 and some others; Martinborough district, Wairarapa region; hand picked 31 March–13 April 1991; 14–16 months in French oak, 25% new, 75% old.
Winemaker: Clive Paton
Best drinking: 1996–2005

A healthy, purplish red wine, savoury and spicy with moments of smokiness, suggestions of compost in its pleasant bouquet. The sweet, slightly intense palate has good depth of flavour and hints of milk powder and more of that spicy smoke character, with tannins that are quite assertive. This gives the whole wine an angular feel, especially at the finish, but the essence of fruit fills in the corners and hangs on until the end to give a balancing flavour. Just at a difficult age, but with enough tidy bits to suggest that it could mature into a more mellow, attractive personality.

1992

13% alc/vol; 100% Pinot Noir, 70–80% Abel clone, balance Pommard, 10/5 and some others; Martinborough district, Wairarapa region; hand picked 1 April–19 April 1992; 14–16 months in French oak, 25% new, 75% old.
Winemaker: Clive Paton
Best drinking: 1996–2002

Very attractive, dark red wine that is deep and glossy with purple-cerise highlights and a superbly fragrant, perfumed softness suggesting violets and warm summers. Smells of liquorice and warm, spicy oak complement this perfume, and the clear sweetness of fruit flavour that just leaps into your mouth, mildly viscous, deep and juicy with ideas of ripe cherries and a hint cinnamon. Another beautiful wine, not big but layered with sensuous fruit, spiced oak and warm, mellow tannins like some exotic pastry, delicately rich and oh so tempting. With more bottle age, it should gain in complexity and subtlety to become a very special wine indeed, having a fine structure for the satisfaction of technocrats, and enough sensual charm to titillate the most demanding hedonist.

1993

13% alc/vol; 100% Pinot Noir, 70–80% Abel clone,
balance Pommard, 10/5 and some others; Martinborough
district, Wairarapa region; hand picked 18 April–4 May
1993; 14–16 months in French oak, 25% new, 75% old.
Winemaker: Clive Paton
Best drinking: 1997–2001

Moderately dark, deep young red with a fragrant bouquet showing the perfume of Pinot Noir, and just a touch of minerals, compost and some savoury spice. The fruit characters of both aroma and flavour form a patina of intensity for a wine that is generally cool and light, and this intensity, along with a dash of earthy, mushroom nuances, imparts a certain warmth, a cosy sweetness that harmonises with the furry tannins and oak spiciness. Pleasant, attractive wine, quite fragrant, it lingers fresh and clear while showing some very sophisticated winemaking that would have been a great benefit to earlier vintages.

DRY RIVER
PINOT NOIR

PINOT NOIR
1993
DRY RIVER
Martinborough
UNFILTERED
№ 2029

BOTTLED BY DRY RIVER WINES LTD, PURUATANGA RD, MARTINBOROUGH
PRODUCE OF NEW ZEALAND
℮ 750ml   CONTAINS PRESERVATIVE (220)   12.5% VOL

Pinot Noir does not have the role of standard bearer for this winery that it has for the other Martinborough producers, and it has become a part of the Dry River repertoire after the winery's reputation was already established with an excellent sequence of Pinot Gris and Riesling wines. However, although Dry River Pinot Noir does not have as long a pedigree as the other leading Martinborough Pinots, it has quickly asserted itself as an worthy member of the Pinot Noir élite in New Zealand, an active, enthusiastic and competitive collection of talented winemakers who believe they are unravelling the Pinot Noir mystery.

1989

13.5% alc/vol; 100% Pinot Noir, 10/5 clone;
Martinborough district, Wairarapa region; hand picked
24 March 1989.
Winemaker: Neil McCallum
Best drinking: 1996–99

A remarkably youthful-looking red of moderate depth, bright and clear with a blue flush. The pretty, floral-cherry, faintly spiced bouquet enhances this sense of youth, as does the big, soft, sweet palate. A fruit-based wine, although not overtly fruity, it has an abundance of sweet fruit character and cherryish flavours that are merely seasoned by spicy oak, char and a furry coating of tannin that lingers on at the end. Warm and straightforward, this lively red seems to be a mere 10 minutes old, rather than the mature five years it is.

1990

12.6% alc/vol; 100% Pinot Noir, 95% 10/5 clone, 5%
Pommard; Martinborough district, Wairarapa region; hand
picked 29 March 1990.
Winemaker: Neil McCallum
Best drinking: 1995–97

A bright, cheery, shiny red with a smoked cherry and spice nose that is fresh yet tempered with some bottle age nuances. A soft, sweet, cherry-like mouthful that is supple and developing savoury complexities to complement the juicy body of cherry-flavoured fruit. It has some neat tannin fur in the middle that builds nicely towards the end, giving the palate an extra dimension, an astringency which also relieves and modulates the sweet fruit texture. Moderately light but very even wine, it has an excellent, fragrant finish that lingers delightfully, all fruit and mellow harmonies which precisely reflect the wine.

1991

13.8% alc/vol; 100% Pinot Noir, 85% 10/5 clone,
15% Pommard; Martinborough district, Wairarapa region;
hand picked 30 March 1991.
Winemaker: Neil McCallum
Best drinking: 1997–2002

This wine has an even, cautious red-purple colour and a clear, softly fruity fragrance, mellow and spiced with oak to a point of sensuous grace. Although not an abundant wine, it has a warm heart and fine, soft flavours that are quite deep and penetrating, contributing to its charm, which is enhanced by a nice balance, with all its various parts in graceful harmony. It still needs to gain a measure of richness and mellow flavour, which should happen with more bottle age, but it is already shaping up to be a wine for the boudoir—sweetly fragrant, made for seduction with delicacy.

1992

13% alc/vol; 100% Pinot Noir, 80% 10/5 clone,
20% Pommard; Martinborough district, Wairarapa region;
hand picked 23 April 1992.
Winemaker: Neil McCallum
Best drinking: 1996–2000

A light cherrywood-coloured wine, bright, with a savoury, spicy bouquet that has some lovely nuances of soft, smoky oak, and a gentle whiff of cherry. Very cherry-flavoured on first taste, sweet, supple, with a trace of concentration and pretty softness that fades off at the finish. Pleasant, appealing wine, quite fine with a neat taste of fruit right at the end, it suggests that more bottle age is needed for greater complexity, but it certainly has all the grace of a young thoroughbred.

1993

12.5% alc/vol; 100% Pinot Noir, 75% 10/5 clone,
25% Pommard; Martinborough district, Wairarapa region;
hand picked 20–30 April 1993.
Winemaker: Neil McCallum
Best drinking: 1995–98

Dark, cherry-red wine, the sort that winks at the brim given half a chance, it also has cherry in abundance on the nose, with a hint of mushroom and some delightfully spicy oak. Mellow and charming, this has oodles of sweet fruit, quite juicy, certainly promising, and the advantage of some pleasant tannins that

gradually make their presence felt towards the end. Altogether soft, fruit-textured wine that is larded with tannins and attractive oak. Not big wine, it never overstates itself, the mark of a good winemaker.

MARTINBOROUGH VINEYARD PINOT NOIR

Martinborough Vineyard

PINOT NOIR

1993

13% VOL 750ml

PRODUCED AND BOTTLED BY MARTINBOROUGH VINEYARD LTD, PRINCESS STREET, MARTINBOROUGH, NEW ZEALAND.

PRODUCE OF NEW ZEALAND

Martinborough Vineyard Pinot Noir is the wine that showed it was possible to make respectable Pinot Noir in New Zealand, even as it was proving that the original wine pioneers' faith in Martinborough's potential to grow high-quality Pinot Noir was well placed. Ever since the first vintage in 1984, this wine has attracted the attention of wine enthusiasts, first for its obvious fruit quality, and then for the increasing sophistication of its making, an ongoing refinement of style and technique that has turned it into one of the most talked about wines in the Pinot Noir world, a community that stretches from Burgundy to Victoria, via Oregon, Washington and Carneros. For many people, Martinborough Vineyard Pinot Noir is the shape of New World Pinot Noir to come.

1984

13% alc/vol; 100% Pinot Noir; Martinborough district, Wairarapa region; hand picked from 22 April 1984. Winemaker: Russell Schultz

A wine of moderately deep, dark mahogany colour with a slight haze through it, it has a very restrained, sullen nose, but there is a still a sense of the fresh fruit flavours this wine once had. Sweet and astringent, with quite a hard finish, there is still some feel of fruit in a palate, a light juiciness that remembers when it was a more beautiful wine.

1985

12% alc/vol; 100% Pinot Noir; Martinborough district, Wairarapa region; hand picked from 3 April 1985. Winemaker: Larry McKenna Best drinking: 1995

Dark red, bright and clear, with a remarkable touch of purple amid the mahogany. Spicy and stewed prunes aromas are features of the bouquet, which is somewhat one-dimensional, sturdy rather than fragrant. The stewed fruit character is also a part of the palate, although it tastes fresher and has a pleasant, soft, quite smooth texture. This gives way to some hard astringency at the finish, which roughens the wine up somewhat, leaving a coarse, austere impression, somewhat at odds with the pleasing flavours at its heart.

1986

12.2% alc/vol; 100% Pinot Noir; Martinborough district, Wairarapa region; hand picked from 9 April 1986. Winemaker: Larry McKenna Best drinking: 1995

Bright and tawny-mahogany in colour, this wine also has a tawny bouquet that is ripe with round, gamy, leathery aromas kept alive by an edge of freshness. Soft to taste, it has a mild sweetness that combines with mellow flavours and mature warmth to make a tender wine, gently attractive, comfortable to drink.

1987

11.4% alc/vol; 100% Pinot Noir; Martinborough district, Wairarapa region; hand picked from 11 April 1987. Winemaker: Larry McKenna Best drinking: 1995

With the colour of polished mahogany, and a bouquet fragrant with matured, smoky oak and suggestions of raspberries, this is a wine with immediate promise that is mostly satisfied by its supple, easy palate. Raspberries can be found here, and a good measure of charred oak that has been mellowed by bottle age, kept fresh and juicy by lively fruit characters almost to the end. The finish, however, is somewhat astringent, drying out to a dusty end without any shadow of that lovely fruit.

1988

13.5% alc/vol; 100% Pinot Noir; Martinborough district, Wairarapa region; hand picked from 30 March 1988. Winemaker: Larry McKenna Best drinking: 1995–96

A lightish-coloured wine, red with a hint of cherry-wood to show its age, but serious from then on, with a deep, subtle nose and closely worked palate that is quite fine. Investigation of that dark bouquet brings up touches of charred, gently spiced oak, sweetness but not fruitiness, and even a vague suggestion of chocolate. Lovely sweet fruit on the warm palate, undefined, but even, soft and fat, almost chewy were it not for its smooth texture, and deftly embellished with a dab or two of fine oak and quietly swelling tannins that give a mellow, grainy texture to the finish of the wine, balancing its natural softness, and giving it a bit of a kick right at the end. An excellent bottle, intriguing, satisfying, quietly complex.

1989

12.5% alc/vol; 100% Pinot Noir; Martinborough district, Wairarapa region; hand picked from 10 March 1989. Winemaker: Larry McKenna Best drinking: 1995–97

Bright in colour, healthy and red, with a bouquet that is a neat balance of fruit and oak which is aromatic rather than fragrant and, in spite of the fine oak and obviously sweet fruit, quite simple. Very soft and fruity to taste, with chocolate and coffee characters and a plump, suave texture. Attractive right through to its gentle finish it shows plenty of sweetness which combines with that succulent feel to make a very pleasing wine, even if it lacks a little freshness and astringency to keep its flavours lively.

1990

11.5% alc/vol; 100% Pinot Noir; Martinborough district, Wairarapa region; hand picked from 28 March 1990; unfiltered.
Winemaker: Larry McKenna
Best drinking: 1995–97

A good, solid red colour that is turning to mahogany at the edges. The light, fresh bouquet is a fragrant collection of enchanting aromas, slightly sweaty, leather, earth, mushrooms, char, five spice powder and even a suggestion of lanolin, all embedded in a cloth of sweet fruit. Delightfully light and fresh to taste, it has a nice pattern of intricate flavours and some gently aroused tannins that hold on to the flavour right to the finish, which retains its fragrant, almost perfumed character. Very deft use of oak and tannin in this wine turn it into something better than the sum of its parts.

1991

13% alc/vol; 100% Pinot Noir; Martinborough district, Wairarapa region; hand picked from 8 April 1991.
Winemaker: Larry McKenna
Best drinking: 1995–99

A tinge of magenta brightens up the moderate red colour of this wine, giving it a youthful glow. The bouquet is warm with animal aromas and a hint of earth and mushrooms, giving it a carnal air enhanced by the suave feel. Flavours of mushrooms and some concentrated fruit are enhanced by lovely, spicy oak and some really fine tannins that serve to build a long, lingering, vaguely earthy, fragrant finish which completes a very satisfying wine. Beautifully made, alive with sensual suggestions and a light fruit intensity that maintains its presence throughout, it has a certain rogue earthiness, a rustic, unrefined dimension. Very good drinking in 1995.

1991
RESERVE

12.5% alc/vol; 100% Pinot Noir; Martinborough district, Wairarapa region; hand picked from 8 April 1991; unfiltered.
Winemaker: Larry McKenna
Best drinking: 1996–2000

Moderately dark, deepish red wine with a magenta cast and a deep, perfumed bouquet rich with fragrant notes that build up like layers of leaves in a pile: spice, fine oak, char, fresh berryfruit, a faint essence of black cherry, mushrooms, damp earth and coffee, all mingled and yet still slightly separate. The palate is based on a very fine concentration of fresh berry fruit flavour, non-specific but sweet and lingering, neatly laced together with lovely savoury-spicy oak and charred coffee flavours, and a hint of mushrooms and earth. These are absorbed by a lovely robe of texture which begins sweet and easy, builds up smooth, soft, dripping with juice before the fine-grained tannins provide a furry texture that lingers on, supporting a very long, fragrant finish. This is not big wine, but it has depth and is very graceful, poised, with all the parts in harmony and an entrancing balance between earth and fruit characters.

1992

12.5% alc/vol; 100% Pinot Noir; Martinborough district, Wairarapa region; hand picked from 28 April 1992; unfiltered.
Winemaker: Larry McKenna
Best drinking: 1996–98

This wine is red and tinged with magenta, and its bouquet has an interesting meaty tone, somehow bloody and sweet, with fragrances of mushrooms and raspberries amid the oak. Complex and light, with pretty fruit flavours and a distinct violet dimension that lingers from bouquet to palate to finish, giving a floral charm to the wine. Fresh, light, attractive, with tidy complexities, very supple, almost soft feel, neat use of oak and a fine tannin texture that becomes a feature as the finish lingers on and on. Beautifully crafted wine, perfectly balanced in spite of its lightness.

1993

*13% alc/vol; 100% Pinot Noir; Martinborough district,
Wairarapa region; hand picked from 4 May 1993;
unfiltered.
Winemaker: Larry McKenna
Best drinking: 1996–99*

Attractive dark cherry-red colour with a soft, sweetly mellow, fragrant bouquet that has a fresh edge of fruit aroma hinting at violets and raspberry, and some tasteful oak-spice. Fresh, clear, quite fruity wine, with moderate, raspberryish intensity in spite of its general lightness and fresh acidity. Quite softly textured within the border of freshness, supple, cool, with a coating of gentle tannins right through and a return of intensity as a tidy flavour suggestion at the very end. Very pleasant, attractive wine.

NEUDORF PINOT NOIR

The Neudorf winery has been vinifying Pinot Noir grapes from its Upper Moutere vineyards for over a decade now, but it is only recently that winemaker Tim Finn has decided to make a Pinot Noir from them. The reason for this is that the clone of Pinot grown at Neudorf was originally known in New Zealand and California as Gamay Beaujolais and, under such a misnomer, Finn used it initially to make a light, fruity, highly successful wine called Young Nicks Red.

Latterly these grapes had been part of the blend for Blackbird Valley Claret, but in 1988, after planting some clone 10/5 Pinot for future Pinot production, Finn took off a portion to make a serious attempt at Pinot Noir for the first time. The results were encouraging enough for the project to be continued, and in a very short time Neudorf Pinot Noir has become one of the finest examples of New Zealand Pinot.

1988

12% alc/vol; 100% Pinot Noir, (Gamay Beaujolais) clone; Moutere district, Nelson region; hand picked 21 April 1988; aged in used French oak for 8–9 months.
Winemaker: Tim Finn
Best drinking: 1995–96

Light mahogany red, this wine has a charry oak and fragrant, slightly perfumed bouquet that is a bit lean. There is an initial rush of sweet fruit in the mouth, and round, juicy characters, with caramel and cherry flavours. Nice wine, succulent, if rather simple and straightforward, it has a very pleasant, easy feel and perfumed character.

1990

13% alc/vol; 100% Pinot Noir, 50% Gamay Beaujolais, 50% 10/5; Moutere district, Nelson region; hand picked 31 March, 17 April 1990; aged in used French oak for 8–9 months.
Winemaker: Tim Finn
Best drinking: 1995–98

Light, cerise-edged mahogany wine, with colourful deep red tones. More sappy aromas here, with hints of minerals, cherry and forest floor characters suggestive of mushrooms, clay and damp leaves. Fragrant, with a measure of weight behind it that is also apparent on the palate, which is slick, suitably warm, with sweet cherry and sweaty, perfumed characters. Heaps of ripe fruit texture, complemented by sweaty, musky, earthy overtones, a flash of bright cherry and nicely furry tannins. Fruity, steady, pleasant wine, just a touch short on silky texture for top-class Pinot.

1991
MOUTERE PINOT NOIR

13% alc/vol; 100% Pinot Noir, 60% Gamay Beaujolais, 40% 10/5; Moutere district, Nelson region; hand picked 15 April 1991; 25% whole bunch fermented; aged in French oak, 15% new, 85% used, for 8–9 months.
Winemaker: Tim Finn
Best drinking: 1995–99

Magenta-tinted red with a cheeky splash of true pink, this wine is a delight to look at, and to inhale, for it has a pervasively soft, perfumed aroma seasoned with char, hints of earthy mushrooms and flickerings of sweet cherry fruit. Ripe and glossy, it has the sensual

texture to match its animal and fruit aromas, warmly recalling Christmas cake, musk and cherry sweet delights. Nicely weighted, with depth and a rub of furry tannin that helps juicy flavours and intimate texture to linger on beautifully at the end. Fine, sexy wine, with a neat touch of elegance.

1992
MOUTERE PINOT NOIR

13% alc/vol; 100% Pinot Noir, 70% Gamay Beaujolais, 30% 10/5; Moutere district, Nelson region; hand picked 21 April 1992; 25% whole bunch fermented, long fermentation on skins; aged in French oak, 20% new and 80% used, for 8–9 months.
Winemaker: Tim Finn
Best drinking: 1996–2000

Perfumed, fresh aromas redolent of hand cream, charcoal, mushrooms and cherries gurgle up from this dark crimson-purple wine. These are matched with slick, warm, strokable texture, depth and weight suitable for fine wine, allied to ripe, black cherry-flavoured tannins that give the wine resonance and momentum right through the palate and on into a lingering finish. A glossy beauty, it already has a fine amalgam of characters that seem to be whole, rather than a collection of parts, but it is still young and vigorous, with hints of green among the fruit. Already impressive, particularly its texture, and it will be even more so with some bottle age character complexities to add to its energetic gathering of fruit and forest floor flavours.

1993

12.5% alc/vol; 100% Pinot Noir, 80% Gamay Beaujolais, 20% 10/5; Moutere district, Nelson region; hand picked 29 April, 11 May, 14 May 1993; 25% whole bunch fermented, long fermentation on skins; aged in French oak, 20% new and 80% used, for 8–9 months.
Winemaker: Tim Finn
Best drinking: 1996–99

Bright, shiny cerise with dark, deeper pools of colour, this is a fragrant wine, but lacking in the perfume that marked earlier vintages. Sweet oak on the nose, but also a smooth blend of animal, musky, mushroom and cherry aromas, characters that are found in the palate as well, where they seem immersed in a sweet well of fresh fruit. Savoury mushroom and fruit tones linger on through soft, mellow-flavoured tannins to the very end, which is long and persistent. A medium-weight wine, cool, slightly concentrated and less silky in texture, but full of flavour and tension to suggest it will grow with age into a very pleasant bottle with more than enough sex appeal.

RIPPON VINEYARD PINOT NOIR

As with some of the other leading Pinots, Rippon is a recent development, as indeed is the whole wine-growing phenomenon in Central Otago, which has a particularly short growing season. Rippon is without doubt one of the most spectacular of all vineyard sites, tucked into the shore of Lake Wanaka with magnificent views across to the Southern Alps. It also seems to be a micro-climate suited to ripening Pinot Noir, and its wines of the 1990s are among the best made from this variety in New Zealand. As experience is gained, and there are more warm vintages like 1990,

Rippon could establish itself as one of the élite producers of New Zealand red wine.

1990

13.8% alc/vol; 100% Pinot Noir, various clones; Wanaka district, Otago region; hand picked from 19 April 1990; aged in 225-litre French oak, new and one year old.
Winemaker: Rudi Bauer
Best drinking: 1995–96

A darkish, deep mahogany-coloured wine, bright and glossy with blackish lights, it is most attractive, complemented by an inviting, mellow bouquet that has the smell of old oak furniture, char and a certain savoury intensity. The taste is based on a warm core of fruit-like intensity, although the wine is no longer fruity, and a supple, mild richness that suits its soft feel. All this mellow maturity does not run away, however, and there is a fresh boundary to the flavours, and a fresh finish, but the overall effect is made rather awkward by clunky tannin textures and rough flavours that tangle up the finish. Not big, but attractive, open, generous wine that promises conviviality.

1991

13% alc/vol; 100% Pinot Noir, various clones; Wanaka district, Otago region; hand picked from 29 April 1991; aged in 225-litre French oak, new and one year old.
Winemaker: Rudi Bauer
Best drinking: 1995

Lightish red that is mellowing without showing any mahogany colours yet, but with a slightly composty fruit and mineral bouquet which is pretty and fresh. There is a trace of fruit sweetness on the palate which is quite supple, soft and clean, with savoury characters and a mellow cast that substitutes for real warmth. Pleasant, well-made, light red.

1991
'SELECTION'

13.5% alc/vol; 100% Pinot Noir, various clones; Wanaka district, Otago region; hand picked from 29 April 1991; aged in new 225-litre French oak.
Winemaker: Rudi Bauer
Best drinking: 1995–2001

Pretty, light, cherry-toned red, fragrant with a fine oak-dry straw aroma to it, and some hints of cherry amid the char and subtle compost. Very supple, fresh, lively fruit flavours with candy characters dominate the palate, although there is a balancing measure of oak, and a pleasant feel of tannins as the wine fades. Attractive, warm, even charming wine, made smart by good crafting that softens, deepens and shapes the palate, and provides nuances of flavour that keep it interesting.

1992

13% alc/vol; 100% Pinot Noir, various clones; Wanaka district, Otago region; hand picked from 12 May 1992; aged in new 225-litre French oak.
Winemakers: Rudi Bauer and Clotilde Chauvet
Best drinking: 1996–99

Moderately deep, glossy, black-edged cherry colour, ripe in appearance and very pretty. Pretty, too, on the nose, which has a sappy-edged fragrance that is quite highly strung and showing lifted aromas of concentrated fruit and oak, and a kind of fresh clarity. On the palate the fruit intensity strikes right through, fresh and berryish, giving the wine a sense of essence that submerges the complexities somewhat, but the oak manages to fight its way through, and very fine oak it is. Pleasant wine that would be very attractive if it were a little less fresh in character.

1993

13% alc/vol; 100% Pinot Noir, various clones; Wanaka district, Otago region; hand picked from 14 May 1993; aged in 225-litre French oak, new and one year old.
Winemaker: Clotilde Chauvet
Best drinking: 1996–99

Cherry-ruby red, healthy and bright with a fragrant bouquet that has cherry candy and mushrooms among the delicate tracery of oak. Starts with a fresh mouthful of cherry fruitiness and some mellow compost-mushroom complexities, but it lacks fruit sweetness, and the tannins are just a little tough for the lightness of the wine. Finishes dry, with a bit of fire in its tail.

1993
'SELECTION'

13% alc/vol; 100% Pinot Noir, various clones; Wanaka district, Otago region; hand picked from 14 May 1993; aged in new 225-litre French oak.
Winemaker: Clotilde Chauvet
Best drinking: 1995–2000

Bright cerise-red of moderate depth, shiny and new like a carnival toffee apple. The bouquet is clean, fresh with the tang of mineral water, a touch of candy cherries and some subtle oak for warmth. Light but supple fruit that is sweet to the middle and overlaid with a mellow, earthy, mushroom savour, in perfect harmony with softly furry, flavoury tannins which support the fruit-touched finish right to its fragrant end. Very finely balanced wine, still fresh, young, but neatly crafted with oak and suave tannins.

SYRAH

S YRAH WAS PROBABLY ONE OF THE VERY FIRST GRAPE VARIETIES PLANTED IN New Zealand, in James Busby's vineyard at Waitangi in the 1830s, for Busby was impressed by the variety on his visit to Hermitage in France in 1832 when he was collecting vines for Australia. From this collection, planted at the Botanic Gardens in Sydney, he acquired plants for Waitangi, but the demise of the vineyard during the 1845 war with Hone Heke ensured that his efforts did not foster wider enthusiasm for winegrowing in New Zealand.

By the end of the century, however, other colonial winemakers had planted Syrah in various sites around the country, and both the crops and the wine they made were commented on favourably at the time by Bragato.

The ultimate demise of the infant fine wine industry under prohibitionist pressure early in the 20th century soon eliminated any future Syrah might have had, and the fine wine movement of the last 20 years had little success with the variety until Alan Limmer stuck his neck out and planted vines he had secured from the government viticultural research station at Te Kauwhata. His efforts with Syrah on the stony soils west of Hastings are the sole reason for renewed interest in the grape as a serious red wine variety, and at least seven other producers are now making experimental Syrah.

The original source of the Te Kauwhata Syrah remains unknown, but recently new, improved clones have been introduced from France. Their influence will not be known for at least another decade.

STONECROFT SYRAH

Deep, dark, cherry-cerise, ripe red leads to an impressive spice and fruit bouquet that is almost as deep and dark as the colour. Quite reserved, apart from the juicy tang of cherry-plum fruit that wafts up, there is a meaty dimension about the wine as soon as it hits your taste buds—meat and huge wads of sweet, ripe fruit that tower up, tinged with a velvet, floral tone and supported by pillars of tannin. Behind this a complex network of flavours is just building with bottle age, mellowing the wine's youthful vigour, but it still hides behind a paradoxical facade of sweet, fresh fruit and mellow warmth. This paradox, warmth and freshness, is the key to the wine's class, a feature so intriguing that when combined, as it is, with such breathtaking fruit, it makes a non-issue of the slightly clunky oak characters.

1990

13% alc/vol; 100% Syrah; Mere Road/Gimblett Road district, Hawke's Bay region; hand picked 15 April 1990; aged in once-used 225-litre French oak barriques for 18 months.
Winemaker: Alan Limmer
Best drinking: 1996–99

Opaque, dark cerise and purple red that is shiny on the surface and almost impenetrable. A peppery nose, with a hydrangea-floral note backed by sweet oak and juicy fruit aromas that slip easily into a palate full of juicy flavours, full and sweet, and lined with grainy tannins. Warm, lively, fresh-tasting wine, with a measure of warmth, pleasant flavours, and a toughness that promises to soften with time, it is less brawny than its companions, but equally seductive in its fruit-sweet-floral fragrance and velvet promises.

1991
HAWKE'S BAY SYRAH

13% alc/vol; 100% Syrah; Mere Road/Gimblett Road district, Hawke's Bay region; hand picked 12 April 1991; aged in once-used 225-litre French oak barriques for 18 months.
Winemaker: Alan Limmer
Best drinking: 1997–2016

Deep, ripe black cherry and lively red colours with a glossy sheen and dark heart. The bouquet is fine, fresh, aromatic-fragrant with floral high notes and a richness of ripe fruit that has just a touch of oak. Fruit-laden wine with mouth-filling sweetness that is ripe and

Stonecroft Winery remains the only producer to have a consistent record with Syrah wines. Produced from fruit grown on the proprietors' property in Mere Road, west of Hastings, where conditions in the extremely stony soils are very dry and warm throughout the growing season, Stonecroft Syrah is notably alive with ripe, rich, juicy fruit, around which winemaker Alan Limmer has developed superb winecraft. These are wines made to age, and it will only be with time that the real value of Stonecroft Syrah will be known, but they are already among the most impressive reds being made in New Zealand.

1989
MERE ROAD SYRAH

13.5% alc/vol; 100% Syrah; Mere Road/Gimblett Road district, Hawke's Bay region; hand picked 21 March 1989; aged in once-used 225-litre French oak barriques for 18 months.
Winemaker: Alan Limmer
Best drinking: 1996–2004

supple in its juiciness, welling up like a wave of succulent, seductive flavour embroidered with floral tones, a trace of oak and the hearty substance of tannin and alcohol in its dark depths. A delicious thing, long and lovely, made to last and to mature in the bottle, it lacks just a dimension of sophistication to be superb.

1992

13% alc/vol; 100% Syrah; Mere Road/Gimblett Road district, Hawke's Bay region; hand picked 10 April 1992; aged in 225-litre French oak barriques for 18 months; 70% new, 30% once-used.
Winemaker: Alan Limmer
Best drinking: 1997–2005

Bright, moderately deep, dark, cerise wine with a lifted, peppery-spicy aroma modulated by touches of sweet oak and a pinch of char. Sweet, soft, attractive palate, laden with fine fruit and an entrancing fruit fragrance that is almost like violets in character and texture, all of which is backed by quietly furry, ripe, solid tannins, oak trimmings and warm depths. All charm and spice, even at this youthful stage, but loaded with enough tannic spine and vigour to promise age with grace, when young fragrances will mellow into seductive bouquets of silk and velvet. As well as the delicious fruit characters and sturdy tannins, this wine has the advantage of some fine winemaking that has added texture and structure to its cause, sophisticated qualities that will emerge fully as it ages.

THE WINEMAKERS

JOE BABICH

Conservative Joe Babich is one of the most respected winemakers in the country, both as a producer of old-fashioned fortified wines on which the Babich company was once based, and as a craftsman of the solid and increasingly fine varietal table wines that have kept this staunchly family firm abreast of the quality revolution. His favourite wine is Chardonnay, and it is with this variety that he has made his best wines, invariably restrained, cool styles that respond well to bottle age. This reserve and subtlety is also becoming apparent in rapidly improving Cabernet-based reds and in Sauvignons that seem to be made to sit at the table, wines that are following a slightly different direction from most other winemakers in the use of the pure fruit characters that typify New Zealand-grown grapes.

JOHN BELSHAM

Belsham made his mark first at Matua Valley and then with Hunter's in Marlborough, producing wines for both that consolidated each company's quality image. Responsible in recent years for an incredible collection of medal-winning wines under various labels as a result of his contract winemaking at Vintech, Belsham's own white wines are notably balanced, graceful renditions of New Zealand fruit, beautifully aromatic and finely detailed. They have set standards for reflection of fruit quality in an almost minimalist sense, fruit character that is the substance as well as the basis for each wine, a style that is epitomised by Hunter's Marlborough Sauvignon Blancs made during his tenure as winemaker there.

MICHAEL BRAJKOVICH

Panache, with its French connotations and implications of effortless style, is the description that best suits this winemaker. As son of one of New Zealand wine's most influential patriarchs, and a precocious graduate from Roseworthy's winemaking programme who took every prize available in his final year, followed by experience on the illustrious Moueix estates in Bordeaux, Brajkovich began his career with a ready-made reputation in waiting. He could have been excused for beginning with tentative conservatism, but after two years he had established himself as a high-risk performer with a great feel for the natural harmony of wine. By letting his winemaking follow a natural course as far as possible, he deviated from the accepted New Zealand practice of strict scientific control in the winery and showed drinkers the persuasive qualities of natural yeast fermentation, malolactic bacteria and small French oak *en masse*. With few exceptions, he has managed to create wines that have the advantages of fruit sophisticated by a kaleidoscope of other flavours, all finely tuned to a complex, intricate harmony. He has also pioneered Merlot and Cabernet Franc as valuable varieties in their own right, and has matched his consistently stunning Chardonnays with an equally elegant, poised procession of Merlot/Cabernet reds and increasingly influential, cosmopolitan Sauvignon Blancs. It is not surprising that his wines are as well respected in North America as they are in Britain.

DANIEL LE BRUN

Le Brun gave himself the incredibly difficult job of reproducing his Champagne-based family's winemaking tradition in the untried Marlborough region with little capital and few, if any supporters. His success, making wines that have more yeast influence than any other local sparkling, has shown that Marlborough's future may be as much in the ethereal sphere dominated by Champagne as it is with Sauvignon Blanc. Unequivocally independent, in style as well as in their proprietors' attitude, le Brun's meaty, strongly fruit-based, assertively yeasty wines have gained a wide following with their bold character. They have also gained for their maker a grudging respect from New Zealand sceptics, and from his family and one-time neighbours back in France.

BRUCE COLLARD

One of the big men of New Zealand winemaking, Bruce Collard has an impressive record as a winemaker — in the show ring, where his wines have been winning trophies for almost 25 years, and in the marketplace, where Collard labels are highly regarded by trade and consumers alike. Harmony is a popular word with Bruce, his brother Geoff, and his father Lionell, who between them have developed a regime of careful viticulture and attention to winemaking detail that has consistently produced wines of considerable artistry — carefully wrought, painfully honest, long-lasting whites that for many are the archetypal New Zealand styles. The basis for this excellence could be as much in Bruce's finely tuned palate, long a feature of wine competitions, as it is in the beautifully manicured Collard vineyards. Now the subtlety of detailed nuance and grace are being seen in red Collard wines as well, particularly in the exciting realm of Pinot Noir, of which Bruce Collard has long been an admirer but has only recently become a participant. The promise of Pinots that match the fragrance, clarity and tranquil beauty of Collard Chardonnays is a tempting prospect for all wine enthusiasts who have long followed this winemaker's illustrious career.

ALWYN CORBAN

Corban's individualism has not been respected by critics in New Zealand, but his restrained, long-flavoured, complex wines have a strong following among wine enthusiasts who are as supportive of structure and balance as they are of the more obvious charms of fruit flavour. Not that Corban's wines are lacking in fruit; it is just that they represent a style that is more concerned with balance and subtlety than it is with homage to full frontal fruit. Both with his red wines and Chardonnays, Corban's restraint is not caution, it is more a commitment to the long-term evolution of his wines, and to the use of wine as an important part of cuisine. It is not surprising that this wider vision should also find time to consider the intricate world of botrytised sweet wines, which Corban also makes with subtlety and the careful power of thoroughbred: graceful, elegant, memorable.

PETER COWLEY

Cowley came to Te Mata from Delegat's at a time when Te Mata already had a reputation as the leading red wine producer in the country, having given up a career in the restaurant trade to study winemaking at Roseworthy College, where he was the top post-graduate student of his year. At Te Mata he has not only maintained the company's red wine reputation but has advanced it to the point where their top wine has the sophistication and detail of a completely international style, and the whole range is notably balanced and refined, coupling Hawke's Bay fragrance and deep fruit flavours with a remarkably light winemaking touch. It is this sure, subtle craft that elevates Cowley's wines to such a high quality, a skill that brings to bear the full advantage of Te Mata's impressive collection of palates that includes proprietors John Buck and Michael Morris, as well as Cowley. As well as the consistently outstanding Coleraine and Awatea reds, Cowley has also made a series of Elston Chardonnays that are the epitome of the power and subtlety that this variety is capable of, moderating deep fruit flavours with a seasoning of careful oak and fermentation nuances. They are wines of vigour that are accentuated by a style that invites elegance as it ages.

TIM FINN

Finn makes wine with dexterity, often in the past shaping something beautiful from ordinary fruit but, as his viticultural knowledge has advanced, producing wines that are a superb balance of fine fruit, winemaking texture and excitement and have few peers in New Zealand. Recently his Rieslings have been as gracefully beautiful and piercing as any, his Sauvignons juicy and fresh with bell-like clarity, and his Chardonnays marrying cool fragrance, deep flavour and edge with ripe, creamy texture. He never allows the natural freshness of his wine to be more than a cutting edge for substance and sensuality, and has defined a cool-climate style that has set an example for many of his contemporaries. His presence in Nelson has given the district a reputation for quality that far outweighs the size of its wine industry.

KIM GOLDWATER

It was Goldwater who began the Waiheke experience and who continues to sustain its credibility with red wines that are consistently fine textured, flavourful, and liberally sprinkled with fruit. With a pedigree of vintages that stretches back to 1982, he has established a reputation for consistency subsequently grown to a sophistication that is more than a simple reproduction of fruit flavour washed with oak. By attending to harmony within his wines, Goldwater has developed a style that has the delicacy Waiheke's fruit characters seem to demand, adding grace to both bouquet and palate, without subverting the deep, long flavours that are the heart of his wines.

JOHN HANCOCK

Australian-born and trained, Hancock is one of the most flamboyant characters in the New Zealand wine industry, and his assertive wines, particularly Chardonnays, attracted many winemakers to the advantages of small oak. Hancock made his name at Delegat's with a series of attention-grabbing, if unsubtle, Chardonnays in the early eighties, before taking his skills to the new Morton Estate company, where he remains, and where the Chardonnays have gradually been refined to a point of elegance, a graceful representation of clear fruit, suave texture and attention to detail. Along with a sequence of fruit-driven, deeply flavoured sparkling wines, these Chardonnays have an arresting combination of strength as well as style.

PETER HUBSCHER

Hubscher is not so much a style master as a wine philosopher, one whose belief in the rightness of making the best possible wines for the lowest possible prices has set very high minimum standards for the rest of the industry. As winemaker and now managing director of Montana, the largest wine producer in the country, responsible for some 40 percent of total industry production, Hubscher's views are unavoidable, and Montana's seminal Marlborough Sauvignon Blancs and Marlborough Rieslings have become standards for these now international wine styles. He has also instigated serious consideration of bottle-fermented sparkling wines as a viable option for the New Zealand industry by making successful mass-produced wines using this technique, and with most premium grape varieties has defined the public's knowledge of them with simple, purely flavoured styles that are direct reflections of their natural, local-grown characters.

KEVIN JUDD

Judd's Cloudy Bay Sauvignon Blancs are the most complex, cosmopolitan versions of the Marlborough Sauvignon Blanc style, fresh, lively wines whose energy is moderated by very subtle flavour nuances and textures imparted by Semillon, oak, and other winemaking refinements that begin in the carefully managed vineyards. They are wines that exude class, and in recent vintages have been joined by equally stylish, carefully textured Chardonnays that are the excellent examples of finesse. They are always wines that suggest considerable attention has been paid to every detail, and are remarkably consistent, in quality if not character, whatever the vagaries of vintage.

ALAN LIMMER

Limmer has emerged from nowhere as a producer of powerful but poised wines, particularly reds and Chardonnay, and his contribution to the rapid progress of Syrah in New Zealand conditions has been a feature of the last decade. His wine has presence above all, making its mark with richly pervasive fruit aromas and flavours before they turn to subtlety and balance to finally persuade the drinker.

NEIL McCALLUM

As producer of the finest Gewürztraminer and Pinot Gris, as well as very high-quality Pinot Noir, Riesling and botrytised sweet wines, McCallum has a presence in New Zealand far greater than his tiny winery suggests he should. His style is invariably cautious, restrained, and intent upon elegance as well as pure fruit character, frequently resulting in great depth and length of flavour, and an enthusiastic band of followers.

ALAN McCORKINDALE

One of the quiet men of the wine industry, McCorkindale has considerable influence through the widespread success of his wine. He has maintained Corban's Marlborough winery's reputation for fine, delicate Stoneleigh Sauvignon Blancs and Rieslings, and Corban's similarly structured Private Bin Chardonnays, and has also given a similar sense of fine balance and delicacy to a series of experimental reds that suggest a healthy future in the district for Merlot and Pinot Noir.

LARRY McKENNA

His invigorating effect on Pinot Noir production in New Zealand is as much to do with McKenna's enthusiasm for sharing developmental success as it is with his own considerable success with the variety in Martinborough. Arriving at the bleak, tiny town from Delegat's in Auckland, McKenna set about changing the reputation of Martinborough Vineyard with a series of politically correct Chardonnays, Rieslings and Pinot Noirs that reflect mainstream New World winemaking with a high degree of skill and keen fruit character in the New Zealand mould. His experimentation with Pinot Noir, however, and his quest for a more sophisticated, oak-matured style has put him offside with the purists but offers exciting prospects for those who believe the future for New Zealand Pinot Noir is in the high profile, high-risk regions dominated by the luxurious French producers.

BRENT MARRIS

Marris has kept Delegat's abreast with the quality trend across the country, and with sound technique and reliable fruit sources in Hawke's Bay and Marlborough has maintained a range of well-made, fruit-based wines that conform to all expectations of New Zealand wine standards. Reds and whites are mid-weight, well-crafted and balanced wines with moderate complexity and cellaring potential.

JAMES MILLTON

When James Millton first talked of his commitment to winegrowing without reliance on chemical insecticide and botrycide regimes, most people in the wine industry thought he was crazy, but his wines have been very eloquent in support of his approach, their inevitably soft, charming, perfectly balanced style showing what is possible outside the bounds of mainstream science. He makes both Riesling and Chardonnay with a comfortable sense of proportion, and Chenin Blanc that is never less than intriguing in its complex array of flavours. All are wines that invite further investigation and leave behind an air of satisfaction.

KYM MILNE

Milne made an amazing number of medal- and trophy-winning wines during his years at Villa Maria, and his artful use of barriques and undoubted blending skills made him one of the popular gurus of New Zealand winemaking before he left for Europe. His wines have a freshness and an expensive feel to them, laced as they are with clear fruit and rich oak. They are really delicious at a young age — comely, supple, long-flavoured. Whether they will survive for as long as their reputation suggests they should is yet to be proven, but they certainly illustrate the advantages of top-class oak when making top-class wines.

CLIVE PATON

A proponent of red wine in a district that seems more naturally attuned to whites, Paton has consistently produced sensitive reflections of the character of Martinborough fruit, and as he has learned more about this character with succeeding vintages, so his wines have been more subtle, more responsive to fruit character and structure. Above all else he makes attractive wines, all more or less beautiful according to the character of fruit, but each one underscored by charm and mouth-watering appeal. It is a style that is perfectly suited to Pinot Noir, which in Paton's hands produces a gorgeous, soft sensuality, a come-on quality that it is difficult to ignore.

DAVID PEARCE

Fruit, fruit and fruit are the memories left by Pearce's wines, whether experimental Pinotages, intense Gewürztraminers or extravagantly fragrant Rieslings. It is a character that fits perfectly with Marlborough's propensity for growing grapes with amazing flavour, and is something that Pearce has turned to his advantage, building a reputation as one of the most reliable Marlborough winemakers. Now he has fashioned Chardonnay to match the flashing flavour and delicious texture of his Rieslings, Pearce has made his mark as a winemaker worthy of respect.

MARK ROBERTSON

The pleasure of simple things done well is a somewhat misleading impression given by Robertson's Matua Valley Wines, because while they appear easy they have a complexity and intricate structure that facilitates this effortless style but does not intrude. It is a development of the honest, fruit-based styles that was once the Matua style, to more sophistication without pretence, and as such is widely popular and at its best good enough to meet the demanding standards of fine wine.

PETER ROBERTSON

Warm, convivial wines, red and white, are typical of Peter Robertson, himself an engaging personality for whom wine seems as much an enjoyment as it is a business. His approach is conservative yet not dogmatic, and the wines always reflect honest attention to ripe fruit and good oak, made with resilience and substance, and a significant edge of comfort.

GLENN THOMAS

Refinement is what marks Glenn Thomas' wines, from his days at Corbans to his present acclaimed position at Vavasour, where he has made Chardonnays, Sauvignon Blancs and Cabernet-based reds of fine quality, carefully made, fragrant and long. His is neither a powerful, nor an assertive style, rather its qualities creep up on you with texture and detail that is so intricately wrought it is almost seamless. Working with fruit from the untried Awatere Valley east of Blenheim, Thomas's success has been such that there is now a lot more interest in this district from other producers seeking to repeat his success.

THE WINERIES

ATA RANGI VINEYARD
PO Box 43
Martinborough
UK AGENT
Fine Wines of New Zealand
PO Box 476
London NW5 2NZ

BABICH WINES LTD
Babich Road
Henderson
UK AGENT
Deinhard & Co. Ltd
12a Brick Street
London W1Y 8DJ

BROOKFIELDS VINEYARDS
(1977) LTD
PO Box 7174
Taradale
Hawke's Bay

CELLIER LE BRUN LTD
PO Box 33
Renwick
Blenheim
UK AGENT
Hedley Wright & Co. Ltd
10–11 Twyford Centre
London Road
Bishop's Stortford
Hertfordshire
CM23 3YT

CLOUDY BAY VINEYARDS
LTD
PO Box 376
Blenheim

UK AGENT
Cloudy Bay
Fifth Floor
79 Knightsbridge
London SW1X 7RB

COLLARD BROTHERS LTD
303 Lincoln Road
Henderson
Auckland

CORBANS WINES LTD
(COOKS, ROBARD &
BUTLER, STONELEIGH)
PO Box 21183
Henderson
Auckland
UK AGENT
Caxton Tower Wines Limited
4 Harlequin Avenue
Brentford
Middlesex TW8 9EW

COOPERS CREEK
VINEYARD LTD
PO Box 40
Kumeu
Auckland
UK AGENT
Ehrmanns Group PLC
29 Corsica Street
London N5 1JT

DELEGAT'S WINE ESTATE
LTD
(OYSTER BAY)
Hepburn Road
Henderson
Auckland

UK AGENT
Geoffrey Roberts Associates
430 High Road
London NW10 2HA

DRY RIVER WINES LTD
PO Box 72
Martinborough

GIESEN WINE ESTATE
CANTERBURY LTD
PO Box 11066
Christchurch

GOLDWATER ESTATE
18 Causeway Road
Putiki Bay
Waiheke Island
UK AGENT
House of Hallgarten
Hallgarten Wines Ltd
Dallow Road
Luton
Bedfordshire
LU1 1UR

GROVE MILL WINE
COMPANY LTD
PO Box 67
Renwick
Blenheim

HUNTER'S WINES (NZ)
LTD
PO Box 839
Blenheim
UK AGENT
AH Wines Ltd

West Camel
Nr Yeovil
Somerset
BA22 7QB

KUMEU RIVER WINES LTD
PO Box 24
Kumeu
Auckland 1454
UK AGENT
Boxford Wine Company
Spring Cottage
Butchers Lane
Boxford
Sudbury
Suffolk CO10 5EA

MARTINBOROUGH
VINEYARD LTD
PO Box 85
Martinborough
UK AGENT
Haughton Fine Wines
Chorley
Nantwich
Cheshire CW5 8JR

MATUA VALLEY WINES
LTD
PO Box 100
Kumeu
Auckland
UK AGENT
Mentzendorf & Co Ltd
8th Floor
Prince Consort House
27 - 29 Albert Embankment
London SE1 7TJ

MONTANA WINES LTD
PO Box 18293
Glen Innes
Auckland
UK AGENT
Seagram (UK) Ltd
Pinnacle House
25 Hartfield Road
Wimbledon
London SW19 3SE

MORTON ESTATE LTD
State Highway 2
RD2
Katikati
UK AGENT
Berkmann Wine Cellars Limited
12 Brewery Road
London N7 9NH

NEUDORF VINEYARDS
RD2
Upper Moutere
Nelson
UK AGENT
Haughton Fine Wines
Chorley, Nantwich
Cheshire CW5 8JR

NGATARAWA WINES LTD
Ngatarawa Road
RD5
Hastings
Hawke's Bay
UK AGENT
Walter S Siegel Ltd
Regent House
123 High Street
Odiham, Hampshire
RG25 1LA

RIPPON VINEYARD
Mount Aspiring Road
Wanaka 9192
Central Otago
UK AGENT
Fine Wines of New Zealand
PO Box 476
London NW5 2NZ

SEIFRIED ESTATE
(REDWOOD VALLEY) (UK
only)
PO Box 18
Upper Moutere
Nelson 7152
UK AGENT
Fine Wines of New Zealand
PO Box 476
London NW5 2NZ

STONECROFT WINES
Mere Road
RD5
Hastings
Hawke's Bay
UK AGENT
Bibendum
113 Regents Park Road
London NW1 8UR

TE MATA ESTATE WINERY
LTD
PO Box 8335
Havelock North
Hawke's Bay
UK AGENT
Michael Druitt Wines
136 - 142 New Kent Road
London SE1 6TU

THE MILLTON VINEYARD
PO Box 66
Manutuke
Gisborne
UK AGENT
Bottle Green Vinceremos Wines
261 Upper Town Street
Leeds
LS13 3JT

VAVASOUR WINES LTD
PO Box 72
Seddon
Blenheim
UK AGENT
AH Wines Ltd
West Camel
nr Yeovil
Somerset
BA22 7QB

VILLA MARIA ESTATE LTD
PO Box 43046
Mangere
Auckland
UK AGENT
Hatch Mansfield Agencies Ltd
Old Bank House
Thames Street
Windsor
Berkshire SL4 1PZ

(VIDALS)
Fine Wines of New Zealand
PO Box 476
London NW5 2NZ